Blacks against *Brown*

Blacks against *Brown*

The Intra-racial Struggle over Segregated Schools in Topeka, Kansas

Charise L. Cheney

The University of North Carolina Press CHAPEL HILL

This book was published with the assistance of the John Hope Franklin Fund of the University of North Carolina Press.

Complete Cataloging-in-Publication Data for this title is available from the Library of Congress at https://lccn.loc.gov/9781469681641.

ISBN 978-1-4696-8164-1 (cloth: alk. paper)
ISBN 978-1-4696-8165-8 (pbk.: alk. paper)
ISBN 978-1-4696-8166-5 (epub)
ISBN 978-1-4696-8167-2 (pdf)

Cover art: Brown v. Board of Education, 347 U.S. 483 (1954); 08) *Topeka's African American Teachers, 1949*, National Parks Gallery.

Dedicated to the Mann sisters: Angela, Valerie, and Cheryl

Angela Mann (author collection)

Valerie Mann in cheerleading uniform
(author collection)

Cheryl Mann (author collection)

Contents

List of Illustrations ix

Acknowledgments xi

Introduction 1

CHAPTER ONE
Over John Brown's Dead Body 16
White Supremacy and White Liberalism in Kansas

CHAPTER TWO
The Alchemy of Race and Rights 39
Separate but Equal in Topeka Public Schools, 1861–1954

CHAPTER THREE
Reading, Ri(gh)ting, and Resistance 69
*Racial Uplift Ideologies and Practices in Topeka's All-Black
Schools, 1929–1954*

CHAPTER FOUR
Graham v. Board and the Clash of the Black Counterpublics,
1941–1948 102

CHAPTER FIVE
Harrison Caldwell 130
The Unsung Black Antihero of Brown

CHAPTER SIX
Blacks against *Brown* 150
The Final Chapter, 1948–1954

Conclusion 181

Notes 211

Index 245

Illustrations

Lucinda Todd's Family 65

Third and fourth graders at Monroe School, 1892 74

Mamie Williams with students at Buchanan School 79

Mamie Luella Williams, 1944 80

Topeka's Black educators, 1949 166

Linda Brown and her sister Terry Lynn on train tracks 182

Linda and Terry Lynn Brown on school bus 184

Linda and Terry Lynn Brown in front of Monroe School 184

Mamie Williams's Monroe School classroom, 1953 185

Acknowledgments
Confessions of a High School Cheerleader

I was a standout junior varsity cheerleader my sophomore year at Topeka High School. I was a great tumbler, a solid flyer, and base. I had excellent jumps and a loud voice. I could even dance and choreograph routines. I had varsity aspirations for my junior year. There were ten positions on the squad, and I knew I would score in the top ten. But to be promoted, I would have to outperform two athletes, Shalice and Jeannette. Shalice was already a varsity cheerleader with an amazingly high toe touch and tremendous flexibility. She was a shoo-in. I would be in direct competition against my JV teammate Jeannette because only two of the ten slots on the Trojans' varsity cheer team were reserved for Black students. After *Brown*, Topeka High School implemented a quota system to ensure integrated cheer, dance, and flag teams. There was an additional spot on the cheer team set aside for an "other"; that is, a nonwhite, non-Black cheerleader. The rest of the team would be white. But at the end of my sophomore year in 1987, three strong, qualified Black athletes prepared to try out for varsity cheer. A policy instituted with antiracist intent would have a racist outcome.

That is, until Mrs. (Marian) Douglas intervened. Mrs. Douglas was a member of the varsity cheerleader selection committee that year. She was a highly respected Black security officer who was no stranger to the interplay among race, racism, and sports at Topeka High. During the mid-to-late 1940s, she was a cheerleader for the segregated Black basketball team the Ramblers. Forty years later, Mrs. Douglas successfully lobbied to liberate the cheer team's racial arithmetic from the school's racial demographics. She brokered a compromise that shifted the varsity's racial composition from a seven-two-one quota to a policy that guaranteed a place on the team for one white, one Black, and one "other" cheerleader. The rest of the team would be determined by the next seven highest scores.

No one ever talked about *Brown v. Board of Education* during my childhood years in Topeka. Until I conducted research for this project, I was unaware of how the racial landscape I traversed as a student in Unified School District No. 501 was shaped by the landmark Supreme Court case that originated in my hometown. There was no discussion of *Brown* in the mandatory state history curriculum designed for elementary and middle school students nor in my high school AP US History course. But the silence around the city's racist role in the most significant civil rights case in American history did not negate the fact that racism persisted. Sixteen years after *Brown*, my aunt Valerie Mann was the second Black student to become a varsity cheerleader for Topeka High School Trojan teams. On April 20, 1970, during her junior year, approximately 100 Black Topeka High School students staged a walkout to protest the racism of white teachers and administrators. Four days later, Black students at Highland Park High School set the school auditorium's curtains on fire to express their frustrations with discriminatory treatment.

Nine years later, I attended Lowman Hill Elementary School, one of the most contested educational sites in Topeka's civil rights history. The first lawsuit brought against the Topeka Board of Education by a Black resident was in response to the city's stealthy segregation of Lowman Hill in 1902. When I attended the elementary school between 1979 and 1982, the racially diverse student population reflected the demographics of the neighborhood. My third-grade teacher at Lowman Hill was the only Black teacher I would ever have as a student in Topeka. I had no idea that twenty-two years earlier in 1957 Mrs. Jean Price had been one of the first Black teachers to integrate a white school in Topeka.

The first cohort of Black students and teachers who integrated public schools in the mid-to-late 1950s had to negotiate the implicit and explicit racism of white students, teachers, and administrators. Not much had changed for Black students in predominantly white schools during the 1970s and '80s. In 1977, I was the only Black first grader at Maude Bishop Elementary School, an almost all-white school with an all-white teaching staff in a mostly white neighborhood of West Topeka. I was regularly called "nigger" on the playground by white classmates who also blocked me from playing games with other students during recess. There was no intervention by white teachers or administrators. When my English teacher recommended me for the Gifted, Talented and Creative program that year, my homeroom teacher revoked it. She assessed that the lone little Black girl wasn't smart enough for the accelerated curriculum. I wish I remembered her name. She deserves special recognition.

But my doubter deserves less of a shout-out than my believers. My fourth-grade Lowman Hill teacher Susan Stickley and my Topeka High School journalism teacher Susan Patrick pushed me to strive for greatness. Miss Stickley encouraged my love for reading, and Ms. Patrick stoked my love for writing.

This book is a personal and professional homecoming for me. I am a native Topekan, who studied under groundbreaking historian of education Dr. James D. Anderson as a history graduate student at the University of Illinois. I hope this book makes him proud. I started this research thirteen years ago with the intent to write a manuscript on the aftermath of *Brown* in Topeka public schools. But the archives at the Kansas State Historical Society led me in a different direction. It has been a long road of starts and stops, but I'm grateful for the process. The product is much better because of the time it took to complete it. My only regret is that my Aunt Val is not here to see it, but I know she's smiling down on me.

The support I've experienced from my University of Oregon community has been unparalleled. My friends and colleagues in the Indigenous Race and Ethnic Studies Department have supported me and advocated for me through the good, the bad, and the ugly. I am forever thankful for the intervention of Laura Pulido, who gave me a swift kick in the butt when I was stuck in the quicksand of productivity. She also introduced me to the simple yet profound phrase "geography matters," which revolutionized how I thought about "Why Kansas?" Ernesto Martinez's gift of conceptual clarity guided my theoretical approach to *Blacks against Brown*. I don't know what I would have done or how I could have done it without Lynn Fujiwara, who sacrifices the most to keep us all grounded. Thank you for constantly reminding me what is real and what is not. Brian Klopotek was always in my corner with an eye iron so I could see clearly, even when on the ropes. My colleague Jerry Rosiek in education came in clutch in the eleventh hour with the conceptual framework I needed to end this manuscript with a "bang" versus a "pop." And thanks to my former student (and one of my favorites) Zoë Haakenstad for editing my first draft.

I have had several financial supporters over the past thirteen years. The University of Oregon (UO) Women of Color Project and the Center for the Study of Women in Society provided support for writing workshops and outside readers. The UO Division of Equity and Inclusion went above and beyond to provide funding for research trips, editors, and release time to complete this manuscript.

On a more personal note, big ups to my OGs Lynn Hudson and Jane Rhodes and to my ride-or-dies Joy Williamson and Alicia Young for always having my personal and professional back. And to Annette Willsey Liebhardt and Dee Gribbin for cheering me on. And there are not enough words to express the gratitude I have for my mom Angie Davis and children Safiya, Soleil, Saire, and Siel for keeping me a balanced human being.

Blacks against *Brown*

Introduction

In the shadow of the fortieth anniversary of *Brown v. Board of Education of Topeka*, US district court judge Robert L. Carter reminisced about his days as an NAACP Legal Defense Fund (LDF) lawyer arguing the case before the Supreme Court. "The stakes were personally enormous." Because the case could prove monumental for African Americans, Carter felt responsible for the "fate of black people in this country." Despite his racial burden, Carter was convinced that the NAACP had a unique strategic advantage. "I didn't think we could lose because we had nothing to lose," Carter asserted. "Separate but equal was on the ballot and that was the best they could do. They couldn't make it any worse so that there was nothing to lose."[1]

Carter's recollection of the landmark desegregation case has the makings of a legendary story. The national NAACP's legal approach to *Brown* was risky but necessary. Its outcome was uncertain, but its radical potential was unquestionable. *They couldn't make it any worse so that there was nothing to lose.* And yet Carter's reflection represents willful historical revisionism. The Supreme Court case made Black Topekans a national symbol of the desegregation movement, but in reality, they were in conflict over the issue of integrating schools. As one of the lead lawyers in the *Brown v. Board of Education* Kansas Supreme Court case in 1951, Carter knew two things to be true: there was no universal anti-Black segregationist practice or unanimity about its resolution.

The NAACP LDF chose to represent the Topeka plaintiffs because the defendant deviated from segregationist norms. Unlike most white school boards, the Topeka Board of Education managed separate-but-relatively-equal elementary schools.[2] The school board's unorthodoxy did not deter members of the local NAACP, who decided to pursue a lawsuit in 1950. When they contacted the national office for legal assistance, Robert Carter and his cohort were intrigued. Months earlier, the NAACP LDF had secured two Supreme Court victories against segregated educational spaces in Texas and Oklahoma. After *Sweatt v. Painter* and *McLaurin v. Oklahoma*, they decided to shift their legal strategy from contesting schools that were separate and unequal to a direct assault on the constitutionality of *Plessy v. Ferguson*. With the Topeka lawsuit, they found the perfect test case to argue that separate-but-equal schools were inherently discriminatory. It "should be much easier for us to win cases and get favorable precedence in both areas and states like Kansas where the pattern is not as definitely and rigidly set as it is in the deep South," Robert Carter wrote to a colleague in 1950.[3]

But what attracted the national NAACP to *Brown* repelled local Topekans. Members of the NAACP LDF were notoriously inattentive to the nuanced racial dynamics that faced local branches, and Carter was no exception. His conclusion that "we had nothing to lose" with *Brown* may have been true for Black students in underfunded, overcrowded Jim Crow schools. But segregated elementary schools in Topeka had comparable resources, equitable facilities, and similar curricula as well as compassionate, qualified, well-paid Black faculty and administrators. So when the Topeka NAACP staged an intervention against the local school board in 1948, many Black parents, educators, and alumni actively engaged in obstruction of justice. They preferred all-Black schools to predominantly white ones. Black elementary students had affirming educational experiences in all-Black schools, and the subject-to-object positioning of Black children transitioning into integrated classrooms was a legitimate cause for concern to Black residents. In their cost-benefit analysis, these Black school advocates anticipated the price paid for "freedom" and fought vehemently to maintain all-Black schools. This unique set of circumstances presented a significant challenge for the local NAACP during the late 1940s and early 1950s.

Blacks against Brown: *The Intra-racial Struggle over Segregated Schools in Topeka, Kansas* documents the intra-racial conflict among Black Topekans over the city's Jim Crow education system. The "hidden history" of Blacks against *Brown* disrupts the metanarrative about one of the most significant moments in America's racial history.[4] School integration did not signify racial progress for all African Americans during the Jim Crow era. In the historical shadow of *Brown v. Board,* Black resistance to integrated schools occurred at one of the most surprising times in one of the most unsuspecting places. *Blacks against* Brown is a community study that centers controversy over Topeka public schools to demonstrate how racial geographies and embodied geographies of race shape histories of white domination and Black resistance.

Blacks against *Brown*: Racist Structures and Racial Subjectivities

The first objective of *Blacks against* Brown is to study the symbiotic relationship between race and space. It is vitally important to recognize the "temporal and spatial" dynamics that informed Black political activism for and against desegregating Topeka public schools from 1929 to 1953.[5] White domination and discourses of whiteness vis-à-vis Blackness have regional and local specificities. These distinctions are rooted in histories of settler colonialism, immigration, and slavery or proximity to the enslaved. A secondary objective of *Blacks against* Brown is to explore how those histories of white supremacy are internalized by and inscribed on the bodies of racialized "others." I interrogate how the body figures in the production of racial consciousness and the performance of racial politics. My work then surveys the cast(e) of Blacks against *Brown*, mapping correlations between personal identity and political expression relative to color, class, gender, and generation.

Blacks against Brown contributes to a body of literature that signals new directions for the writing of Black histories, breaking the regional ties that bind civil rights movement literatures.[6] Like many places in the American West, racial restrictions in the Sunflower State were complex, inconsistent, and elastic. The true historical legacy of "Bleeding Kansas" was not white racial enlightenment, it was an internal conflict over the limits of Black freedom. From the post–Civil War period to the post–World War II period, white policymakers legislated both civil rights and racial segregation because they favored political equality over social equality. Kansas state laws regarding public education were a primary example. An 1861 statute only permitted school segregation in cities with populations over 15,000, as long as local school boards secured "equal advantages" for Black and white schoolchildren. Segregation in high schools was prohibited.

The Topeka Board of Education complied with the state's legal parameters. Since it was unable to maintain parallel schools for Black and white schoolchildren, the board had an optional enrollment policy throughout the late nineteenth and early twentieth centuries. Some Black students went to all-Black schools, while others attended integrated schools. That racial flexibility changed in 1929, when a "dual" education system became economically viable due to the passing of an $850,000 bond. For the next twenty years, the Topeka Board of Education semisuccessfully operationalized the "separate-but-equal" *Plessy* standard. Therefore, the Topeka NAACP's desegregation lawsuit was radically different from the others subsumed under *Brown*. Black schoolchildren in Topeka did not experience overcrowded classrooms like those in Washington, DC, nor were they subjected to dilapidated school buildings like those in Delaware or Virginia. While Black parents in Delaware and South Carolina petitioned their local school boards for bus service, the Topeka school board voluntarily provided buses for Black children.

The roots and routes of anti-Black racism in Topeka help to explain the divergent antiracism strategies of Black Topekans. When the Topeka NAACP launched their desegregation campaign in the late 1940s, they struggled to mobilize Black residents. Unlike in many southern localities, Black reluctance toward or resistance to NAACP efforts did not stem from Black fears or anxieties about a white backlash. The Topeka school board's anti-Black racism inadvertently subsidized Black resistance to antiracism activism. Because its privileging of whiteness did not include divestment in Black schools, schools it created to enforce interracial exclusion unintentionally fostered intra-racial inclusion. By creating a semiparallel school system for Blacks, the Topeka school board facilitated economic opportunities for Black educators, insured instructional parity for Black children, and reinforced racial pride in Black communities.

White Topekans' unusual segregationist approach implemented Kansas state law, which was also remarkable. Kansas state law mandated the *Plessy* standard and prohibited perpetual school segregation. All Black schoolchildren in Topeka matriculated from all-Black elementary schools to predominantly white junior and senior high schools. The transition from a familial learning environment with compassionate Black faculty and administrators into racially mixed schools with indifferent or racist white faculty and administrators was harsh and alienating. "It wasn't the grade schools that sunk me," recalled Black resident Richard Ridley. "It was the high school."[7]

The nuances of individual and institutional racism in Topeka public schools complicated Black political projects in relation to educational rights. When civil rights proponents successfully pursued legal intervention against segregated junior high schools in 1940, Black parents and educators launched a countermovement. Following the 1941 Kansas Supreme Court decision in *Graham v. Board of Education of Topeka*, the school board fully integrated its junior high schools despite organized Black opposition. Tensions between pro- and antidesegregation activists remained so high throughout the 1940s, the local NAACP consciously avoided the issue. But when McKinley Burnett was elected president of the local branch in 1947, he set his sights on the city's remaining Jim Crow schools. Within months he appeared at a school board meeting and demanded the "full and complete integration of both pupils and teachers." Membership in the organization plummeted.

Without the resilience and resourcefulness of three local NAACP members, there would have been no *Brown v. Board of Education of Topeka*. Historians fail to question the motivations of these historical actors because the ends justify the means. But the fact that they were a minority voice in a minoritized community calls into question historical assumptions about Blacks before *Brown*. Not only was there no Black united front, but more Black Topekans advocated for race-based school policies than protested against race-based school policies during the 1940s and early 1950s. *Brown v. Board of Education of Topeka* was the culmination of a decade-long struggle of a few local civil rights activists. But that small cohort of NAACP members kept pushing against all odds even when at odds with most Black residents. Their dogged determination deserves some explanation.

As previously stated, the second objective of my book is to interrogate the symbiosis between political structures and political subjectivities. For example, without suggesting causation, there is a clear correlation between the corporeality and consciousness of the Black Topekans who were for and those who were against *Brown*. The architects of the desegregation campaign, McKinley Burnett, Daniel Sawyer, and Lucinda Todd, were fair-skinned. The Burnett family could pass for white, and the Sawyers were listed in the 1910 and 1920 federal censuses as "mulatto." Their destiny was bound not by class or color but by racial inheritance. By contrast, the most vocal advocates for the city's all-Black schools, Harrison Caldwell, Ezekiel Ridley, and Mamie Williams, were prominent dark-skinned educators with no illusion of inclusion. It was not uncommon for Black Topekans to reference the phenotype and physicality of Caldwell and Williams when discussing their accomplishments. In fact, Williams's intelligence was often juxtaposed to her skin color and/or hair texture, exposing Black internalization of the interrelated systems of white supremacy and heteropatriarchy.

But complexion was not the only connection among pro- and anti-school integrationists. The civil rights activists were native-born Kansans firmly situated in elite, if not elitist, social circles in Black Topeka. These not-white-but-light Black Topekans' demand for equal access was unequivocal and undaunted by other Black residents' concerns about interracial learning environments, Black teachers, or the Black community at large. On the other hand, many of the outspoken proponents of all-Black schools were the children of Southern migrants who articulated their racial uplift politics through race pride, racial self-determination, and bourgeois respectability. *Blacks against* Brown uses these personal and political patterns to explore (1) the intersections of race, color, gender, and generation; and (2) how this identity complex informs individual and collective racial subjectivities.

Blacks against *Brown*: An Alternative Historical Narrative

Scholarship on *Brown* is wide-ranging and prolific. During the past generation, historians have assessed its place in the civil rights movement, legal scholars have debated the case and the Supreme Court's role in social reform, and social scientists have analyzed its legacy and the persistence of racial segregation in America's schools.[8] Despite considerable attention and analysis, scholarly writings on the landmark case tend to neglect the local stories behind the national symbol.[9] Given the historical importance of *Brown*, it is remarkable that few researchers have interrogated the origins or outcome of the local case that provided its namesake. The social and political significance of *Brown* was obviously more far-reaching than any one of the five local lawsuits involved in the groundbreaking decision. However, there was something special about the case against the Topeka school board.

By foregrounding Blacks against *Brown*, my work engages and expands ongoing historical debates about the modern civil rights movement. Over the past twenty years, scholars have successfully challenged conceptions of the civil rights movement as a linear, ideologically unified period of antiracism activism that started with *Brown* and ended with the Voting Rights Act of 1965.[10] My monograph bears witness to the "Long Movement" school of civil rights history by expanding the interpretative framework and descriptive language used to examine Black social activism before the 1954 Supreme Court decision. *Blacks against* Brown contributes to a body of literature that insists upon recognition of the heterogeneity of Black communities and the historical realities of coexisting subaltern Black counterpublics. Using Black Topekans as a case study, I survey the political battle between civil rights activists who wanted to abolish segregated schools and educational advocates who fought to protect the city's all-Black schools. This tension over equity and equality demonstrates divergent perspectives within Black communities about what constituted educational justice for Black communities in the era of Jim Crow.

As a community study, my book complicates conventional tropes in civil rights movement histories. The *Brown* Supreme Court decision represents a pivotal moment in American racial mythologies that project our national history as an evolution from racist evil to racial good. The story of Blacks against *Brown* presents an "alternative narrative."[11] Black students' experiences with integration into predominantly white schools, usually a signifier of racial progress, was one motivation behind Black Topekans' opposition to the local NAACP. Although Black resistance to desegregation is present in public records, it is absent in historical accounts. The well-documented but unwritten story of Blacks against *Brown* epitomizes the "erasure of historical voices, actors, and debates" in civil rights movement studies that do not affirm the "virtues of democratic liberalism."[12]

Richard Kluger's classic 1975 book *Simple Justice: The History of* Brown v. Board of Education *and Black America's Struggle for Equality* is a primary example. *Simple Justice* is known as a comprehensive history of local and national events leading up to the Supreme Court decision. It has been described by scholars as "magisterial" and "masterful."[13] In 2004, education professor Robert Lowe wrote that after almost thirty years, *Simple Justice* remained "the most important as well as the most exhaustive book on *Brown*."[14] Kluger's 789-page opus includes two chapters on the Topeka case but barely mentions Black Topekans' support for all-Black schools. This omission is noteworthy because his interview transcripts clearly bear witness to Black opposition to school integration. Kluger invalidated those who mobilized for all-Black schools, not only because they interrupt his story arc but also because he dismissed their racial logic. His treatment of seventy-four-year-old Mamie Williams is a case in point.

In the decade before *Brown*, Williams was a well-known proponent of all-Black schools within Black communities. As such, she was a person of interest to Kluger. Williams taught in Topeka for forty-two years. Her teaching career began in 1918 and ended in 1960 when she was forced to retire alongside the closing of Buchanan Elementary. Not only was she a veteran of Topeka public schools, but she was also a principal actor in the drama surrounding segregated schools. She even testified on behalf of Black schools in a 1941 Kansas Supreme Court desegregation case. Williams believed that Black schools with Black teachers were key to Black student success. In the 1940s she wrote, "Those who are socially informed about people can help them best."[15] It was clear that her position had not changed when Kluger interviewed her in 1970. Racially separated schools were "best for the children," she contended.[16]

Kluger's interview afforded Williams the opportunity to address what she perceived to be a miscarriage of justice. His handwritten and typed transcripts document her conscientious objection to public perceptions about the inferiority of Jim Crow schools. Sixteen years after the Supreme Court overturned *Plessy*, Williams held Chief Justice Earl Warren in contempt for his claim that segregated schools caused psychological, mental, and educational harm to Black children. Black children "were not damaged by being in separate schools," she insisted.[17] As counterevidence, Williams shared a personal anecdote involving a negative interaction she had had as a student with a white teacher who was "picking on her" in an integrated school. In all-Black schools, she rationalized, Black students received "Black enrichment," not the racism of white teachers.

Williams's restorative narrative eluded Kluger. "INTERPRETATION: MAMIE WAS HOSTILE TO INTEGRATION," he editorialized on her interview transcript. Through the lens of white liberalism, Kluger envisioned two Black political camps, civil rights activists, or "militants," and those he called "conservatives." Not only did he conclude that Williams was "no militant," but he also grossly mischaracterized her political standpoint. Her "attitude," he wrote, "would now have her pegged as an Aunt Jemima."[18] The "minor subtext of African American pathology" in *Simple Justice* is also clear in Kluger's notations of interviews he conducted with Black Topekans.[19] His racial paternalism rendered him unable to appreciate Black politics and practices nonaligned with his narrow definition of civil rights. Mamie Williams was an active member of the Republican Party, who defended her rights as an American citizen and supported equal access. She also championed separate schools because, as an educator, she was a firm believer in racial uplift. Twenty-five years before "Black Power" was articulated, Black Topekans like Williams institutionalized race pride, racial solidarity, and self-determination in segregated schools. But Kluger failed to grasp the nuances of Williams's political philosophies and could not reconcile her opposition to school integration with her racial self-determination. She was "not at all apologetic for her conservative position," he wrote, "yet [had] a clear belief in Black Is Beautiful."[20]

In Kluger's estimation, "conservatives" like Williams threatened to undermine "real" social change enacted by Black "militants." Black political diversity was a diversion from "black America's struggle for equality." Kluger summarily dismissed proponents of all-Black schools as an impediment to racial progress, but their cause was much more complex. The competing interests of Blacks against *Brown* defy his neatly packaged categories. Advocates of all-Black schools were neither "militant" nor "conservative." They prioritized equity over equality in Topeka's public school system because they found agency within the confines of a parallel Jim Crow educational system. But they were also critical of white segregationists. Their political pragmatism reveals an ideological flexibility over the message and method of civil rights activism.

When it came to Topeka's public schools, there was no "simple justice." And yet, Kluger's work continues to be widely acclaimed as the "definitive history" of *Brown v. Board of Education* over forty years after its publication. There is no question that the breadth and depth of Kluger's research and his extraordinary attention to "people at the bottom of the process" was remarkable.[21] But Kluger secreted his discovery of a "hidden transcript" in Topeka's desegregation struggle.[22] His extensive research materials, archived at Yale University, contain interviews he conducted with Black and white Kansans involved in the local case. NAACP members, Black educators, and attorneys on both sides of *Brown* all bore witness to strong antidesegregation mobilization among Black residents. Kluger's work was also heavily reliant on NAACP correspondence, which clearly recorded Black resistance to school integration in Topeka. Kluger deliberately minimized the significance of Blacks against *Brown* by muting their voices and discrediting their concerns. Despite this sin of omission, his story became the history of *Brown v. Board of Education*.

This critical exercise is not intended to cannibalize Richard Kluger or his legacy, but to demonstrate the standardization of a certain type of knowledge about *Brown v. Board of Education*. Kluger is not the only historical observer whose ideological bias affected their conclusions about Black school advocates. Jean Van Delinder's *Struggles before* Brown: *Early Civil Rights Protests and Their Significance Today* (2008) is one of few publications that acknowledged Black opposition to the Topeka NAACP's battle against the board of education. Van Delinder's book draws attention to the regional specificities of civil rights histories by focusing on border states. She argues that scholarship on civil rights has neglected the activism of local change agents in places like Kansas and Oklahoma because of scholars' fixation on social movements, formal organizations, and charismatic male leadership. In situating "Border Campaigns" in contradistinction to the "Master Narrative," Van Delinder attempts a historical corrective. She argues that Black residents in border states engaged in political mobilizations that were smaller in scale because white domination was unevenly enforced. More often than not, their goals were not to dismantle segregation but to create "a better immediate reality" within the boundaries of segregation, she wrote.[23] Their political legacies were not spectacular but were nonetheless significant and worthy of scholarly consideration.

In many ways, *Struggles before* Brown was ideally situated to highlight the plight of Black school preservationists in Topeka. Not only did Van Delinder's thesis speak directly to the motives of Black school advocates, many of whom were women, but she was also one of few researchers who was intimately aware of the local story behind the national case. As a University of Kansas graduate student in the early 1990s, she was part of an oral history project commissioned to record Black Topekans' remembrances of *Brown*. Despite her familiarity with the subject, proponents of all-Black schools were only a brief mention, not a subject of exploration in *Struggles before Brown*.

When studying Blacks against *Brown*, the question is not "can the subaltern speak" but "how are the subaltern are silenced?" Neither Kluger or Van Delinder were African Americanists nor did they benefit from epistemic privilege. Both authors failed to fully appreciate the Afro-pessimism that informed Black Topekans' opposition to school integration. For example, Van Delinder grossly underestimated Black intelligence in her attempt to explain why some African Americans supported separate spaces, concluding that the "value of equal rights" had yet to be recognized prior to the modern civil rights movement. Although she acknowledged that "racial separation" was embraced by some as a form of "black empowerment," she mistakenly indicated that Black separatism mirrored white supremacy.[24] In the end, both Kluger and Van Delinder largely attributed school antidesegregation activities to the economic anxieties of a single group with a singular cause: Black teachers who feared integration would lead to job loss.[25] Kluger even reduced Black teachers' cause to racial insecurities, or as he speculated, an "unspoken fear that they might not measure up in open competition with their white counterparts."[26]

Concern for Black teachers was a motivation but not the only motivation behind Black advocacy of all-Black schools. That is a matter of fact. But the fact of the matter is that these scholars and others were less interested in explicating the complexities of Blackness than they were in telling a tale of a triumph of good over evil. All too often the histories of *Brown v. Board* read much like simplified histories of the Montgomery bus boycott, providing a portrait instead of a panoramic view. Mythical tales of the trials of Rosa Parks and Linda Brown, Black females endangered by segregation, are patriarchal appeals to a collective sense of moral wrong. Despite access to a spectrum of Black political standpoints, scholars like Kluger and Van Delinder missed opportunities to provide meaningful critical analysis of the intra-racial debate over school integration in Topeka. My work seeks to push past racial liberalism, in recognition of W. E. B. Du Bois's 1935 warning about "the perennial difficulty that comes in trying to make a general statement which will cover any such complicated matter as the segregation of races in the United States."[27]

Over eighty years ago Du Bois's "philosophy of race segregation" contended that individual and collective Black subjectivities—deeply influenced by racial geographies—inevitably produce multiple, sometimes contradictory and conflicting, political practices and discourses. Such was the case among Black Topekans in the pre-*Brown* era. Proponents and opponents of school desegregation were not only positioned in opposition to each other but also against white segregationists. In fact, Black school advocates provide an opportunity to explore African American political practices that both collude and collide with white domination. Their opposition to school integrationists was a public stance on behalf of Black children that also aligned with a public stake in whiteness as property. Although their interests converged with the white school board, Black school activists desired internally defined racial separation, not externally imposed racial segregation. They fought to preserve safe, antiracist educational spaces that nurtured the psychosocial and cultural development of Black students.

While historical observers may fail to acknowledge the logic of Black anti-integrationists, there is much to learn from biblical scholar Avaren Ipsen's warning that the only way to "adjudicate conflicting liberation reading is . . . through acceptance of multiple valid liberation readings."[28] This is just as true for the feminist scholars Ipsen challenged in *Sex Working in the Bible* as it is for Black liberation scholars. Advocates for all-Black schools have been wildly misunderstood and grossly underrepresented in the literature on *Brown*. Scholarly misperceptions that the Topeka case, when compared to other *Brown* lawsuits, was "the least eventful in terms of organic grassroots activism" can only be deduced when histories of Black political organizing are skewed toward formal organizations and direct action.[29] Black responses to the strange career of Jim Crow in Topeka represent the very essence of bottom-up organizing, even if they defy scholars' expectations of or desire for Black political uniformity.

Over the past generation, social movement theorists have transformed scholarship on politicized actions and political activism by highlighting the multifaceted, sometimes veiled, ways that the oppressed resist oppression.[30] Marginalized communities create counterpublics to strategize against and around dominant groups. By necessity, that infrapolitics occurs in "free spaces" or "protected spaces," the physical or social sites in marginalized communities that operate outside the view and purview of dominant publics and institutions. In African America, Black churches, Black schools, and the Black press are frequently cited as historical centers of development for racial identity formation, community building, and a politics of resistance. This interpretative framework is critical to understanding the shadow work of Blacks against *Brown*. But the intra-racial conflict over Topeka's segregated schools evidences a need to study how opposing Black political groups inhabited and navigated the same "free social spaces." Although scholars acknowledge that marginalized communities use protected spaces to deliberate discontent and dissent, many fall short of examining what happens in these places when conflicting viewpoints fail to end in compromise or consensus.

Multiple Black counterpublics existed in Topeka, but their visibility to outsiders was relative and relational. When it came to resistance for and against separate schools, sites that typically operated as organizational bases became contested spaces. Black school advocates and school desegregationists were members of the same churches, so Black ministers were unwilling to risk alienating their congregations by taking a political stance. Black school preservationists and desegregationists commingled in civic organizations and social networks. They lived in the same neighborhoods. Black schools were critical spaces of political mobilization in other Black communities, but in Topeka they were off-limits for opponents and too risky for proponents. Black educators were vulnerable to the retaliation of a segregationist superintendent and his Black overseer, despite their interest convergence.

Consequently, Black school advocates' interventions in the conflict between the NAACP and the Topeka school board were intentionally executed under the proverbial radar. And yet, traditional forms of political dissent were not necessary for these Black dissidents. Defenders of all-Black schools deployed horizontal weapons of resistance aimed at their dominant threat, not the dominant group. This "subterranean world of political conflict" was dominated by women who were mothers and teachers, so most attempts at resolution occurred in the social arena.[31] Lobbying, informal or "submerged" networking, and other covert forms of mobilization were powerful tools at their disposal, alongside retributive justice like social ostracism, verbal threats, vandalism, and harassing mail and phone calls.[32] These "nonheroic" gendered forms of racial resistance can be elusive to researchers using traditional methods and theoretical frameworks.[33]

By contrast, the civil disobedience of the Topeka NAACP is legible because of their direct engagement of dominant publics, as evidenced in archived correspondence, petitions, school board minutes, newspaper articles, and oral histories. And yet, their presence in the dominant public sphere was disproportionate to their influence in the subaltern. Black residents' strong sympathies for Black teachers and commitment to Black schools prevented the local NAACP from gaining political legitimacy or moral authority in "local movement centers."[34] In fact, the issue of segregated schools was so contentious in the city's Black communities that the Topeka NAACP avoided addressing it from 1941 to 1947. Faced with formidable Black opposition and a dismissive white school board, local NAACP members appealed to the national office, which already had its sights on the US Supreme Court. Aligning with the vision of the national NAACP enabled the Topeka branch not only to transcend subaltern political struggles but also to launch their local crusade to the national stage.

The Topeka NAACP was privileged in the historical moment and, in turn, through historical memorializing. Black anti-integrationists may have been written out of scholarship on the landmark case, but their contemporaries in the NAACP knew they were a force with which to be reckoned. Ironically, their testimonies and Richard Kluger's research materials were critical for recovering the story of Blacks against *Brown*. Despite Kluger's partialities, his extensive interview notes archived in the Brown vs. Board of Education Collection at Yale University were a valuable resource for unveiling the "hidden transcript" of Black supporters of all-Black schools. This infrapolitics is also evident in the Brown v. Board of Education Oral History Collection at the Kansas State Historical Society. This oral history project recorded the memories of local residents who were connected to the *Brown* case, including NAACP members, Black educators, Black community members, and attorneys on both sides of *Brown*, many of whom bore witness to antidesegregation mobilization.

Blacks against *Brown*: An Overview

My historical resurrection of Blacks against *Brown* begins with a racial geography of the state of Kansas and the city of Topeka. The logic and logistics of Blacks against *Brown* are best understood when situated within the peculiar institution of the state's anti-Black racism. Although official state histories fetishize the militant abolitionist John Brown, anti-Black racism was codified in local and state laws. Chapter 1, "Over John Brown's Dead Body: White Supremacy and White Liberalism in Kansas," explicates the dissonance between the racial ideals and the racist practices of white Kansans. Despite their mythologies of white exceptionalism, white Topekans privileged whiteness through real estate policies and practices, employment restrictions, segregated public spaces, and schools and social conventions. The end of the chapter surveys Black Topekans' experiences with variable forms of racial discrimination during the early-to-mid twentieth century.

The second chapter continues to expose contradictions between official narratives and state laws by focusing on educational policies and practices.

"The Alchemy of Race and Rights: Separate but Equal in Topeka Public Schools" examines the discursive and material practices of race-making through school segregation during the early-to-mid twentieth century. It begins with a comparative and relational study of the city's Black and "Mexican" elementary schools. The school board's differential racialization of people of African and Mexican descent provides both a panorama of Topeka's racial geography and a telescopic view into the social location of Blacks in the city. This chapter not only questions how race was inscribed on the bodies of "others" but also begins to examine how Black Topekans internalized and rejected those "racial scripts."[35] The chapter concludes by mapping Black residents' resistance to segregated schools in Tennessee Town, a neighborhood originally settled by Exodusters that became home to a self-described "better class of colored people."[36] A close inspection of Black school integrationists reveals intra-racial formations within Topeka's Black community along lines of class and color.

While chapter 2 discusses the routes of antisegregation school activism, chapter 3 examines the roots of anti-integration school activism. "Reading, Ri(gh)ting, and Resistance: Racial Uplift Ideologies and Practices in Topeka's All-Black Schools" contextualizes Black opposition to school desegregation by focusing on the infrastructure and infrapolitics of the city's all-Black schools. Whites established Jim Crow schools for socialization into subordination, but Topeka's segregated schools functioned as crucial spaces for resistance to anti-Black racism.[37] Black educators and administrators were producers of situated knowledges and conduits for Black emancipatory projects. Chapter 3 surveys the mission, pedagogy, and curriculum of Black teachers to evidence Black schools' centrality to Black racial formations. One of the "unintended consequences"[38] of school segregation in Topeka was the creation of semiautonomous Black educational institutions with an explicit racial agenda: "Through education we rise."[39]

Chapter 4, "*Graham v. Board* and the Clash of the Black Counterpublics, 1941 to 1948," documents the historical moment Black residents were forced to confront the question of race and rights in Topeka public schools. In 1941 the family of a twelve-year-old Buchanan Elementary School student successfully challenged the constitutionality of the city's segregated junior high schools in *Graham v. Board of Education*. Although historical observers memorialize the Kansas Supreme Court case as a sign of racial progress, the *Graham* lawsuit and its aftermath revealed Black Topekans' legitimate, yet divergent, definitions of educational justice. This chapter chronicles the period between 1941 and 1948, when subterranean tensions among Black Topekans over all-Black schools erupted into the public domain. The political drama between Black school preservationists and school desegregationists played out before the Kansas Supreme Court, in school board meetings, and in the Black press.

Chapter 5 introduces a little known but pivotal character in the story of Blacks against *Brown*. "Harrison Caldwell: The Unsung Black Antihero of *Brown*" outlines the contributions of the city's director of colored schools. *Brown* architects McKinley Burnett, Daniel Sawyer, and Lucinda Todd identified Harrison Caldwell as the instigator of the breakthrough civil rights moment of the late 1940s. This chapter interrogates how a Black man became the antihero in the *Brown* story and questions how one of the most critical catalysts for the city's desegregation campaign has been virtually absented in the narrativizing of the *Brown* backstory.

"Blacks against *Brown*: The Final Chapter, 1948–1954" details the beginning of the end of Topeka's segregated schools. Building on historian Vanessa Siddle Walker's body of work, this chapter intervenes on the scholarship concerning Black teachers and Black school activism during the Jim Crow era.[40] *Brown* scholars' fixation on the NAACP has effectively erased Black teachers' struggles for educational equality. But Black teachers and their allies were central to the local story of *Brown*. Chapter 6 highlights the public crusades and political strategies of these Black Topekans. It situates Black school preservationists as freedom fighters and their shadow work as a legitimate struggle for educational justice. Their "submerged" networking and acts of social retribution made it virtually impossible for the Topeka NAACP to get community support for its case against the Topeka school board. By broadening the conversation from a singular focus on civil rights activism to alternative forms of political advocacy, chapter 6 attempts to create more inclusive definitions of racial justice and education.

Black Topekans' battle over all-Black schools was only resolved after outside intervention by the national NAACP and the US Supreme Court. The conclusion of *Blacks against* Brown assesses the local consequences of the historic Supreme Court decision. Despite the best efforts of Black preservationists, history was not on their side. And yet, their predictions about the impact of integration on Black students and teachers were accurate. Chapter 6 bears witness to the desegregation experiences of Black students and teachers during the 1950s and '60s. It concludes with reflections on the lessons and legacies of Blacks against *Brown*.

CHAPTER ONE

Over John Brown's Dead Body
White Supremacy and White Liberalism in Kansas

As news spread throughout the state of Kansas in 1953 that a Topeka school was named in a segregation case to be heard by the Supreme Court, white public officials responded in a manner that could be described as collective shame. That sentiment was summed up in an oft-cited letter written to Governor Edward Arn in 1953. "I am surprised and I must say chagrined to learn that Kansas now classifies itself as one of the White Supremacy states as indicated by the case now before the United States Supreme Court," wrote Augusta, Kansas, school superintendent H. H. Robinson. "As I review those historical events which caused us to be called 'bleeding Kansas,' I wonder how we suddenly find ourselves represented before the Supreme Court opposed to those human rights for which our early settlers bled."[1]

Scholarly writings about the local *Brown* lawsuit use Robinson's letter to highlight white Kansans' contempt of court proceedings.[2] Within his literary protest lies the key to understanding the constitutive process of and discursive approach to whiteness in Kansas. Dating back to the period of statehood, white officials carefully cultivated an image of racial liberalism, replete with stories of a famous militant abolitionist, Jayhawkers, and "Bleeding Kansas." White racial formation in Kansas was dependent upon a distancing, both real and imagined, from the "White Supremacy" states of the American South. But the *Brown* case exposed an uncomfortable truth: in the "Free State," an uneasy but undeniable combination of white liberalism and white supremacy developed over John Brown's dead body.

This chapter calls into question white Kansans' commemorative race-making and reveals contradictions between white racial phantasms and Black racial realities. The Black movement against school integration in Topeka is unintelligible without understanding the peculiar institution of anti-Black racism in Kansas, a state that simultaneously celebrated its abolitionist roots *and* preserved racial apartheid. Black Topekans on both sides of the public school debate experienced the (dis)advantages of these conflicting visions and versions of whiteness. This chapter bears witness to how racial geographies inform racial resistance.

Critical geographers of race have made significant contributions to scholarly understandings of the coconstitutive process of race and place, but much of that discussion focuses on minoritized populations.[3] The study of racial formation in Kansas provides an opportunity to de-essentialize and visibilize whiteness, a racial category that is often un- or underexamined by scholars outside of whiteness studies. The intent of this chapter is not to rewrite Kansas state history or Black histories in the state of Kansas, but to reframe those historical narratives using critical race theory and methodologies. It contextualizes local Black freedom struggles by analyzing white scripts and Black proscriptions in the land of John Brown.

The White Man's Burden: White Racial Formation during the Territorial Period

The ontology of whiteness in Kansas is intimately tied to the history of white settlement. The territorial dispute following the Kansas-Nebraska Act of 1854 dominates scholarship written about Kansas state history, but little attention is paid to how that conflict shaped emergent discourses of whiteness. Although a semidiverse group of whites were drawn to Kansas Territory, official state histories reduce multiplicity to a duality: proslavery and antislavery militants. The repeal of the Missouri Compromise meant that white settlers would determine Blacks' fate, sparking an intra-racial battle that foreshadowed the Civil War. As "North" and "South" clashed in the West, white male subjectivities pivoted on the limits of Black objectification. Consequently, the "sociospatial elaboration" of whiteness in "Bleeding Kansas" was not rooted in white distancing from Black bodies but in white men's divisiveness over Black bodies.

Whereas the relational subjectivity of whiteness is usually situated against the projection of a racialized other, in Kansas the "axes of negation" are race *and* region.[4] As many Kansas historians have noted, white supremacy in the state was defined not only against Blackness but also against "Southern" whiteness. For Northern settlers of Kansas, "the South" was an imagined community that did not account for the diverse and varied structures and symbols of whiteness in American slave states. During and after the internecine territorial conflict, "a vigorous, aggressive minority" associated with the New England Emigrant Aid Society rose to power.[5] This group of Northern abolitionists influenced white racial formations in Kansas in a manner that was disproportionate to their numbers. As a result, the "zero-point of [white] orientation" in Kansas bears the imprint of white Anglo-Saxon

Protestantism, a racial-ethnic ideal bound by virtue and reason, conscience and morality, and respectability and responsibility.[6]

Historical writing on the territorial period reflects this WASP-inspired racial subjectivity and political standpoint, evolving into what historian Brent M. S. Campney called the "Free State Narrative."[7] The tale of "Bleeding Kansas" becomes a racial allegory of "good whites versus bad whites," a story of the abolitionist antiracist "self" who triumphs over the racist proslavery other. "Free Staters" were "men of principle," the "moral heroes" whose antislavery militance was governed by benevolence and gentility. By contrast, proslavery white Missourians were deemed guilty by Southern association. Defined by "fiendish rage and savage cruelty," their racial deviance is indicated by the label "Border Ruffians."[8] This dichotomous framing of the state's origin story reveals much about white normativity in Kansas. It is the phenomenological structure of whiteness, the "relationship to place and to placement," that became habitual knowledge through generations of discursive repetition.[9]

This not-South/not-racist relational racial subjectivity was the inheritance of white Kansans who had an existential crisis over *Brown.* Augusta school superintendent H. H. Robinson was one among many white Kansans who censured state officials for "throwing the influence of our state against those principles for which we have always stood."[10] And an oft-cited *St. Louis Post-Dispatch* editorial reprinted by the Topeka *Daily Capital* in 1953 asked, "Why Kansas?" An unidentified writer wondered why a state founded "on the belief in equal rights" would appear before the Supreme Court alongside states that "are Southern in outlook . . . and all practice racial segregation by law." Like Robinson, the editorial chastised state officials who were defending a practice most past and present Kansans would oppose.[11] A year later, a small-town journalist held Kansas state attorney general Harold Fatzer personally accountable for sullying the reputation of the state. "If Topeka, or any other community, wants segregation, let them look out for themselves," wrote F. J. Cloud of Kingman. "You know—or should know—that your action was contrary to the sentiment of a vast majority of Kansas and exposed the state to unjustifiable ridicule."[12]

White Kansans' resistance to defending a seventy-five-year-old state law before the US Supreme Court reflected an epistemological framing of whiteness that was unique to Kansas. A new generation of historians like Brent M. S. Campney, Nicole Etchison, and Kristen Tegtmeier Oertel have critically examined the metanarrative of anti-Black white radicalism that obscured whites' execution of anti-Black racism in Kansas.[13] The dissonance between discursive formations of whiteness in Kansas and the institutionalization of anti-Blackness originated during the territorial period. Abolitionists prevailed and the Border Ruffians failed, but both shared a belief in white supremacy and white domination.[14] Antislavery sentiments and anti-Black antipathies coexisted in many states, a fact confirmed by the histories of abolition and racist exclusion in Ohio and Oregon.[15] In Kansas, Free-Soilers also wanted a "Free State"—that is, a state without slavery and without Blacks. "We never fancied the idea of having free Negroes colonized among us," a white citizen wrote to the *White Cloud Kansas Chief* in 1861. Within months of the outbreak of the Civil War, the author bemoaned the migration of fugitive and freed slaves from Missouri to Kansas. "Wherever our armies march, we trust they will leave the traitors niggerless."[16] Exclusionist opinions and practices were passed down from generation to generation and were most apparent in southern and western Kansas, where some Black Topekans recalled local whites issuing the warning "don't let the sun catch you here."[17]

The Whims of Whiteness: Codifying Black Rights and Anti-Black Racism after Statehood

The diverse and divergent ideologies of white domination that were pervasive during the territorial period were also present within the legislative record of early statehood. White legislators' negotiation of the sociospatial situatedness of whiteness is evident in the persistent conflict over the limits of whites' rights over Black bodies. Early laws protecting and restricting Blacks' civil rights vacillated, reflecting whites' reservations about Blacks' presence. During the Wyandotte Convention of 1859, delegates were evenly divided over a constitutional ban of Blacks from the state's public institutions. In the end, the measure was defeated by one vote. While some of the state's settlers believed in racial equality, most Free-Soilers extended certain rights to Blacks to maintain political power over their adversaries, not because they were antiracist.[18] Nevertheless Kansas was comparably favorable toward its Black citizens. State law, more often than not, established formal equality for African Americans. White Kansans did not resist granting Black residents the right to vote after the ratification of the Fifteenth Amendment in 1870. The Kansas state legislature voted to allow Blacks to serve on juries in 1874. And ten months before the federal government passed the Civil Rights Act of 1875, the Kansas legislature enacted a civil rights statute that prohibited racial discrimination in public accommodations that required municipal licenses. This statute made it illegal to "make any distinction on account of race, color or previous condition of servitude" in primary and secondary schools, state colleges and universities, places of lodging, and places of "entertainment and amusement" as well as public transportation.[19]

These political promises are noteworthy. Black Kansans benefited from legal recognition denied their counterparts in other parts of the country, even if they were subject to the whims of whiteness. The boundedness of Blackness fluctuated because of white conflict over the boundaries of Black social and spatial imaginaries. The contradictory congressional activity of 1867 provides a prime example. State legislators endorsed Blacks' civil rights by ratifying the Fourteenth Amendment and then restricted those rights by passing a law that permitted school segregation in the state's smaller cities. In the same session, lawmakers extended equal protection to Black students by levying fines and threatening to imprison local school boards that denied Blacks access to public education.

The instability of Blacks' civil rights was a product of empowered whites' divergent political subjectivities. For example, the same year that voting rights were conferred to Black men, a group of legislators set out to disrupt an already tenuous racial infrastructure. Using a familiar trope of benevolent whiteness, segregationists introduced a bill to mandate Jim Crow schools. They argued that separate schools were in the best interest of Black schoolchildren because Black students in integrated schools would inevitably be exposed to racial discrimination. In advocating for the proposed legislation, a subcommittee issued a dismal warning: integration could provoke a statewide collapse of the public education system. "It is a notorious fact that in many districts of the State, the public schools have been broken up and discontinued the moment that an attempt was made to force colored children into such schools with white children, and that in such districts the schools have been discontinued entirely, or replaced by subscription schools."[20] The subcommittee's polite articulation of institutional violence masked the aggression involved in a threat of white withdrawal from public schools. Although this bill was eventually defeated, the mass migration of Black bodies across state lines in 1877 ushered in a new era for public education. During the Exodusters movement, state legislators amended the Kansas school code and legalized all-white schools in cities of the "first class," or those with populations of 15,000 or more.

Even though white officials waffled over Black containment and exclusion, the option was theirs to exercise. The flexibility of white power demonstrates the "ethos of dominion" that is integral to whiteness, even in the absence of a history of enslavement. It is "the sense of unchecked proprietorship

W. E. B. DuBois locates in the very 'souls' of white people."[21] Despite a constant unresolved ambivalence toward Black circumscription, Blackness in Kansas, like elsewhere in the country, was created and maintained through its subordination to whiteness. Debates over school integration reveal the true historical legacy of "Bleeding Kansas." The birthright of white Kansans' is not racial enlightenment but an internal conflict over the limits of Black freedom. From the post–Civil War period to the post–World War II period, state and city legislators advocated both civil rights and racial segregation because they favored political equality over social equality. The social location of Blacks was a persistent dilemma for many whites. Debates over antimiscegenation bills in 1913 and 1916 demonstrate how white Kansans' commitment to racial justice was complicated by a steadfast belief in white supremacy, even though those bills were eventually defeated. From the mid-nineteenth century throughout the twentieth century, the driving force behind white Kansans' politics of ambivalence was a racialized dynamic George Lipsitz called the "possessive investment in whiteness."[22]

White over Non-Black: Disrupting the Myth of Benevolent Whiteness, 1830–1930

Despite its abolitionist roots, white domination and a culture of white supremacy were an integral part of the racial landscape in Kansas. Settler-colonial discourse frames the state's origin story as a dispute between whites over Blacks, but it obscures the displacement of Indigenous peoples by whites. The geographical area originally inhabited by the Kansa, Osage, Pawnee, and Wichita became a destination for tribes directly impacted by the 1830 Indian Removal Act. Less than a generation later, the federal government forcibly removed most of these emigrant tribes when it opened Kansas Territory for white settlement in 1854. Whites' battle over "free soil" was costly for Native American inhabitants, who rarely appear in historical accounts of "Bloody Kansas." Despite that historiographical omission, the 1838 Potawatomi Trail of Death shares more than geography with the 1856 Pottawatomie Massacre of proslavery whites by "Osawatomie" Brown. The irony of whites' appeals for "popular sovereignty" is that squatters' struggle over slavery was made possible by local and federal dispossession of Native people. So contrary to state mythology, the history of Kansas was not driven by a racially enlightened white citizenry but by white settlers who were unapologetic for and unequivocal in their possessive investment in whiteness, particularly in relation to non-Black people of color.[23]

The Free State narrative did not protect nonwhite/not-Blacks from the blunt force of institutional violence. The incongruities between whiteness-as-concept and whiteness-in-practice in Kansas are further signified by the racialization of Mexican immigrants. While the sociospatial making and marking of "Indians" was effectuated, in part, through assimilation, extermination, and relocation policies, for "Mexicans" that constitutive process included assimilation, segregation, and repatriation. During the first three decades of the twentieth century, Mexican immigration to the state grew alongside the need for railroad, agricultural, and industrial laborers. In fact, Kansas had the nation's seventh-largest population of people of Mexican descent by 1930.[24] Over 40 percent of those residents were American-born, but citizenship did not protect them from the spike in anti-immigrant resentments that resulted from economic crises in the 1920s. During the summer of 1921 white demands for repatriation led to the forcible removal of approximately 2,300 residents of Mexican descent from Topeka and Kansas City.[25] After the crash of 1929, white demands for Mexican expulsions intensified once again. So in 1930 Kansas senator Henry J. Allen capitalized upon the wages of whiteness, lobbying railroad companies to "dismiss Mexican aliens" for the sake of struggling white workers and campaigning to impose legal restrictions on Mexican immigration.[26] A spike in anti-"Mexican" sentiment during the 1930s was the catalyst for another wave of mass deportations from Kansas, during which the state reportedly lost almost half its residents of Mexican descent.

Mexican immigrants weren't the only newcomers targeted by white legislators during the 1920s and '30s. As anti-Asian antipathies heightened in other western states like California, the Kansas state legislature passed its own alien land laws. Even though there were few Asian immigrants in the Plains state, Asians were banned from owning land in 1925. Eight years later, that law was amended to prohibit people of Asian descent from inheriting land.

These racial violations against people of Indigenous, Asian, and Latinx descent are obscured by a collective imagining of "benevolent" whiteness that pivots on degrees of anti-Blackness. The metanarrative of white racial liberalism privileges a narrow, albeit existent, advocacy for Blacks' civil rights that also marginalizes histories of anti-Black racism. As previously stated, the relational racial formation of whiteness in Kansas was contingent not only upon Blackness but also upon a demonized and mythologized white "South." But this comparison is counterfactual. Whites in Kansas also benefitted from exclusive access to all-white schools, restaurants, movie theaters, lodging, and swimming pools. Despite these significant similarities, anti-Black racism in much of Kansas evolved in ways that were more Northern than Southern in both style and substance. The ontology and epistemology of whiteness—that is, the emergence of whiteness as a mode of being, seeing, and doing—was predicated upon Northern abolitionists' nonviolent white racial imaginary during the territorial period. While antislavery militants viewed their use of violence as situational, they deemed it an "invariable and fixed property" of Southern whiteness.[27] Consequently racial hierarchies in the state were not maintained by violence (or the threat of violence), and interracial interactions were informed more by code of civility than a code of chivalry. "Blacks and whites moved about in deceiving air, seeming to avoid any sort of relationship that might somehow damage their pride," wrote native son and famed Black artist Gordon Parks.[28]

White Souls Undressed: The Emergence and Evolution of Normative Whiteness in Topeka

The capital city of Kansas was founded in 1854 as a Free State town by antislavery advocates, many of whom were members of the Massachusetts Emigrant Aid Society. As such, Topeka enjoyed a favorable reputation among African Americans during the antebellum and postbellum periods. Before the Civil War, the city's rural Highland Park area housed an Underground Railroad station. During Reconstruction, Topeka was the site of the Kansas Freedman's Relief Association. Consequently, the city attracted the attention of Benjamin "Pap" Singleton and other Exodusters who migrated to Kansas in response to Southern redemption. Although many Kansans, regardless of race, expressed concerns about the thousands of poor Black Southerners crossing into the state in 1879, the Topeka *Colored Citizen* welcomed them. "If they come here and starve, all well," the writer stated. "It is better to starve to death in Kansas than be shot and killed in the South."[29]

The author's juxtaposition of deprivation and death was a critical distinction for Southern Black migrants, because the execution of anti-Blackness in Topeka did not depend upon racial terrorism. The performance and production of normative whiteness derived from the white Anglo-Saxon Protestantism of its New England founders. Violence was a consequence of passion, and passion was antithetical to a version/vision of whiteness that valued respectability, responsibility, and antisensuality. Brent Campney's 2013 article about the 1889 hanging of a white transient provides insight into how normative whiteness in Topeka was negotiated and re/iterated vis-à-vis violence. The mob lynching of Nat Oliphant was retributive justice meted out against the alleged murderer of a man and attempted murder of his wife. The spectacle of violence was deemed uncharacteristic for a community the *Topeka State Journal* described as "generally conservative, seldom excitable and generally slow to act."[30] While support for the vigilantes was widespread, some of the "best citizens" began to express regret over the incident once news about the "disgraceful" event spread throughout the region. The local press was univocal in its condemnation. An "aroused" populace threatened not only the state's reputation but also dominant cultural values. Lynching was "not in harmony with later civilization and self control," the *Topeka Daily Capital* editorialized. "It is something left over from barbarism."[31]

According to Campney, the spontaneous collective act of violence that led to the death of Nat Oliphant confirms that normative whiteness in Topeka was not stable but contested, transgressed, and negotiated by marginalized whites. The hanging of Oliphant became a cautionary tale for white Kansans, a dangerous deviation from the discursive and material practices of whiteness inherited from the territorial period. In its aftermath, public officials and law enforcement successfully conspired to intervene in mob violence, in part, because it did not reflect the desired racial/cultural ethos of the dominant class. Their efforts were largely successful. Collective and individual violence were rarely used as forms of social control in Topeka, even when the target was Black. The virtual absence of mob violence was significant not only to Black residents but also to empowered whites who imagined that "the problem of race" was something that happened elsewhere. "Race feeling has not been acute in Topeka at any time," the *Topeka Daily Capital* concluded in 1919 during the rash of racial terrorism known as "Red Summer." "On the whole we may say that the colored race has been more fairly treated in Topeka than in most places."[32]

Although white overseers of exclusive spaces did not need threats or intimidation to protect the property in whiteness, it was always an option. In the summer of 1933, Black residents met white resistance at city parks informally prohibited to nonwhites. NAACP attorney Raymond Reynolds told a local journalist that police officers twice responded to interracial disturbances by "mistreating and embarrassing the colored citizens of this community."[33] An attorney for the City of Topeka acknowledged that the unofficial segregationist policy violated Blacks' constitutional rights, but the city's park commissioner Harry Snyder was resolute. He would not concede Blacks' presence at parks reserved for white residents. The *Topeka Daily Capital* summarized the segregationist park commissioner's combative stance in the title of a June 1933 article: "May Close City Parks to Avert Race Trouble Com. Snyder Says Negroes Threaten to Invade all Parks." Harry Snyder used a militant tone to assure white readers that he would not tolerate the integration of public recreational spaces. "I may not be able to order Negroes out, but I can keep everyone out," he threatened. Snyder then warned Black protestors that he would not surrender to political pressure. "My enemies believe they can 'put me on the spot' in this manner, but they don't know me."[34]

Snyder's impassioned anti-Blackness deviated from conventional performances of whiteness in Topeka. But he was an equal opportunity offender who also had a reputation among white residents for his tyrannical rule over the city's parks.[35] The mayor's comments on the park controversy were more representative of the constant unresolved tension between performances of whiteness and the privileging of whiteness in Topeka. In an interview with the *Topeka Daily Capital*, Omar B. Ketchum simultaneously acknowledged Black residents' civil rights and white residents' birthrights. "I recognize the right of the colored citizens of Topeka to the free use of the public parks and cannot deny them that privilege," he equivocated. "I also recognize that public opinion is the power behind all laws and regulations and it must be taken into consideration."[36] Despite differences in tone, both Snyder and Ketchum communicated a commitment to protecting the wages of whiteness. In a manner that echoed the *Dred Scott v. Sanford* ruling, empowered white Topekans relied on the widespread belief that the descendants of American slaves had "no rights which the white man was bound to respect." Or as Black resident William Mitchell Sr. succinctly stated, "White folks do what they want to do."

Despite these exceptions, there was some degree of alignment between whiteness-as-concept and whiteness-in-practice with respect to anti-Black violence in Topeka. When observed through a relational lens, anti-Blackness in Topeka could be illusory, especially for those who were not familiar with its peculiarities or particularities. That was intentional, for the performance of benevolent whiteness obscured the practice of white supremacy, even in glaring instances of discrimination. The national NAACP's response to the city's decision to enforce segregation in public parks in 1933 is a primary example. Despite Black residents' reports of police harassment and intimidation, NAACP assistant secretary Roy Wilkins wrote to the *Topeka Daily Capital*, "Topeka has been free of bitterness between the races and enjoys a tradition of fair play and equality."[37] For an outsider looking in, anti-Black racism in the capital city may have appeared to be a benign institution. "Topeka is a town that has a very strong, at least surface, friendliness to it," observed Chris Hansen, a white American Civil Liberties Union (ACLU) lawyer who represented the plaintiffs in *Brown III*. "I've never seen outspoken sort of raw ugly racism in Topeka. But it's there and it's hidden below the friendliness."[38]

As Hansen intimated, white civility and anti-Black racism were interdependent in Topeka. Take, for example, one Black resident's story of his junior high school tennis team tryouts in 1965. After winning his final match, the young athlete felt confident that he had earned a spot on the team. But instead of affirming the student's performance on the court, the white tennis coach told him that most competitions were held at the Topeka Country Club, so he needed his parents' permission to join the team. The Black teen excitedly ran home to relay the message to his mother. "Can I be on the tennis team?" he asked. "Boy you didn't make the team," she responded. "They don't let Negroes play at the country club!"[39]

This story is a microcosm of how a property in whiteness was protected by white Topekans. While state law protected the Black student's right to try out for the tennis team, local custom prevented him from competing on the team. When the young student naively crossed a racial boundary, the tennis coach did not confront or censure him. Because the legacy of whiteness in Topeka was WASP in nurture, the coach's defense mechanism was passive racial transgression. He allowed the teen to complete his tryout but then sent the student home with a coded message. By deferring disclosure to the student's mother, the coach was able to simultaneously evade an impolite conversation about racial restrictions and avoid accountability for racialized harm. A decade after the Supreme Court decision in *Brown*, Gordon Parks's writings about the double bind of Blackness in Kansas still rang true. "Here, for the black man, freedom loosed one hand while custom restrained the other."[40]

Behind the Veil: White Civility and Black Refusal in Topeka, 1910–1950s

Through experience and socialization, Black Topekans learned to tolerate and transgress a color line that was somewhat flexible and not always transparent. Their interface with white domination may not have required strict dissemblance, but their navigation of the "Souls of White Folk" involved a self-preservative dance. Black insiders could see what many outsiders did not, a fact that attests to W. E. B. Du Bois's theorizations on the clairvoyance that is forged through racism.[41] This epistemic privilege is reflected in the testimonies of Black residents like Lena Burnett. The wife of civil rights activist McKinley Burnett estimated that Black families "coming from the South" were "perhaps better off than they had ever been." But the Burnetts were native Kansans who moved to Topeka in 1922 from a small town just east of the city. Lena found white Topekans "patronizing" and was under no illusions about their intention to "keep [Blacks] in their places."[42] Black Topekans' ability to see white "souls undressed" was also evidenced in William Mitchell Sr.'s admonition to his son during the mid-1920s. William Mitchell Jr. attended his neighborhood school for a year before he was suddenly and inexplicably transferred to an all-Black school. When he asked his father for an explanation, the elder Mitchell answered plainly. "I don't know. White folks do what they want to do."[43]

William Mitchell Sr.'s matter-of-fact recognition of and resignation to white power is an antecedent of Afro-pessimism, a reminder to scholars that the dehumanizing force of anti-Blackness is an invitation "to think . . . about the position of the exslave without recourse to the consolation of transcendence."[44] The performance of white civility did not mitigate the "social death" inherent in white supremacy.[45] Blackness was a state of beingless-ness, a fact confirmed by the stories of white-passing Black Topekans. For these fair-skinned Blacks, the property line between whiteness and Blackness was drawn not by color but by the legacy of enslavement.

The phenotypical presentation of McKinley Burnett's family simultaneously disrupted myths of racial transparency and affirmed Black racialization. US census takers classified Lena as "white" in 1940, and *Simple Justice* author Richard Kluger was color struck by her proximity to whiteness in 1970. He wrote that she "could pass for white but instead gives off the most militant noises."[46] Kluger's manuscript notes situated Lena's corporeality against her consciousness, but naivete was not a luxury fair-skinned African Americans could afford. Degrees of lightness did not confer the privileges of whiteness. For example, when McKinley Burnett defiantly applied for a deliveryman position at a local bakery, the manager was frank. "He told me that he could not hire a Negro for such a job." Not only had the bakery never considered hiring a Black employee, but it had also never had a Black applicant before Burnett.[47]

Burnett's children also found that the burden of anti-Blackness operated independently from the spectacle of Blackness. His oldest daughter Maurita was hired, then abruptly fired, at Hallmark Cards in the mid-1940s because her interviewer mistook her for white. The breach of protocol was exposed when another Black woman called inquiring about a job after hearing about

Burnett's employment at the company. The company's investigation into Burnett's records found that she had attended segregated Monroe Elementary School. "They told me they were sorry," Maurita Davis remembered. But the policy was clear. "We cannot hire you, because we don't hire Negroes at Hallmark." Incensed, Davis called the white woman's attention to the absurdity of hypodescent. "I'm just as white as you, so what difference does it make?" But Davis understood her pigment was a figment in the racist imagination. "It made a difference, and I could not work anymore."[48]

Like the Burnetts, other fair-skinned Black Topekans who crossed the color line were quickly reminded of the city's racial boundaries. As a grade-schooler during the 1920s, William Mitchell Jr. and his younger brother went to the "white show" to see the movies. As he recalled, "A show was a show to me." Unaware of the city's de facto segregation, the Mitchell brothers unwittingly passed for white for six weeks. When an employee finally inquired about their "nationality," the boys told the truth. Mitchell remembered the young white man seemed apologetic when he turned them away. "We are sorry," he said. "We think you've got the wrong theater." After the employee corrected the boys' apparent mistake, he directed them toward the all-Black theater. Mitchell's memory of the exchange was pleasant, not punitive. "They were very nice to tell me what I was supposed to do." Although introduced to advantages of passing at an early age, Mitchell never experimented with its possibilities. "When I found out I was supposed to go where the colored people were at, that's where I went."[49]

Anti-Black racism in Topeka may not have been identified as Jim Crow in name, but it was Jim Crow in function. Black resident Barbara Gibson was born in Topeka in 1925. "It was awfully strange what happened in Topeka," she explained. "Topeka always had a permissive law."[50] The impression of flexibility was facilitated by state laws that provided Blacks with certain civil rights protections. But the 1933 park controversy is one of many examples of how easily local whites could evade state directives because whiteness, by its very nature, is predicated upon racial differentiation. The facade of benevolent whiteness was undermined by the fact that racial segregation in public accommodations was standard practice in the capital city. Not only were people of African and Mexican descent segregated in parks but also in swimming pools, movie theaters, and some forms of transportation. They were also barred from many restaurants, stores, and hotels. Richard Ridley returned from a stint in the Air Force in 1953 with a stark realization. "I remember coming home as a first lieutenant with $1,000 in my pocket and I couldn't eat on Kansas Avenue."[51] A few residents spoke of signs that directed

Blacks, and sometimes "Mexicans," to be served in sacks at some eating establishments.[52] "That hurt just reading those signs," Mexican American resident Ed Rangel recalled.[53] But by most accounts, segregation in public spaces was maintained through custom. "We just more or less knew and understood what we could do and what we couldn't do and went by those guidelines," explained Claude Emerson.[54]

Dissemblance may have characterized some Blacks' response to strict racial apartheid in many parts of the Deep South, but as Emerson indicates, Black Topekans' reactions to anti-Black racism varied because white domination in the capital city was more discreet and variable. Maurita Davis believed that a "more subtle" style of racism lulled Black Topekans into a sense of complacency. "That's one reason why in the South I think they made more progress than we did up here, because they told you right out what you couldn't do."[55] While not a wholly accurate assessment of regional differences, Davis's assumption is shared by some historians.[56] However the linearity of Davis's argument was correct: A symbiotic relationship between white domination and Black resistance is quite evident in Topeka. White Topekans' dissimulative approach to white supremacy influenced the multitude of ways that Blacks responded to anti-Black racism.

Blacks' historical memories of Jim Crow in Topeka were dissonant because their experiences with individual and institutional racism were inconsistent. Yet despite their disparate impressions of white supremacy in the capital city, quotidian resistance is evident even when collective action was sparse and sporadic. For example, Lucinda Todd and McKinley Burnett challenged the racist policies of Topeka theaters, not as NAACP members but as private citizens. In the mid-1940s Topeka police escorted Todd out of the Grand Theater at gunpoint. She had refused to move from the space reserved for whites because the segregated section was at capacity. "They made me leave, but the theater gave me my money back," she declared with pride.[57] Burnett's method of protest was more indirect than Todd's. He forbade his children from patronizing local theaters because he opposed separate seating policies. "My father resented that and he did not want us to go," recalled his daughter Maurita.[58]

Burnett's willful, but covert, evasion of white supremacy points to the "subterranean world of political conflict" that animates political scientist James C. Scott's body of scholarly work. It is a strategy of resistance that "left scarcely a trace in the public record."[59] The practice of refusal was a viable alternative to direct or collective action. Burnett and his daughter protested the imposition of white power in their day-to-day lives when they knowingly applied for employment exclusively reserved for whites without denying their Blackness. Although passing was an unexplored option, the Burnett family leveraged lightness for themselves and others in attempts to escape anti-Blackness in the job and housing markets. And yet, their refusals were an assertion of racial agency that was "neither utopic nor autonomous, and neither pessimistic or futuristic."[60]

Individuals' boycott of segregated restaurants is another example of Black Topekans' practice of refusal. Not only was this form of racial dissidence imperceptible to whites, but it also went unrecognized by some Black children. One Black resident reflected on the fact that his family did not eat at restaurants during the 1910s and '20s. As a child he deduced that it was because "my folks had food at home."[61] Deborah Dandridge's parents also preferred eating in during the late 1940s to early 1950s but never provided an explanation to their daughter. "As a kid, I couldn't figure out whether it was [because] we didn't have the money or if it [was] because there was some reason we couldn't be there," she recalled.[62] By contrast, Claude Emerson was under no delusion about many Black residents' preference for home cooking: "We just more or less knew we couldn't [go], so we didn't. Instead of being humiliated, we just didn't go."[63] This circumvention was an affirmative action that simultaneously challenged and sustained white domination. The legacy of those unarticulated acts of self-preservation is present in how Black residents consistently reframed their memories of racial segregation in terms of choice instead of compulsion. "I thought we sat in the balcony at the Jayhawk Theater because that was the best place to see the movie," Topeka resident Lance Murphy recalled of his childhood in the mid-to-late 1950s.[64]

Making Lemons Out of Lemonade: Segregation and Black Sociality at Topeka High School, 1935–1949

Like Murphy's recollection of segregated movie theaters, the oral histories of Black Topeka High School alumni from the 1930s and '40s evidence the racial situatedness of historical memory and how Black Topekans reimagined and reclaimed spaces designed for racial containment. Classes at the city's high school were integrated from its inception in 1871. However extracurricular activities, including certain athletics and social events, were segregated until 1949. "We had a Black king and a white king, a Black queen and a white queen. We had the white basketball team and a Black basketball team. It was very segregated, but you know, I enjoyed it," recalled Maurita Davis.[65]

Black sociality eclipsed anti-Black racism in the memories of these former Trojans. It is a reminder of Black Studies scholar Fred Moten's *consent not to be a single thing*, or the "practices of an alternative sociality or life form that 'animaterialises' both a constant underpresence, 'the dynamic hum of blackness's facticity' and the white racial fantasies and projections that constitute the series of figures for sensuality and indiscipline."[66] Take, for example, Topeka High School's segregated basketball team the Ramblers. Anti-Black policies barred Black athletes from playing with or against white athletes on basketball courts, but the Ramblers' games became places of Black joy that defied racial containment. That escape was inappreciable both in the moment and in retrospect to white alumni like Dean Smith. The former University of North Carolina men's basketball coach became "very agitated" during a 1981 tribute to the Ramblers. As a senior in 1949, Smith had advocated for Black inclusion on the Trojan team. Thirty-two years later, he felt like his classmate Jack Alexander's commemoration of the Ramblers overshadowed the anti-Black discrimination that had created the segregated team. "Why don't you tell it like it is?" he snapped.[67] But Smith's frustration was a product of whiteness. He was unable to see that which he was not structurally intended to see. He was not alone. Former Trojan basketball player Bill Bunten attributed the "de facto segregation" to student choice, not social regulation. "The Black kids wanted to play on the Ramblers and the white kids wanted to play on the Trojans."[68]

Black students' reality was more complicated than what their white counterparts could perceive. The Ramblers team was founded in 1935 by a group of Black male students who were prohibited from playing on the official men's basketball team. "The young men with whom I worked had all of the necessary endowments except the right complexion," declared the Ramblers' final coach Merrill Ross. The Ramblers could not wear school colors or play in the school's gym, although the school supplied team uniforms. It also provided buses so the Ramblers could compete on the "Chitlin' Circuit" against other Black high school teams in Kansas and western Missouri. On these road trips, the team would stay in the homes of Black residents, who also provided them with meals.[69] But the Ramblers were never allowed to compete against the Topeka High Trojans. "I think we would have won if we played the white boys, but the administration discouraged this," boasted Ross, who was recruited from Fort Scott, Kansas, to lead the team in 1944.[70]

Despite its racist origins, the segregated basketball team was a source of racial pride for Black Topekans. Former Ramblers flipped the script on narratives of white supremacy and celebrated the athleticism of Black ball-players. Like Ross, former team captain Jack Alexander believed that the official team's competitive capabilities paled in comparison to the Ramblers'. White students "played the game, but they weren't basketball players," signified Alexander. "Had there been a [white] coach who looked at the talent we could have bigger trophy rooms at Topeka High School."[71] Black Topekans held the Ramblers in such high regard that several young Black men wanted to play for the Ramblers, not the official Topeka High basketball team after integration. When Topeka High School sports fully integrated in 1949, some Black male residents lamented the loss of the all-Black basketball team. Don Oden enrolled in Topeka High in 1950. "Those were my heroes, the Ramblers," he said. "I was devastated when they integrated the team—I didn't want to play for anyone but the Ramblers."[72]

It took a formal policy to overturn an unsanctioned practice, but as former Ramblers' center Richard Ridley noted, "Any time separate is not equal, there's chicanery."[73] The purpose of the chicanery in extracurricular activities was to protect the property of embodied whiteness. White racial logic vis-à-vis Blackness pivoted upon fears of interracial bodily contact and contamination, especially regarding sexuality. Black students were barred from the school swimming pool. The high school football, baseball, and track and field teams were integrated, but the basketball teams were not. After Trojan basketball games, Black and white students attended separate parties called "varsities." White students would host school dances in the cafeteria with live bands, while their Black peers were provided a record player and a classroom on the second floor. Despite this marginalization, Black sociality at Topeka High School thrived, and Black students' memory-making centered Black desires. For example, as a teen, Jack Alexander thought that school dances were racially separate due to music preferences. As an adult, he wondered if he was engaging in self-preservation. "Maybe I was just trying to con myself that it was not by design," he said.[74] Richard Ridley also believed that Black students' embrace of separate social spheres may have been a defense mechanism. "There was bitterness, but we took lemons and made lemonade," he said.[75]

Creating Race through Space: Real Estate and White Racial Formation, 1900–1960s

The creation of race through place is common white practice in the United States, and Topeka was no exception. Between *Plessy* and *Brown*, public

schools became critical sites of race-making in a city where residential segregation was not strictly enforced. Real estate policies and practices designed
to ensure racially homogenous neighborhoods were intentional but inconsistent. In turn, although elementary schools were segregated after 1929, the
city's junior high and high schools were enrolled according to neighborhood,
not race. So, most Topeka schools were predominantly white, not only
because of segregationist school policy but also because they reflected the
racial demographic of their neighborhoods.

White residents, bankers, and real estate agents worked in concert to sustain a relational value of whiteness in housing, elevating it through racially
exclusive residential areas. In Topeka most Black residents were concentrated
in one of four neighborhoods: downtown in The Bottoms, Tennessee Town
on the west side of town, Sandtown on the north side, and Mudtown in the
east. However, white neighborhoods were not impenetrable despite the racist conspiracy among homeowners, agents, and bank lenders. Civil rights
advocate Charles Baston was able to purchase a home in a predominantly
white neighborhood after he returned from World War II. When his Realtor
asked, "Why don't you try to find something in your own neighborhood, in
your own community?" Baston countered, "All of Topeka is my community
and all of Topeka is my neighborhood. Wherever I can afford to buy or
wherever I can afford to live, that is my neighborhood."[76]

Not all white Topekans were compliant with the spatial imperatives of
whiteness. One Black resident, Frances Ridley, discovered a restrictive covenant in the deed of her parents' house after it was sold. "I thought it was
kind of funny," she said.[77] In 1932 the NAACP represented a white man
named George Moore who was sued by his neighbor for allowing a Black resident to occupy his property. The neighbor claimed that Moore violated the
property's contract, which stated that the "premises should not be sold, conveyed, mortgaged, leased, let nor occupied by any natural person not of the
Caucasian race" for twenty-five years after date of purchase. Moore's case
caught the attention of Black Topekans. "Colored citizens of this city are very
much aroused over this action and are up in arms against the enforcement
of the discriminatory covenant herein before set out," civil rights attorney
Raymond J. Reynolds wrote to NAACP president Walter White.[78]

Despite the Topeka NAACP's legal efforts, racial discrimination in housing persisted. So in the early 1950s, Richard Ridley and his future wife
Frances launched a covert operation. They wanted to buy property in an all-
white section of East Topeka, so they enlisted the assistance of "a very light
fair-skinned friend." Their secret agent was a relative of McKinley Burnett

who could pass for white. But the seller grew suspicious of the emissary's racial identity during the transaction. He canceled the transaction when the Ridleys' coconspirator confessed that she was Black. "I'm sorry," he said. "I can't sell it you."[79]

White Topekans designed discriminatory covenants and loan practices to safeguard white neighborhoods, but Realtors were the gatekeepers to the property of whiteness. Steering was the most direct form of racist real estate fraud. In 1948 Lillian Gooden's real estate agent restricted her search for a new home to economically disadvantaged, racially mixed neighborhoods. "This is all we can show you people," he rationalized.[80] The practice continued through the 1960s. White "realtors just wouldn't sell to you in certain areas of town," reminisced Black resident, educator, and former Tuskegee Airman Merrill Ross. Instead, they would direct Black buyers toward East Topeka.[81] Ross's wife Barbara remembered one Realtor who expressed interest in working with the couple over the phone, but her enthusiasm changed when she met Barbara in person. "She looked at me and said, 'You are part colored!'"[82]

Despite whites' best efforts at carving out exclusive geographical spaces, residential segregation was not strictly enforced in Topeka. And yet, it is how "probationary" whites like Russian Mennonites were extended the property rights of whiteness.[83] During the 1870s, the Santa Fe Railway company recruited Russian-Germans to Kansas to attract settlers, create consumers, and employ laborers. However, native-born whites took issue with the variegated whiteness of these newcomers. Discussions of white distinctions centered upon the corporeality of Russian immigrants. The Hays City *Sentinel* described their presence as an assault on the senses in August 1876. "They are here; they are there; and at every corner they may be seen gathering, jabbering about this and that no one knows what. Their presence is unmistakable; for where they are there is also something else—a smell so pungent and potent as to make a strong man weak."[84] The mainstream press counterbalanced the perceived aural and olfactory offenses of Russian-Germans by projecting upon them an exceptional physicality. A "Russian can shovel more pure dirt in a day than a white man can in two," a journalist for the Topeka *Commonwealth* wrote in 1876.[85]

These narratives of hypersensuality served as public reminders of how dominant whiteness was predicated, in part, upon a disassociation from the body. In fact, it became an axis of negation by which the Russian newcomers were dehumanized and othered. As "constitutive outsiders," Russian-Germans were cast alongside racially marginalized Kansans. For example, in March 1876 the Hays City *Sentinel* deployed class and gender narratives to characterize their racial deviance. "They are strong looking animals, and seem capable of any work, especially the women, who seem to perform as much menial labor as the children, which are numerous," a journalist wrote. "It is refreshing to see one of these females with a small child slung to her in a pouch, in very much the same manner in which the American Indians carry their young, harnessed to a yoke with a bucket of water at each end [to] get down to business!"[86]

The imagined social proximity of Russian-Germans to minoritized Kansans continued into the twentieth century. Topeka resident Tom Rodriguez recalled Seymour Foods' exclusive hiring practices during the Great Depression. People of Russian and Mexican descent worked side by side as "pickers" at the North Topeka egg-processing facility. "Russians, although white skinned, were treated the same as Mexicans," he wrote.[87]

While Russian-Germans experienced prejudice and discrimination, they also benefitted from the wages of whiteness. Their children attended white schools, and they were allowed in white restaurants and hotels. They also received the privileges of whiteness in the workplace. Santa Fe was one of the few local businesses that regularly hired Black men prior to desegregation, but the company prohibited people of color from competing with white workers for skilled jobs. McKinley Burnett moved to Topeka to capitalize on the job openings created by the Great Railroad Strike of 1922. Prior to the strike, white unions had an agreement with the company that banned Black, Mexican, and Mexican American laborers from the repair shops. During the strike, Santa Fe violated that racial contract but fell short of completely abandoning the wages of whiteness. Strikebreakers were still barred from skilled positions, but jobs defined as "unskilled" provided better earning opportunities for men of color than service or agricultural work.

In addition to advantaging white laborers in the workplace, Santa Fe established a whites-only, company-sponsored housing development. Black resident Berdyne Scott grew up in North Topeka during the 1920s. She dreamed of living in one of the "pretty little houses" located across the railroad tracks from her childhood home. When Scott discovered that Santa Fe had created the community to entice Russian-German laborers, she reflected upon white limits of Black mobility. "My family could have afforded to live some place other than next to the railroad tracks on Jefferson Street, and those things made me unhappy, even when I become older."[88]

The Santa Fe Railway company's hiring and housing policies contributed to the racial formation of people of Russian and Mexican descent. It affirmed whiteness as property by creating "pretty little houses" for white-by-law, not-white-in-theory Russian immigrants and denying residential access to white-by-law, not-white-in-practice Mexican immigrants. In the early twentieth century, the company recruited Mexican immigrants to Topeka to fill unskilled, low-wage job openings created first by the 1882 Chinese Exclusion Act and then by World War I labor shortages. Most of these workers and their families settled on or near the city's rail yards in old boxcars.[89] "They got coal free, and there was no utilities so they only had to worry about food and clothes," explained Jane Rangel, whose family immigrated in 1921 so her father could find work at Santa Fe.[90] As Mexican residents began to move out of "La Yarda," many relocated to Oakland, a community in northeast Topeka that evolved due to anti-Mexican racism, ethnic preferences, language barriers, and economic necessity.

Although white supremacy influenced the creation of these residential clusters, as previously mentioned, the City of Topeka did not legislate boundaries between whites and nonwhites in housing. That was the prerogative of white citizens. When Rangel and her husband bought a house in Oakland during the late 1940s, they were the first Mexican American family on their block. Most of their new neighbors were of Russian-German descent, some of whom were so alarmed by the presence of a nonwhite family, they campaigned to have the Rangels removed. When that failed, white flight ensued. Unable to enforce their desire to live in an all-white neighborhood, many whites chose to abandon their homes.[91]

Despite white resistance to integration, racially and ethnically diverse working-class neighborhoods developed throughout Topeka. Consequently, several children of color, particularly Black children, grew up in integrated neighborhoods. "Until I got to [Washington,] D.C. I never lived on a street that was all Black," recalled Berdyne Scott.[92] A few Black residents recall racial incidents, but most describe amicable social relations between whites and nonwhites. Joseph Douglas lived in East Topeka as a child during the 1930s when it was still predominantly white. When the economic anxieties of the Great Depression fueled racial tensions in other parts of the country, Douglas recalled a communal ethos among neighbors in East Topeka. William Mitchell Jr. shared similar stories of resource sharing during that time of economic hardship. "There were not a lot of racial problems because people were more concerned about survival then," he stated. "Everybody was in the same boat." According to Mitchell, whites, Blacks, and "Mexicans" shared foodstuffs and disciplined one another's children. "Them white women would grab your butt and whip it just like they would theirs," he asserted. "And the Black [women] would whip their kids butts just like that."[93] White and Black residents who grew up in integrated neighborhoods recall integrated social experiences in public and private spaces—some even had sleepovers. White resident Rev. Maurice J. Lang III spoke of having "very close, very intimate" friendships with Black children in his North Topeka community during the 1930s and '40s.[94]

And yet, elementary school students who lived in racially diverse neighborhoods attended racially segregated schools, a fact of life that did not go unnoticed by white and nonwhite children. "I used to play with white kids, yet you'd find yourselves on school days going to separate schools," *Brown* attorney Charles S. Scott Sr. said of his childhood during the 1920s and '30s. "We often wondered why that happened."[95] Black children like Scott who lived in Tennessee Town were assigned to Buchanan Elementary School while many of their white friends attended Lowman Hill. Claude Emerson was one of those students. As a child during the late 1940s and early 1950s, he questioned the absurdity of his "long walk" to Buchanan when Lowman Hill was located six blocks from his house. In his estimation, the answer was illogical. "We were told that Blacks could not go to school with whites there. But we played together after school."[96] Charles Scott's daughter Deborah spent one year at Buchanan before Lowman Hill was integrated due to *Brown v. Board*. "Our block was predominantly Black but right across the alley was predominantly white," she explained. "My brother played with this little boy across the alley but when Monday came, they went to separate schools." Like her father, Scott remembered being confused as a child by the dissonance between integrated play and segregated schools. "We spent the night with each other and our mothers knew each other but we were kind of forced to go to different schools and we never understood that."[97]

These interracial interactions were not unique to Tennessee Town. The Reverend E. B. Hicks grew up across the Kansas River in a predominantly white area of North Topeka and attended all-Black McKinley Elementary School. "I came home in the evenings and played with the white children and went to school in the day and played with the Black children," he reminisced of the 1910s.[98] Across the racial divide, white children like Maurice Lang also noticed the discrepancy between their socializing and their school lives. Blacks were "all over" North Topeka, he said, but they were not present in his neighborhood school. "Everything else went there but Blacks," he recalled.[99] Similarly when Lupe Perez's parents enrolled her in the "Mexican" school in the early 1940s, she questioned the logic of white supremacy. "I did not know why, when the neighborhood was a mix of white, Black and

Mexican, we had to go to different schools," she said. When she asked her mother why white and Black kids walked past her school to get to theirs each day, her mother simply responded, "That's the way it is."[100]

The segregation of white, Black, and "Mexican" schoolchildren may have seemed unavoidable by the early 1940s, but it was not inevitable. School segregation was not mandated by Kansas state law. However, schools became a crucial site of racial formation for whites, Blacks, and children of Mexican descent. The concerted efforts of state lawmakers, district courts, local school boards, and private citizens to create and maintain all-white schools further evidences the coconstitutive relationship between race and space. Therefore, the following chapter, "The Alchemy of Race and Rights: Separate but Equal in Topeka Public Schools," continues to explore the tension between white liberalism and white supremacy in the Free State.

CHAPTER TWO

The Alchemy of Race and Rights

Separate but Equal in Topeka Public Schools, 1861–1954

When *Brown v. Board of Education* became national news, Kansas state attorney general Harold Fatzer found himself in the unenviable and undesired position of being the public face of white segregationism in Kansas. He was scapegoated by the ideological descendants of white Free Staters, some of whom made it publicly clear that defending *Brown* defendants was unconscionable. Days before the case was argued, Fatzer tried to assure his detractors that he was only fulfilling his professional duties. "My personal views are not involved" in this case, he told the Topeka *Daily Capital*. "I have never advocated or championed segregation and will not do so before the Supreme Court. The argument will solely be on the constitutional question." The centripetal force of Fatzer's whiteness was evidenced by his disclaimer, which relied on a familiar relational trope. The school statute at issue in *Brown* "is permissive," he contended, "and it is not of major importance as it appears to be in the Southern States."[1]

Fatzer's detraction of anti-Black racism in Kansas was indicative of white Kansans' racial solipsism. His personal and professional vindication pivoted more upon associational whiteness than objectified Blackness.[2] How Black Kansans felt about the Supreme Court case was of less importance to Fatzer than the fact that it was a logistical nightmare of optic proportions. *Brown* disrupted the not-South/not-racist relational subjectivity that defined dominant whiteness in the state. And the state attorney general was poised to gain national recognition in a matter that implicated him in Southern-style racism. Fatzer proved an unwilling accomplice. First, he tried to defer responsibility to the Topeka school board. The school board declined. Fatzer then refused to appear before the US Supreme Court, but the Supreme Court forced the issue with a per curium order. With few options left at his disposal, Fatzer successfully sidestepped a segregationist defense of Topeka public schools by sending his new assistant attorney general Paul Wilson.[3]

Harold Fatzer was not the only public official guilty of racial duplicitousness. At multiple Topeka school board meetings between 1948 and 1952, board members ignored, mocked, and physically threatened Black civil rights activists who lobbied against the city's segregated schools. But when the local NAACP's case reached the US Supreme Court, the Topeka Board of Education refused to defend its anti-Black policy. When a white resident asked why, board member Harold Conrad answered, "We feel that segregation is not an American practice."[4] However, a race traitor informed the local NAACP in 1950 that two board members "were bitterly against integration" while the other four welcomed the Supreme Court case to "take the load off of their shoulders."[5] Faced with a public defaming, the board quickly reconfigured. After the replacement of two long-standing staunch segregationists, the Topeka school board voted to dismantle its segregated schools in September 1953, eight months before the Supreme Court's landmark decision. "Be it resolved that it is the policy of the Topeka Board of Education to terminate the maintenance of segregation in the elementary grades as rapidly as is practicable," motioned the newly elected Topeka school board president J. A. Dickinson. The proposal passed five to one.

Brown v. Board of Education of Topeka was an unwelcome public revelation for white Kansans invested in the "good whites versus bad whites" racial allegory of the Free State narrative.[6] The day the ruling was announced, Dickinson spoke to a reporter about the white man's burden. "The historically free state of Kansas was placed in the embarrassing position of leading off in the fight to maintain segregation before the high court in all of its arguments," he explained.[7] The US Supreme Court case exposed white Kansans' racial sanctimoniousness, drawing unwanted attention to the dissonance between the discursive practice of benevolent whiteness and the realities of anti-Blackness. Despite their public protestations, white Kansans were just as committed to preserving the property of whiteness as their Southern counterparts. Harold Fatzer's political standpoint and his personal doings are a primary example. As the state attorney general, Fatzer objected to a prosegregationist argument, but as a father he did not object to segregation's benefits. Months before the *Daily Capital* interviewed him about the Supreme Court case, Fatzer enrolled his kindergartner son in one of Topeka's all-white schools. This discordance between the personal and professional evidences the fact that whiteness is "constituted by discursive practices that order and organize the world to obscure the entitlement many white people experience."[8]

So goes the alchemy of race and rights in Topeka, Kansas. The city's public schools in the decades before *Brown* provide a primary site to examine the discursive and material practices of race-making. The Topeka school board's constant negotiation between the state's civil rights laws and the "wages of whiteness" reveals how educational policies and practices were used to reify whiteness vis-à-vis Blackness. However, the school board's ambivalence toward separate-but-equal all-Black schools provides only one example of its racial politics. White Topekans' "possessive investment in whiteness" becomes much more transparent with a comparative and relational study of its Black and "Mexican" elementary schools.[9] Local school boards' educational approach to non-Black/nonwhite students complicates educational histories of racial discrimination in the era before *Brown*. The story of school segregation in Kansas is often misleading. It was not a dual education system, it was a tripartite one. Local school boards throughout the state did not treat all nonwhite children equally. The differential racialization of Black, white, and Latinx children challenges official state renderings of white exceptionalism because it speaks directly to a concerted effort to preserve whiteness as property.

"Kansas has for many years had a complicated crazy-quilt educational pattern," NAACP secretary Lucinda Todd wrote prior to *Brown*.[10] Because Black-white binaries of race dominate academic discussions of racial segregation, social scientists typically refer to segregated schooling in the era before *Brown* as a "dual education system." However, several scholars have begun to expose that terminology as an inaccurate descriptor of racially segregated schools, particularly in the West. Like elsewhere in the West, Mexican immigrants forced whites in Topeka to reexamine their racial paradigm. As not-Blacks, not-whites, and non-Americans, people of Mexican descent were projected as racialized objects and assimilable subjects. Despite discursive uncertainties about "Mexicans" and their social location, empowered whites developed discriminatory policies and practices that created racial triangulation in public spaces throughout the city. Nowhere is this dynamic more apparent than in the city's segregated schools, where students of African and Mexican descent had different paths to junior and senior high schools. "Not until I went to East Topeka Junior High and I was in the eighth grade did the Black children attend the junior high and other schools with white and Mexican-American students," recalled Topeka resident Lupe Perez.[11]

The "Dregs of Slavery": Legalizing Segregated Schools in the "Free State," 1861–1929

White settlers' first attempts to educate nonwhite students in Kansas took place in schools like the Shawnee Manual Labor School founded in 1839, the Highland Presbyterian Mission erected in 1845, the Potawatomi Mission built in 1847, and the Kaw Mission completed in 1851. Under the guise of benevolence, these whites designed early Indian schools as vehicles for radical racial transformation. But their pedagogical promise of racial inclusion necessitated cultural genocide, or the complete and total erasure of students' indigeneity. These local schools were soon replaced by boarding schools invested in similar outcomes. When the federal "solution" to the "Indian problem" shifted from extermination to assimilation in the 1880s, Native education shifted from private practice to public policy. In 1884, Lawrence became home to the United States Indian Industrial Training School. It was renamed in 1887 to formally recognize Dudley Chase Haskell, the US senator and chair of the Committee on Indian Affairs who lobbied to have the federally funded nonreservation boarding school located in Kansas.[12]

Schools were a key component of the discursive deracination of Indigenous people, but a critical site for reinscribing Blackness in the postemancipation era. At the beginning of the Civil War, thousands of enslaved Missourians crossed the Kansas border in search of freedom behind Union lines. Racial demographics radically shifted with this mass migration of "contraband," especially in abolitionist strongholds in the northeast corner of the state. Black and white reformers from across the nation traveled to Kansas to aid these fugitive-to-free Blacks, including improvising much-needed educational opportunities. Like the early founders of Indian schools, white originators of colored schools were activated by racialist religiosities. However, their mission deviated due to divergent racial scripts. While the goal for Indian schools was assimilation into whiteness, the objective for colored schools was acculturation into Black subordination.[13]

On the heels of a territorial battle over enslaved bodies, empowered white Kansans had a prime opportunity to operationalize their white racial imaginary. Instead, legislators in the newly admitted state formalized racial boundaries between Black and white schoolchildren. Two state statutes in 1861 and 1862 provided for "the separate education of white and colored children" as long as they secured "equal advantages" for all schoolchildren.[14] But internal contradictions between discursive and material whiteness were not limited to the state level. Topeka was founded as a Free State town by Northern abolitionists in 1854, but the city segregated its first public school a year after it was established. Black and white schoolchildren who attended school together in 1865 were separated by floor and assigned different teachers in 1866. When the Topeka Board of Education took over the city's public schools in 1867, it opened Topeka's first colored school. The one-room schoolhouse was located on Kansas Avenue and led by a white teacher responsible for all grade levels and multisubject instruction.

The segregationist impulse of the white majority alarmed racially progressive white educators throughout the state. In 1866, members of the State

Teachers Association spoke out on behalf of integrated schools and announced that they will "use our best endeavors to overcome unreasonable prejudices existing in certain localities against the admission of colored children as guaranteed by the spirit of the law of our state."[15] Two years later the Topeka Board of Education's first superintendent L. C. Wilmarth also resisted situating education as a property of whiteness. Wilmarth believed the inclusion of the formerly enslaved into the state's democratic process was inevitable. "Therefore it behooves us to be preparing not only for him, but ourselves, for the coming changes by freely furnishing them with the best of educational advantages." While Wilmarth was not opposed to segregation, he insisted upon equal access to quality education. "I hope the board will see fit either to establish a graded school for colored children or to admit them with the whites into any of the schools of the city."[16] Republican state senator Jacob Winter was unequivocal about Black inclusion in 1874 when the state legislature revisited the subject of school segregation. With abolitionist animation, Winter called those in favor of segregation "moral dyspeptics who still have the scum and dregs of slavery deeply seated in their unregenerative natures."[17]

Despite Black and white resistance, the majority ruled over minority rights. The public push to create all-white educational spaces grew alongside the Black population. During the late 1870s and early 1880s, the Promised Land turned into a dream deferred for the Southern migrants whose exodus west alarmed many Black and white Kansans. Five years after enacting a civil rights statute that prohibited racial discrimination in public accommodations, state legislators revisited the issue of separate schools. In 1879, they amended the school code to permit segregated schools in cities with populations of 15,000 or more. There was one exception. In a statement that ironically acknowledged the anti-Blackness inherent in school segregation, state legislators determined that "no discrimination shall be made on account of color" in high schools.[18]

Topeka was a city of the "first class," and its school boards exercised their prerogative to create and maintain racially segregated schools. By 1900 Topeka's "colored" schools had transitioned from a one-room schoolhouse led by a white teacher to four multiroom, freestanding buildings led by Black teachers. In the meantime, there were private interventions like the kindergarten Rev. Charles Sheldon established in a Tennessee Town speakeasy for the children of Exodusters in 1892. It was the first Black kindergarten founded west of the Mississippi River and eventually merged with Buchanan School. Black students' attendance in all-Black schools was not formally required by the Topeka school board until 1929. The editors of the *Colored Citizen* suspected that the school board's racial flexibility was a tactical delay. "Just enough colored pupils have been admitted into some of the schools to cover up the measures of the board in forcing the others into separate schools," they wrote in 1878. State law required localities with segregated schools to manage parallel educational systems, which was not possible in Topeka until the city passed an $850,000 bond in 1928. So from 1929 until 1954, the Topeka Board of Education complied with the state's legal parameters and semisuccessfully operationalized the "separate-but-equal" *Plessy* standard in its school district.

Public Schools as Race-Making Places: Topeka's Juan Crow School, 1918–1942

Public education became central to race-making throughout the state because schools were the only public spaces where segregation was legally permitted. Empowered by state law, local school board members became racial arbiters who decided when and where to draw the boundaries of whiteness within their jurisdictions. However, when state legislators penned the 1879 school statute, their racial orientation was white over Black. As a result, non-Black minoritized families were also vulnerable to the vagaries of anti-Black racism. When C. K. Kelly's daughter was enrolled at Buchanan School in 1924, he believed a mistake had been made. Kelly was Indian, not Black, he explained when he petitioned school board members to reassign his daughter to their neighborhood school Lowman Hill. The school board denied his request four years before the Topeka school board enacted its strict segregationist policy.[19] For Native Americans, Kelly's case was a stark reminder of white racial imaginaries. The compulsion to exclude minoritized students would become naturalized and normalized through experimentation upon Black bodies. A wave of Mexican immigration during the first two decades of the twentieth century tested the elasticity of the state's dual education system. Over 13,000 not-white, not-Black residents presented white Kansans with a new racial dilemma as a crisis of whiteness played out in public school systems throughout the state.

The simultaneous administration of Jim and Juan Crow schools speaks to the motility of discursive and material forms of whiteness rooted in anti-Blackness. The discriminatory treatment of Black students diverged from that of Mexican students because of the differential racialization of Black and Latinx people. The state's racial politics emerged from a white dispute over Black bodies, but neither side believed that Blackness was mutable. In Topeka between 1929 and 1941, that racial signification bound all Black students to all-Black schools until the ninth grade.[20] Sixty miles away in Kansas City, Black students never attended schools with whites.[21] Black students were fixed by theories of biological determinism, but white-by-law Mexican students were subject to discursive deracialization. In white supremacist discourse, the distance between people of European and Mexican descent was considered permeable, not permanent. So empowered whites used cultural, not corporeal, distinctions to justify anti-Mexican policies and practices. This fictional fluid relationship to whiteness informed Topeka's educational policy, which integrated Mexican-descended students with whites in the fourth grade, five years earlier than Blacks. This practice lasted from the founding of the "Mexican" school in 1918 until 1942.

The contradictions and complexities of white racial formation in Kansas are evidenced by white citizens' divergent approach to schooling residents of African and Mexican descent. Like other states in the American West, demography influenced local school boards' decisions about the inclusion, semi-inclusion, or exclusion of Black and Latinx students. In smaller cities and rural towns, student enrollment in secondary schools was not determined by race. At a time when the education of Indigenous youth was transitioning to nonreservation boarding schools, state law prohibited separate schools for Blacks but did not mention other nonwhite populations. Whites' racialization of people of Mexican descent, like Native Americans, was situational and spasmodic. For example, Lupe Perez attended kindergarten in 1938 at a school that was "95 percent white and 5 percent Mexican" in Turner, Kansas, located just outside of Kansas City. Perez and her brother entered their neighborhood school without incident, she recalled, because her friend's parents were school board members.[22] But the Perez siblings were fortunate. They had white guarantors and lived in a town with a small Mexican population. White Kansans who lived close to newly formed colonias were less receptive to Mexican immigrants and more likely to resist Mexican integration into all-white schools.

The battle over Emerson Elementary School in Argentine, Kansas, is a prime example. Located on former Shawnee allotment land, Argentine was a Santa Fe Railway company town southeast of Kansas City and on the eastern border of Turner. Mexican immigration into Argentine increased dramatically between 1905 and 1907. It was home to the largest concentration of Mexican-descended residents in the Kansas City metropolitan area until the 1920s.[23] At a time when Black students were restricted to segregated schools, the children of Mexican railroad and meatpacking laborers were permitted to attend their neighborhood school. The school board's semi-inclusive attendance policy integrated Mexican students into Emerson Elementary, but they were confined to separate classes.

As Mexican enrollments at Emerson grew, so did white anxieties. White parents began vocalizing concerns about the obtrusion of nonwhite students and their children being forced to attend school with "filthy and unclean" Mexicans.[24] Although they avoided using explicit racial rationales, white residents consistently employed eugenics rhetoric as their rationale to expel Mexican students from Emerson. When the Seventh Ward Improvement Association of Argentine expressed their discontent in 1917, they were careful to note that Mexican schoolchildren "were not objected to on the account of their color [sic] but because of uncleanliness in person and in dress."[25] The following year, an influenza outbreak escalated whites' anti-Mexican paranoia, and the school board responded by isolating Mexican students in the school basement. These substandard accommodations did not deter Mexican parents from enrolling their children at Emerson. The school's Mexican student population increased from 40 to 100 in 1922, despite losing 65 students to repatriation the previous summer.[26] White parents continued to protest Mexican encroachment upon their children's educational privileges, citing fears of racial "mixing" on the school playground. After a four-year campaign, their reclamation campaign succeeded in pressuring the school board to create a separate school for Mexican-descended students. Clara Barton Elementary opened its doors in 1923.[27]

The story of Clara Barton Elementary School demonstrates how the integration of Mexican-descended students in Kansas pivoted upon the racial anxiety of white residents. In larger Kansas cities with significant immigrant populations like Argentine, Armourdale, and Rosedale, white parents successfully lobbied for all-white educational spaces. School boards protected whites' property in whiteness by establishing racially separated schools. Other Kansas City neighborhoods with fewer residents of Mexican descent were integrated with little or no white resistance.

In the capital city, the school board founded a "Mexican school" in 1918 next to Branner Elementary, an all-white school in East Topeka. Public officials rationalized that a separate school was needed to accommodate "Spanish-speaking" children. Like elsewhere in the western United States, language acquisition was a thinly veiled discriminatory strategy that feigned the promise of delayed racial inclusion. "It was hoped" that by the fourth grade Branner Annex students "would have sufficient mastery of English to proceed in the regular rooms at Branner or Lincoln Schools," said school principal Allen Ecord.[28] Yet students of Mexican descent were assigned to the

"Mexican school" regardless of their nationality or native language. Lupe Perez was enrolled at Branner Annex after moving to Topeka from Turner, even though the only Spanish words she knew were letters and numbers. She and her brother were anxious about attending their first day of school with classmates who "speak nothing but Spanish," she recalled. "But we got along fine."[29] Like many other minoritized Topekans, the Perez family lived in an integrated residential area. So Lupe asked her mother why, when her neighborhood was "a mix of white, Black and Mexican, we had to go to different schools?" Her mother simply responded, "That's the way it is."[30]

Local school boards' confusion over where to place newly arrived Mexican students reflected racial scripts that simultaneously positioned people of Mexican descent as a race, an ethnicity, and a nationality. First-generation Mexican Americans like the Perez siblings experienced racial inclusion, ethnic exclusion, and disregard for their citizenship in public schools throughout the West. Their experiences evidence historian Natalia Molina's 2014 arguments regarding the relational racialization of Mexican immigrants in *How Race Is Made*.[31] Empowered white Kansans struggled with Mexican legibility during the early twentieth century because American racial logics were rooted in white settler colonialism and white supremacy.

Take, for example, the Topeka school board's deliberation over people of Mexican descent as nonwhite/not-Blacks during a May 1942 meeting. With summer quickly approaching, school board members were faced with a dilemma about the city's segregated swimming pools. Throughout the country, white fears of contamination and miscegenation made public swimming pools "contested waters."[32] Topeka was no exception. White residents' concerns about the comingling of white and nonwhite bodies were amplified by the city's park commissioner Harry Snyder. Snyder was a staunch segregationist who vehemently opposed Black presence in all-white parks in 1933. Nine years later, his possessive investment in whiteness targeted residents of Mexican descent and public pools. School board members debated whether to stage an intervention on behalf of "Mexican" students. Snyder's strict exclusionary approach posed a dilemma for board members. "Mexican children will not swim in the same pool with the colored children," they reported. But Mexican-descended Topekans would not receive the privileges of whiteness, even with their internalization of anti-Blackness. The school board deferred to Snyder. The city's all-white pools remained all white.[33]

The Topeka school board's negotiation over the city's swimming pools exposed the interstices of othering. Despite the legal fiction of white inclusion, people of Mexican descent occupied similar structural locations as

Blacks in Kansas's cities. Policies and practices created to restrict the mobility of Blacks served as blueprints for those used to contain Mexican immigrants. People of African and Mexican descent were segregated in parks, movie theaters, restaurants, stores, hotels, and some forms of transportation. Discursive fluctuations in Mexican classifications did not disrupt the function of racialization, which was dehumanization and subordination. In the case of "integrated" city pools, that meant alternating days of play. After the Garfield Pool in North Topeka was drained, the order of service transitioned from all-white, to all-Mexican and Mexican American, and finally to all-Black.[34]

While the city instituted a hierarchical pool attendance policy, white school board members systemized "shifting bottoms and rotating centers" in Topeka public schools.[35] As previously stated, whites throughout the American West demarcated "Mexicanness" using cultural differences, specifically language. The distinction between embodied whiteness and whiteness as property for people of Mexican descent was the illusion of racial permeability. This myth was affirmed by Topeka school board policy, which conferred white privilege upon Mexican-descended students at the start of their fourth-grade year. However, that abbreviated social distancing masked anti-Mexican educational discrimination rooted in nativist paternalism and contagion anxieties about Mexicans.

The segregated learning environment at Branner Annex School paled in comparison to white and Black schools. Former students and staff characterized the school as a site of material and cultural deprivation. "We had just the minimum, as little as possible," said Helen Espinoza Delci, who attended Branner Annex during the mid-to-late 1930s.[36] The school had four portable rooms with no water fountain or lavatory, the latter of which was in another building with an unconcealed row of toilets. Inexperienced white teachers taught classrooms with multiple grade levels. School principal Allen Ecord also reported that the school could not accommodate all its enrollees. "Classes were large, most all of them forty or fifty and, in a few cases, classes of over sixty have been reported."[37] That overcrowding was remarkable in light of the fact that the Topeka school board did not provide school buses for "Mexican" school students like it did for segregated Black students. Many Branner Annex students who lived in the Oakland neighborhood walked over two miles to attend their underfunded, overrun, substandard segregated school.

The most important school board decision affecting the educational well-being of students of color may have been its personnel policy. Since the official rationale for a segregated "Mexican" school was to acculturate Spanish-speaking children, the Topeka school board assigned Branner Annex monolingual white teachers. Lupe Perez recalled one "wonderful" Mexican American teacher at Branner Annex during the early 1940s, but the rest of the teaching staff was white. "None of the teachers had any special training for this type of work, and none of them spoke Spanish," recalled the Branner Annex principal.[38] While Black students at all-Black schools benefitted from the familial environment cultivated by Black teachers, administrators, and staff, Mexican and Mexican American schoolchildren suffered ill-equipped and intolerant white teachers. These agents of assimilation subjected their students to systemic cultural denigration. Perez explained that students were "forbidden from speaking Spanish in school." If they were caught defying these orders, "the teachers would punish them. They would hit them on the hand with a ruler."[39] Corporeal punishment was common in all schools, but Branner Annex students were also abused by the low expectations of white teachers.

Branner Annex alum Helen Espinoza Delci believed that their parents endured these inequities because they "knew things would get better" once they were integrated into Branner Elementary School.[40] Unfortunately, that was not always the case. Once assigned to "all-white" schools, many Branner Annex alums experienced social alienation and stigmatization from their white peers. While some Mexican parents appealed to the Mexican consuls for mediation, others protested by opting out of the Topeka public education system.[41] A significant number of Mexican-descended parents pooled their resources and sent their children to Our Lady of Guadalupe Parochial School, founded in the Oakland neighborhood in 1929. Alum Ed Rangel said there "I was treated like a human being."[42]

After a 1941 Kansas Supreme Court case opened the city's junior high schools to Black students, a delegation from the "Mexican Colony" began asserting pressure on the school board to close Branner Annex. "Mexican children should be treated with equality," they stated. The group supplemented their civil rights appeal with a discursive nod to cultural assimilability. They believed that contact with "other American children would benefit the young Mexican socially."[43] In the wake of antisegregation litigation and lobbying by Black Topekans, students of Mexican descent no longer attended segregated schools in Topeka after 1942.[44]

"A Place for Negroes": Black Topekans v. Topeka Board of Education, 1903–1930

Students of Mexican descent in Topeka were denied many of the educational advantages the school board provided for Black students, despite earlier integration into white schools. Unlike the fluidity that marked Mexicanness in racialized discourses, Blackness was delimited from whiteness by an imagined racial permanence. The discursive formation of an inherent and inheritable Blackness translated into the material reality of Black students attending segregated schools until the ninth grade. They attended one year of junior high before matriculating into Topeka High School. However, Kansas law upheld the value of whiteness vis-à-vis Blackness through exclusion, not deprivation. The Topeka school board's attentiveness to the *Plessy* standard created educational opportunities for Black students that were not extended to their Mexican-descended counterparts. Black schoolchildren were provided bus transportation, the curriculum was shared, teacher-to-student ratios were reasonable, and Black teachers' salaries were comparable.[45] While students of Mexican descent were subjected to inferior facilities, white and Black observers described the city's four Black schools as "modern" structures. In fact, a local NAACP member told members of the national office that some "Negro schools are even better than the white schools."[46]

These accommodations were not bestowed upon Black residents through the goodwill of white school board members. From the early twentieth century, Black residents staged interventions against segregated schools in local school board meetings and in the state supreme court. Black resistance to white school policies in Topeka led to four Kansas Supreme Court cases: *Reynolds v. Board of Education* (1903), *Wright v. Board of Education* (1930), *Foster v. Board of Education* (1930), and *Graham v. Board of Education* (1941).[47] While each case challenged the segregationist policies of the Topeka school board, the first three were allegories of annexation and trails of broken promises.

The first case involved Lowman Hill Elementary School. In 1900, a fire destroyed integrated Lowman Hill Elementary School. White parents, hoping to turn tragedy into triumph, petitioned the Topeka school board for an all-white school. Black suspicions about a covert conspiracy between white parents and white school board members grew after a few Black residents observed canvassing among whites in the neighborhood. But when a small group of Black parents approached superintendent William Davidson, he assured them that the newly constructed brick school would be home to both Black and white students. Within weeks, a local newspaper exposed his duplicity. A January 3, 1902, Topeka *Journal* article made public the school board's proposal to create "A Place for Negroes." An older Douglas Elementary School building previously used for white students was being transferred to the old Lowman Hill site for an all-Black school. Black parents mobilized. A Mississippi-born Black resident cited the origins of that resistance as an article titled "A Place for Niggers," a misnaming that bore witness to the relationship between Black geographies and the phenomenology of Blackness.[48] Three days after the article was published, a delegation of Black parents appeared before the school board to protest the scheme. But it was too late; the school board's plan was in motion. The new eight-room, two-story Lowman Hill Elementary School reopened for white students in February of 1902. Black parents boycotted the Black alternative. A month later, a school board member reported that "the colored people in that district were in open rebellion."[49] The ensuing revolt culminated in *Reynolds v. Board of Education* (1903).

According to his testimony, plaintiff William Reynolds initiated the lawsuit because of the "underground work" of the Topeka school board. Black parents took offense to the deception of the superintendent and a school board member who "strenuously denied" that the new school would be segregated.[50] During the case, however, the defendants maintained that a segregated Lowman Hill Elementary School was foreordained. Members of the Topeka Board of Education insisted that the original school was only integrated because the district did not have the resources to manage a parallel school for Black students, as per state law. Separate schools provided a "material advantage" for all students, they argued. According to school board president William H. Wilson, there would also be collateral benefits for the Topeka school board. Wilson complained that "the race question is something that comes up frequently" and that segregated schools would resolve "considerable irritation."[51]

The Topeka Board of Education's defense in *Reynolds*, like the grievances of white parents, pivoted upon what geographers Owen J. Dwyer and John Paul Jones called the "authoritative and distanced subjectivity" of whiteness.[52] Proximity to Blackness diminished the property of whiteness and exposed the instability of white supremacy. As such, the double-dealing superintendent testified that racial separation was "a desirable condition to obtain in a school system where the colored people are in large numbers."[53] The unstated, but explicit, subject positioning of his testimony called upon a racial covenant, a shared understanding among empowered whites that public spaces free of Blacks were a "desirable condition" for whites. Consequently, the board of education's strategy relied upon a dominant racial framework that naturalized delineations of race and space codified by the 1879 school statute. For example, Davidson's segregationist deposition hinged on essentialist projections of Black deviance. Black and white children "do not harmonize" well in interracial schools, he contended, because of disciplinary issues caused by Black families' lack of "parental control."[54] Not only did the board's racialist logic use behavioral and environmental arguments, but it also included biological determinism. Segregation was mutually beneficial and necessary due to the "somewhat different intellectual requirements" of Black students, they alleged.[55]

Defense attorneys' sociospatial framing of whiteness simultaneously used racial rationales and racial denials. The school board's attorneys claimed that white students were assigned to the new, larger Lowman Hill facility because they far outnumbered Black students in the neighborhood. Although four out of eight rooms in the new school would be unused, they refused to concede the possibility of use for forty Black students. The school board also justified all-white enrollment by arguing that the new building was situated in a predominantly white area while the older building was closer to Black residences. Black parents contested that assertion. But the board's most insidious line of reasoning was cloaked under the guise of white altruism. They claimed that the refurbished one-story, two-room frame building provided Black students was "more sanitary and healthful" than the larger brick one constructed for white students. The "furniture and apparatus" in the Black school "is better and in better condition" than that in the white school, they testified. "In all respects," the relocated, revamped Douglas School was "suitable, useful and modern."[56]

American Studies scholar George Lipsitz wrote that the conspiracy of white supremacy in a democratic society relies on a "cynical combination," the "disingenuous disavowal of racist intent coupled with the conscious deployment of policies that have clear racist consequences."[57] Well aware of the school board's scheme to subvert the *Plessy* standard, Reynolds's attorneys confronted their possessive investment in whiteness. They argued that the Black school's site was a "veritable cess-pool."[58] The plaintiffs' examination scrutinized the structural condition of and water supply to Douglas, its student-to-teacher ratios, and modes of and materials for instruction as well as advanced Black students' access to an equal education.

But Reynolds's legal team went beyond interrogating the local specificities of racial inequities and seized an opportunity to challenge the anti-Blackness of the state school code. Making the case for discrimination, they anatomized its racialization of Black people. The state's definition of "colored" was not about complexion, they contended. The term "colored" solely delineated the not-whiteness of people of African descent. Kansas school code established two categories of separate schools: white schools and colored schools, they explained. The latter were authorized "exclusively for children of African descent." By extension, the term "'white children' can have no other meaning than 'all children *not* of African descent.'" The Kansas school code was inherently discriminatory because it focused solely on one racialized group.[59] Presaging academic conceptualizations of white privilege, Reynolds's attorneys noted that white advantages hinged on Black disadvantages. "*This* discrimination is *against* a particular race," so it stands to reason that the "*next* discrimination may be *in favor* of a particular race," they argued.[60] After their critical analysis of the legal construction of whiteness, Reynolds's attorneys highlighted the absurdity of racial logics. They asked why integrated schools were permitted in smaller towns but not in larger cities when anti-Blackness existed everywhere. "Are the white children whiter or the colored children blacker" in cities of the first class than in cities of the second class?[61] The plaintiffs' argument included critical intersectional humor. Playing the role of the trickster, Reynolds's attorneys pointed out that only one of seven judges seated on the supreme court "hails from a locality aristocratic enough to be legally entitled to give colored children separate schools, and force the 'poor white trash' to stay away from them."[62]

Reynolds v. Board of Education sought to interrupt the liminal space between discursive and material anti-Blackness as Lowman Hill transitioned from integration to segregation. Black parents hoped to secure racial justice by exposing the school board's ulterior motives. The clear inequities between Douglas and Lowman Hill and the board's failure to attain the *Plessy* standard should have triggered state intervention. Instead, the Kansas Supreme Court ruled that white was right. Seven years after *Plessy v. Ferguson*, the Kansas Supreme Court used a New York State precedent and determined that "equality and not identity of privileges and right is what is guaranteed to the citizen."[63]

The school board's victory in *Reynolds* affirmed its prerogative to segregate Black and white schoolchildren, however the city continued to allow a small number of Black students to enroll in the city's predominantly white schools, as it had from the beginning.[64] For almost thirty years the Topeka school board consistently demonstrated flexibility around integration while simultaneously advancing efforts to solidify all-white schools, much to the chagrin of some white residents. White parents registered discontent with the school board's gradualist segregationist policy on multiple occasions. The 1908 boycotts of Lincoln and Garfield Elementary Schools are a prime example of how integrated schools unsettled the relationship between race and place for disempowered whites who lived in diverse neighborhoods.

In September of that year, rumors of a white revolt against Black students ran rampant throughout the city. One site of anti-integration insurgency was

Lincoln School, located in an area of the city called "the Bottoms." Enrollment at this neighborhood school reflected the demographic of the oldest Black settlement in Topeka, with Black students making up a third of the student population. For whites whose racial subjectivities were already compromised by class, this racial ratio was a stark reminder of the relational situatedness of whiteness. On the morning of September 24, the *Topeka State Journal* interviewed Lincoln principal W. S. Magaw about the potential unrest. "There may be a smouldering feeling of discontent among the white children, but it has not yet come to the surface if there is," he said. The principal acknowledged white students' misgivings about sharing space with Black students, but he refuted the notion that there was "personal animosity between the races." That afternoon, sixty white seventh and eighth graders proved him wrong. The student walkout was punctuated by girls' "shrieks of 'Down with niggers' and 'no nigger school for us.'"[65]

News about the demonstration spread quickly, and the following afternoon another strike erupted at Garfield School. Thirty-two white male students rebelled against Black enrollment: "With yells and shouts mingled with sneers they took up the slogan of the children at Lincoln school: 'Down with the niggers[,]' 'No niggers for us.'" A fourteen-year-old Frank Naylor was the most outspoken and defiant student leader. "There are too many niggers in the seventh and eighth grades and they are of the dirtiest kind. Us kids can't stand them and we ain't goin to. We are going to stay out until the niggers are put out." The *Topeka State Journal* was just as attentive to the intersections of white supremacy and heteropatriarchy in its reporting on Garfield as it was for Lincoln, noting that white female students abstained from the protest.[66]

Although the *Topeka State Journal* attributed the segregationist crusade to children, white students' anti-Blackness was clearly inherited. White rebels at Garfield "all declared that their parents were heartily in favor of the idea and they would help them out if anything happened." Perhaps not coincidentally, the fathers of three Garfield protest leaders worked as clerks for the Santa Fe Railroad. But student support extended beyond their households. The *Topeka State Journal* had a stake in the story. The city's mainstream newspaper worked in congruence with empowered whites to produce Black alterity in the public sphere. White journalists centered the grievances of white working-class residents because they were affirming their right to whiteness. In the unfolding school drama, Black residents were the constitutive outsiders, their voices absent and experiences marginalized. The newspaper confined Black students' fear and their parents' anxiety to one paragraph buried in the middle of the article on Garfield School.

In addition to absenting Black subjectivities, the *Topeka State Journal* propagandized the spatialization of race. While public officials like Principal Magaw emphasized the fact that "equal opportunities are granted to all students irrespective of race or color," the *Topeka State Journal* took editorial license and endorsed separate schools. The newspaper concluded that the solution to the race problem would be "larger facilities for colored students where they may be reared and educated apart from the white children." The journalist's racial superiority was imbued with racial paternalism. Separate schools would "secure [Black students] from the race feeling which is liable at times to become bitter and cause no end of trouble."[67]

The Topeka school board refused to capitulate to combative working-class whites despite their interest convergence. The only neighborhood school segregated prior to 1929 was Potwin, situated in an affluent white neighborhood of the same name. The race and class privilege of Potwin residents undoubtedly influenced the forced removal of Black students to segregated Buchanan School in 1921. Although the official reasoning was "to avoid some trouble that had occurred," the ulterior motive was to preserve the relationship between place and power.[68] By contrast, the school board deferred white working-class parents' demands for the removal of Black students from Gage School in 1924, citing overcrowded schools. However, within five years, segregationists' wishes would be the school board's command. As soon as it could, it did. In January 1929, the board of education refused Black students' admission at Gage Elementary and other predominantly white schools.

The move toward absolute Black exclusion incited two 1930 Kansas Supreme Court cases, *Foster v. Board of Education* and *Wright v. Board of Education*. "The negroes of Topeka are no longer going to stand for inequality in school matters," declared *Foster* attorney William Bradshaw. "Why should we?"[69] Bradshaw's battle cry resonated with Topekans who believed in Black civil rights. Three hundred residents attended an NAACP informational meeting about the *Foster* lawsuit in October 1929.[70] The *Foster* and *Wright* lawsuits challenged the reassignment of Black students to Buchanan. Like *Reynolds*, both cases involved Black children who were forced out of a neighborhood school after their district was annexed by the city. But unlike *Reynolds*, neither plaintiff took issue with the accommodations at Buchanan, which the school board expanded and remodeled in 1920. The *Wright* attorney even echoed the defendant's praise for the city's all-Black elementary school. "No contention is made that the Buchanan school is not as good a school and as well-equipped in every way as is the Randolph school," asserted Eugene S. Quinton.[71] Both *Foster* and *Wright* conceded equal accommodation but contested unequal accessibility. The plaintiffs' attorneys argued that busing violated equal protection laws because exposure to inclement weather put the children's health and safety at risk.[72]

Once again in their segregationist defense, the school board not only denied any racial misconduct but also claimed that the spatialization of race was mutually beneficial. "Said defendants acting in the utmost good faith and for what they deemed to be the best interest of both the colored and white children have attempted to separate said races in the lower grades," they countered.[73] The defendants in *Wright* regurgitated the racial claim in *Reynolds* that creating separate educational spaces was an act of benevolence. Racially homogenous learning environments were "conducive to better scholastic attainment and better spirit" for white and Black schoolchildren. The board's denial of racial harm in *Wright* vacillated between race neutrality and racial paternalism. It defended Black exclusion from neighborhood schools by extolling the virtues of the certified teachers it assigned to segregated schools. Buchanan's "excellent" Black teachers were better able to serve the needs of Black children because they were "conversant with, appreciate and understand their problems and difficulties better than white teachers," they insisted.[74]

Like the board of education's line of argumentation, the Kansas Supreme Court position on Topeka's segregated schools had not changed in twenty-seven years. It upheld the city's right to maintain segregated elementary schools in the *Wright* and *Foster* cases. The *Reynolds*, *Wright*, and *Foster* lawsuits attempted to disrupt the transition to absolute segregation in Topeka public schools, but they did not try to dismantle all-Black schools. Windows of civil rights opportunities for Black residents began to narrow once the Topeka Board of Education systematized the *Plessy* standard for the city's Black schools. However, the Topeka school board's consideration for the constitutional rights of descendants of the enslaved gave Black residents some negotiating power vis-à-vis segregated schools, a relative privilege not enjoyed by residents of Mexican descent.

Refusal, Resistance, and Rabble-Rousers: Black Topekans v. Topeka School Boards, 1930–1940

Three years after the *Foster* and *Wright* supreme court decisions, Topeka's NAACP branch secretary wrote a letter to the national office with a list of civil rights complaints. Galena French explained that the city's schools were segregated, but conditions in Black schools were "good" as a result "of colored people asking for them."[75] Black parents began testing the school board's commitment to equalizing segregated schools once the Kansas Supreme Court affirmed the constitutionality of Topeka's Jim Crow schools in 1930. During the 1930s and '40s, Black Topekans leveraged for more or better provisions for Black schoolchildren by raising concerns about inequities in staffing, facilities, and curricula. Under the guise of negotiations, these nontraditional forms of dissent were politicized actions that exposed the legal fiction of separate-but-equal schools.

As the school board began to operationalize the *Plessy* standard in Topeka public schools, there were some elisions not lost upon Black residents, one of which was the lack of a full-time school nurse. To address the lack of parallelism between Black and white schools, a delegation of Black residents appeared at a June 1938 school board meeting. The colored coalition included members of civic organizations, parent-teacher associations, and a Black women's organization called the Ambassadors. But school board members undoubtedly recognized the lobby's spokesperson William Bradshaw, the "negro assistant" to the state attorney general who represented the plaintiffs in *Foster v. Board of Education*.[76] Nine years later, the civil rights advocate and his cohort took a more indirect approach to the problem of unequal access. Bradshaw strategically appealed to the school board's sense of racial altruism. Black schoolchildren would benefit from access to a school nurse because of low wages, poor housing conditions, and high rates of malnutrition, he explained. Using dissemblance, he assured board members that he had "no doubt" that this disparity between Black and white schools "was just an oversight." Bradshaw glibly added that board members either had an unintentional lapse or "the thought just hadn't occurred to them" to provide a nurse for Black schoolchildren. His diplomacy worked. The Topeka Board of Education hired a Black nurse one month later.[77]

Bradshaw's approach, masked as consent to subordination, was an example of what political anthropologist Audra Simpson called an "avenging of a prior injustice and pointing to its ongoing life in the present."[78] Simpson's intervention into the narrative on Natives provides an important framework for understanding varied approaches to institutional racism. In "Consent's Revenge" she problematized scholarly interpretations of the "political" that overdetermine the role of the state in Indigenous lives and histories and, in turn, eclipse Native articulations of agency that opt out of white settler colonialism. She called this dynamic "refusal."

Simpson's conceptual inclusivity resounds in the antiracist performances and productions of Black Topekans. In histories of the American West, scholars tend to interpret Black "silence" in the political sphere as compliance to anti-Blackness, or as a product of more muted forms of anti-Blackness than existed in the American South. But quiet and acquiescence are not homologous. The absence of collective resistance should not always be mistaken for an absence of political intention. When assessing small-scale interventions against school board policies, it is important to note that a significant number were instigated by parents aligned with the local NAACP. So, outsiders' perception of a lack of resistance can sometimes be attributed to Black actors' unwillingness to be seen or detected. Simpson's work provides a language for historical actors who held space between refusal and resistance but who nonetheless exhibited a commitment to the possibility of a different racial reality.

Traditional archival research and historical methodologies can fail to capture the personal and political subjectivities of subordinated or minoritized people in the United States because they are overly reliant on the observations and recordings of people privileged by race, gender, class, sexuality, ability, and so forth. In the case of Black Topekans, "objective" readings of episodic racial negotiations translated into a false impression that concerted efforts were situational responses. The cumulative political and infrapolitical work of William Bradshaw is a primary example. In isolation, Bradshaw's advocacy of a school nurse could be misunderstood as an accommodation to anti-Blackness. But his 1938 appearance before the Topeka school board was not a singular event. Eight years prior, he was a plaintiff's attorney in *Foster v. Board of Education of Topeka*. In 1935, he urged school board members to build an auditorium for Buchanan School. He successfully tried a Kansas Supreme Court school desegregation case against the board of education in 1941. And in 1946 Bradshaw provided legal assistance to the coach of Topeka High School's Black basketball team when the school board terminated him for playing athletes deemed ineligible as punishment for their antiracism activism. Monroe School principal Edward Graham was reinstated after Bradshaw and former NAACP president R. J. Reynolds reminded the school board of the "illegal practice of promoting and maintaining a segregated basketball team on the basis of race and color at public expense, contrary to the laws of the State of Kansas."[79]

Bradshaw left no strategy unexplored in his antisegregation provocations. Tenacity was a family vibe. "The Bradshaws endured slavery, draught, poverty, segregation, and prejudice. They never gave up," his older sister Mattie wrote in her college newspaper in 1907.[80] The family matriarch Eliza was the daughter of a slaveowner, or as Mattie wrote, "she was born Black side out, while he was born Black side in." Mattie believed there would be no redemption for the rapist who begat the Bradshaw bloodline, differentiating between Blackness as "skin" and Blackness as sin. "When Blackness . . . has penetrated beneath the surface, far beyond the range of human vision, there is hardly a chance for purification," she concluded. Whereas Mattie condemned the enslaver's sexual violence, she commended her enslaved grandmother's use of violence as self-defense. "Crazy Eliza" was dubbed so because of her willingness to risk life and limb to protect herself and her children. According to family lore, Eliza threatened both her overseer and her enslaver with boiling hot water after they threatened to beat her and her children.[81] After emancipation, Eliza escaped white terrorism in Kentucky and migrated to "free and bleeding Kansas" in search of legal protections and access to education for her progeny. Her grandson William inherited her by-any-means-necessary political subjectivity and her belief in the transformative potential of Black education.

But William Bradshaw was not alone in his quest for educational access and equity. Daniel Sawyer was an unofficial partner in crime. Both men laid the groundwork for *Brown*, but neither would live to see its outcome. Daniel Sawyer and William Bradshaw were childhood neighbors. From the 1900s through the '30s, the Sawyer and Bradshaw families lived on the 1500 block of Quincy Street, close to segregated Monroe School. Both had been active members of the NAACP since the mid-'20s. In fact, Daniel's father was one of the founding members of the local NAACP in 1913. Nathaniel Sawyer was also an educator for Topeka public schools and an outspoken opponent of its segregation policy. In 1918, he wrote a letter to the state governor imploring him to veto a bill that would extend school segregation to small towns.[82] Four years later, he was forced to retire after thirty-five years of employment, which in turn, triggered a mental health "breakdown."[83]

Antiracism resistance was in Daniel Sawyer's lineage. Like Bradshaw, he was a repeat offender of the Topeka school board. His individual and collective desegregation activism included lobbying school board members in 1938, testifying before the Kansas Supreme Court in 1941, and drafting a protest petition in 1948. Daniel Sawyer started racial troublemaking with the Topeka school board in 1937. It all began with a conflict over school bus policy. In 1928 the Topeka school board initiated a transportation program to coincide with its new segregationist enrollment policy. However, as the number of Black students in Black schools grew according to plan, so did student need for busing. Overcrowding ensued. After prompting by the Buchanan School principal in November 1937, school board members immediately set two new policies to resolve the problem. The first minimized bus ridership to fifty students. The second redefined rider eligibility. Students who lived within ten blocks of Buchanan would no longer be permitted to ride the school bus without the principal's permission. The Sawyers lived two blocks outside of the new parameters, so five-year-old Constance was suddenly and inexplicably denied transportation. To add insult to injury, although Lowman Hill was less than five blocks away from her family home, the kindergartner was forced to walk one mile to Buchanan.

For Daniel Sawyer, the "arbitrary exclusion" of students from Buchanan's school bus exacerbated the racism inherent in segregated schools. In December 1937, a month after the modified policy passed, Sawyer registered his complaint before the school board. The school board had a legal responsibility to provide transportation for Black students, he argued. Regardless of their place of residence, these students "were entitled to transportation" because the school board involuntarily withdrew many from their neighborhood schools.[84] Although the school board left Sawyer's concerns unaddressed, he did not falter and escalated his demands at the following school board meeting in January. "We are facing a condition beyond our control, a condition that is not of our own choosing," Sawyer contended. "We feel that if our children have to pass a white school in order to reach their own colored school, the rights and privileges that you have seen fit to grant should be maintained." Sawyer then took an opportunity to remind school board members that the city's segregationist policy was an evolution, not an inevitability. "There have been times when this condition did not exist, when colored children attended white schools." If white school board members insisted upon all-white neighborhood schools, "you should take care of the children in that particular locality if they are children of African descent."

At least one school board member deciphered Sawyer's subversive subtext. Judge James McClure asked if Sawyer preferred an adjustment in the board's transportation guidelines or its attendance policy. "It would do no harm for white and colored children to be together and together establish their likes and dislikes," Sawyer responded. He concluded his dissemblance with a counterstatement. Discursive practices of white paternalism framed segregated schools as a protective antiracism measure for Black students, but Sawyer emphasized that he did not believe that "white teachers would discriminate" against Black children in integrated schools.[85]

With no immediate progress on the bus issue, Sawyer followed up at the February 1938 school board meeting. But by his third appearance, board members had grown wary and began staging a counterresistance. School superintendent A. J. Stout addressed Sawyer's previous warning about the lawfulness of the city's school bus policy. "There is no legal claim on the part of the petitioners that it is the duty of the Board of Education to furnish bus service at such short distances as ten or twelve blocks." Stout even threatened retributive justice for Sawyer's racial insubordination. Claiming undue financial burden on the Topeka school board, Stout proposed possible discontinuation of school buses for Black students in favor of providing city bus tokens. School board member Julia Kiene joined the Caucasian chorus and turned the tables on Sawyer's charges of unequal access. She "called Mr. Sawyer's attention to the fact" that the city's four Black schools had cafeterias, while the eighteen white schools had no dedicated dining spaces.[86]

The school board may have stonewalled Daniel Sawyer, but his "posture of refusal" was an example of the disengagement of the dispossessed Audra Simpson called "consent's revenge." Empowered whites' circumvention of Blacks' constitutional rights was an illegal act and a social contract that necessitated Black consent to racial subordination. Sawyer was an unwilling signatory. In fact, he attempted to enroll his daughters at Lowman Hill, one in 1942 and the other in 1947. While his actions may not fall under traditional definitions of political activism, they were a protestation of condition that can be elucidated by Simpson's theorization of refusal. "Refusal holds on to a truth, structures this truth as stance through time . . . and operates as the revenge of consent," she wrote.[87]

A "Better Class of Colored People":
Buchanan Elementary School and Black School Protest

Surveying Black provocations from the mid-1920s through the early 1950s, two sites of contention emerge: the whitened Lowman Hill School and all-Black Buchanan School. Located within a half mile of one another, both schools served the residents of Tennessee Town, a neighborhood settled by Exodusters in the 1880s. Buchanan School was built in 1885 in the heart of Tennessee Town. The public school subsumed a private kindergarten founded by Social Gospel minister Charles M. Sheldon in 1890. That kindergarten was the first of its kind built west of the Mississippi River. In 1910 Buchanan parents requested a new school building because they considered the twenty-five-year-old building "unsafe."[88] The school board agreed, but it decided to remodel instead of investing in new construction. It took ten years to fulfill that promise. But by 1920, their commitment was less about Buchanan students than fortifying their segregationist strategy. Nevertheless, the Topeka

Plaindealer celebrated the new Buchanan School as "one of the most modern and complete school buildings in the Topeka school system."[89]

Despite the school's superior exterior, Buchanan parents led the desegregationist charge against the Topeka Board of Education between 1929 and 1954. The physical structure did not distract them from structural racism. Before *Brown*, three out of the four Kansas Supreme Court desegregation cases involved Black students assigned to Buchanan. Two of the three NAACP activists who mobilized *Brown* were the parents of Buchanan students, and seven of the twelve *Brown* plaintiffs were Buchanan students. Mapping that school activism reveals certain Black geographies in Topeka. By the 1930s the Black residents of Tennessee Town were no longer poor Southern migrants. "Most of the negroes that had good jobs and homes [lived] around here," recalled former NAACP branch secretary Lucinda Todd. "This was the area." Consequently, children of the Black professional class were among those who attended Buchanan. "We were the elite," Todd insisted.[90] This sense of intra-racial exceptionalism fueled Black resistance against segregated schools. When William Bradshaw led a delegation to the school board in 1935 to request the building of an auditorium for Buchanan, part of his expressed rationale was that its body politic was "of the better class of colored people" who "use the school as a community social center."[91]

Some of Topeka's most steadfast school desegregationists engaged in articulations of racial rights that pivoted upon class, and sometimes color. For example, Nathaniel Sawyer's 1918 letter to the state governor objected to the racial essentialism that informed anti-Black practices. "The American colored man is robbed of his self-respect by a treatment in schools and public places which accentuates complexion differences and masses all into a single body without regard to personal worth or character."[92] Sawyer's mention of "complexion differences" is interesting because he and his family were listed as "mulatto" in multiple censuses. But even those fair enough to pass for white understood that the principle of hypodescent defined Blackness in strictly binary terms. Distinctions among Blacks in the United States were only conferred meaning among Blacks, not between Blacks and whites. The Creoles of the Gulf Coast region may have been an exception, but as people who embodied a liminal space between Blackness and whiteness, neither gens de couleur libres nor their descendants could fully escape anti-Blackness.

Plessy v. Ferguson is itself a case in point. The Supreme Court decision that defined the segregationist standard began with a lawsuit initiated by a group of New Orleans Creoles called the Comité des Citoyens. Prior to the Civil War, a tripartite racial system shaped Louisiana's racial geography due to a history of French and Spanish colonization. Gens de couleur enjoyed a so-cial and economic semi-inclusion that was not extended to enslaved Black residents or their descendants. But state lawmakers engaged in a concerted effort to close that racial gap after the Civil War. They passed a Separate Car Act in 1890 to segregate all people of African descent, regardless of class, color, or culture. The Comité des Citoyens immediately set out to interrupt the Americanization of Louisiana with its concomitant Black-white racial bi-nary. They recruited thirty-four-year-old Homer Plessy to test the racist statute because he "was white enough gain access to the train and Black enough to be arrested for doing so."[93] Plessy was one-eighth Black, a de-scendent of property-owning Creoles and literate in French and English. But his utility for the civil rights group had less to do with culture than it did with caste. According to the local Black newspaper the *Crusader*, Plessy appeared "as white as the average white Southerner."[94] He was denied equal access only after he informed the train conductor that he was not white.

The civil rights group's strategy was to use Plessy's phenotypical white-ness to "destabilize racial categories."[95] The plaintiff's attorneys even argued that the Separate Car Act deprived Plessy a property in whiteness because he was white by appearance but Black by law. This line of argumentation led some Black leaders to question whether members of the Comité des Citoyens were more interested in maintaining their light-skinned privileges than they were in dismantling anti-Black racism. Their suspicions were merited. While all people of African descent were harmed by anti-Black laws, the push toward racial bifurcation threatened Creoles' privileged intermediary status. In the end, Judge John Ferguson determined that neither skin color nor mul-tiracial origins would mitigate anti-Blackness in public transport. The US Supreme Court reaffirmed Ferguson's ruling in 1896 and established the separate-but-equal standard of segregation that lasted almost sixty years.

Mobilizers of the two most important Supreme Court cases in America's racial history shared similar personal and political subjectivities. Like the Creoles who initiated *Plessy*, the NAACP members who organized *Brown* leaned into the elite status they held in their racially minoritized communi-ties. The entitlement that came with that intra-racial privilege informed their claims to political rights. They were not political outliers among their peers. It was not uncommon for Black elites who advocated for civil rights during the Jim Crow era to call attention to the intersections of race, class, and color. Many did so, not because they desired whiteness or proximity to white people but because essentialized Blackness was used to justify "racialized rightless-ness."[96] "We are all said to look alike, [but] there are as many differences among us as among the whites," Topeka *Colored Citizen* editors lamented a year after the *Plessy* decision. Those Blacks who are "dead to all sense of decency or self-esteem" act as a "millstone around the necks of the better class."[97]

The oral testimonies of *Brown* architect Lucinda Todd provide a primary example of the enduring legacy of classism and colorism in Black Topekans' pursuit of civil rights. Todd's parents were Exodusters who migrated to Kansas from Alabama with her maternal grandparents. They originally settled in Litchfield, a small mining town in the southeast part of the state. But Charles and Estella Wilson eventually moved to another small town to access the best education possible for their twelve children. Their commitment paid off for their seventh child, Lucinda, who was born in 1903. Lucinda Wilson graduated from Pittsburg State in 1932 with a bachelor's degree in education. She moved to Topeka in 1928 and worked in Topeka public schools until she married Alvin Todd in 1935, which disqualified her from her teaching contract. But the catalyst for Todd's political activism was not that gender discrimination; it was motherhood. "I call my wife the first domino," Todd's son-in-law Ramon Noches joked in 2008.[98] Much like her parents, Lucinda Todd was compelled to action for better, and more equal, access to education.

This college-educated granddaughter of enslaved people would become a critical organizer of the school desegregation activism that culminated in *Brown*. In the post-*Brown* era, she emerged as another kind of history maker. Todd was one of the last surviving NAACP members involved in the Topeka case. As such, she had multiple opportunities to create a historical imprint before she passed away in 1996. In over forty years, Todd never deviated in her narrative performance. It is present in *Simple Justice* author Richard Kluger's 1970 notes, in then–graduate student Ralph Crowder's 1991 interview for the Brown v. Topeka Board of Education Oral History Collection, and in various commemorative articles on the case. The consistency of her storytelling arc traversed time and transcended the subject positionality of the interviewer. As such, her body of work invites serious consideration of the "epistemological and aesthetic choices undertaken by the authorial voice in oral history."[99]

Todd's carefully crafted chronicles affirm historian Martha Rose Beard's 2017 argument that oral history is an "ontologically authored narrative subject to the same discursive effects as all other forms."[100] For example, her autobiographical narratives bear witness to the "body as archive," or how histories of white supremacy are not only inscribed on Black bodies but also

Alvin, Nancy, and Lucinda Todd, 1946 (Kansas State Historical Society, Topeka)

are internalized by Black subjects. Todd's intergenerational trauma was reflected in her 1991 description of her father as an "Irishman" who "talked foreign" and "didn't look too much like a colored man."[101] In fact, Charles Wilson was born enslaved in Georgia around 1861 or 1862. He was listed as "Black," not mulatto, in multiple censuses despite being fair-skinned. The observances of white census-takers spoke to the inheritability of Blackness as a structural location. That reality was not lost upon Todd. Her whitewashing of her father was indicative of an intimate awareness of racial determinism and of the social desirability of proximities to whiteness. When Todd married at thirty-two, it was to a college-educated man whose family surveyors once classified as "mulatto." Neither archival research nor oral histories speak directly to causation, but contextualization suggests correlation between complexion and her selection. In 1941, Lucinda gave birth to a daughter she would later proudly describe as a "very pretty little girl with curls."[102]

Lucinda Todd was an intentional woman who understood that phenotypical and essentialized Blackness disrupted a seeing of being in civil society. That epistemological frame influenced her simultaneous consent to heteropatriarchal, capitalist norms and her dissent from white supremacy and domination. Racial spatialization also oriented Todd's memory-making.

During the 1930s and '40s, she conscientiously claimed a position among the "better class" of Black Topekans. Although raised by a Baptist mother and a Christadelphian father, she joined St. John AME after moving to Topeka. St. John's was known among Black Topekans as an elite, if not elitist, church, and members had a reputation for disassociating from "lower-class" and dark-skinned Blacks. "All of those people that went to St. John's Church thought they were a little better," claimed Black resident Thayer Phillips.[103] Todd became a member of Alpha Kappa Alpha sorority because she said it represented the "cream of the colored woman." And before getting married, she taught at Buchanan, which she classified as "'the' school" among segregated schools. The "cream of the teachers were there," she told *Brown* oral history interviewer Ralph Crowder.[104]

Todd's racial subjectivity was highly motivated by righteous discontent, or the intersectional and relational political standpoint Evelyn Higginbotham called a politics of respectability.[105] Respectability politics weaponized tropes of bourgeois culture to contradict discursive and material forms of anti-Blackness. Todd's performance and production of propriety was a form of quotidian resistance observed by *Brown* documentarian Richard Kluger. His transcript notes described Todd as "very warm and earnest, forceful . . . well educated and spoken, extremely neat, her house is spotless."[106] Todd's Black spatial imaginary intertwined racial rights with personal dignity, the latter of which pivoted upon class distinctions. "She had an air about her," according to former Black educator Merrill Ross.[107] She didn't attend the segregated movie theater in the poor and working-class neighborhood known as the Bottoms because she "didn't mix" with "those kind of people."[108] The same class consciousness that inflected Todd's social play informed her social work. Her belief in racial uplift led her to volunteer at the Crittenden Home, a Topeka shelter for young pregnant Black women "in trouble."[109]

But Todd's sociospatial practices could not rescue her daughter from the structural realities of racism. The school board's binary articulation of its racialized segregationist policy assigned students to schools based on whiteness or Blackness; it did not recognize or acknowledge intermediary categories. So Todd may have consciously claimed intra-racial privileges within Black communities, but she still had to enroll Nancy at Buchanan Elementary School in 1946. Todd's political awakening demonstrates how the experience of Blackness is intimately related to anti-Blackness and, in turn, influences Black fugitivities. For her class entitlement transmuted into racial defiance when her daughter was denied access to an event sponsored by Topeka public schools. While reading a local newspaper in 1946, Todd saw an announcement about a spring concert featuring student talent from the city's eighteen elementary schools. There were twenty-two elementary schools in Topeka, but this was no misprint. Although Nancy was training in piano and violin, she and other Black students were not invited to participate due to anti-Black racism. "I hit the ceiling, I was so mad," she recalled. "I had to go to her rescue."[110]

Upon her discovery, Todd launched a one-woman protest and telephoned Black faculty and administrators. Her first call was to Buchanan School principal J. B. Holland. "I got on Mr. Holland [for] not going to bat for the colored children," she recalled. Todd's appeal for patriarchal protection was met with a hint of Afro-pessimism. The depth of her disappointment with Holland was registered in a rare instance of informality with Black interviewer Ralph Crowder, during which she tapped into a shared vernacular. "He said they had tried to make those white people recognize them but that is just the way they were." Todd concluded that Black administrators' lack of persistence was, in fact, racial resignation. "They didn't try."[111] But Todd was undeterred. "She was a pretty forceful person," Nancy Todd Noches recalled. "Things were either right or wrong. There was no in-between."[112] The school board introduced an instrumental music program for Black elementary schools the following year.[113]

Todd's desire to speak the future into the present was mediated through color, class, and gender performativities. Her resistance to anti-Blackness was the kind of political conjuring Tina Campt described as a "politics of prefiguration that involves living the future *now*—as imperative rather than subjunctive—as a striving for the future you want to see, right now, in the present."[114] And yet, Todd's engagement of Black feminist futurities was rooted in intra-racial formations around class and their interrelations with color. She was not alone.

From Containment to Counterpublic: Reclaiming Segregated Schools, 1929–1954

Black resistance to segregated schools before *Brown* evidences how aggrieved communities participate in, resist, and shape discursive and material practices of race, place, power, and empowerment. The following chapter continues that conversation by examining the racial subjectivities of desegregationists' Black political adversaries. While civil rights advocates opposed the racial discrimination inherent in Black exclusion, there were Black residents who fought to protect exclusive Black spaces. They did so, not because they supported anti-Black racism, but because they embraced an alternative emancipatory vision.

Ironically, that resistance to school integration was, in part, a byproduct of the peculiar racist policies of the Topeka Board of Education. The school board inadvertently enabled the development of Black counterpublics within its school system by maintaining a semiparallel educational environment for Black students. Black educators developed counterideologies to white supremacy within their curricula and nurtured the intellectual and cultural development of Black students. Black residents also reclaimed segregated schools, as protected spaces emerged through the confines of white domination. As William Bradshaw noted in 1935, the city's four Black schools were used as "social center[s]" for Black residents; they were sites that facilitated community-building and a politics of resistance, including pro- and anti-Black school activism.

Many Black Topekans had affirming educational experiences in and positive connections to segregated elementary schools that were, for most intents and purposes, equal to all-white elementary schools. This unique set of circumstances presented a significant challenge for the local NAACP when it began mobilizing against the Topeka Board of Education during the 1940s and early 1950s.

The following chapter then contextualizes the intra-racial battle over school segregation by surveying the internal governance of Topeka's four all-Black elementary schools. Black teachers and administrators' comprehensive approach to educating Black children created a tactical problem for local civil rights advocates in the decade leading up to *Brown*.

CHAPTER THREE

Reading, Ri(gh)ting, and Resistance

Racial Uplift Ideologies and Practices in
Topeka's All-Black Schools, 1929–1954

In 1935 W. E. B. Du Bois challenged the presumption that people of African descent in the United States should unilaterally condemn racial segregation. His "Philosophy of Race Segregation" contended that Blacks' response to the illogic of anti-Blackness should be situational, not universal. Du Bois believed that context determined the best course of political action for the "American Negro." So, he refused to endorse the NAACP's official "no segregation" platform, despite being one of the organization's founders. The value of integration was relative to "time and place," he argued. When it came to the nation's public schools, Du Bois strongly advocated for political dexterity. Minoritized students in integrated schools experienced "systematic neglect" in the absence of "close human ties," he wrote. In fact, in 1940 he concluded that, all things being equal, "most Negroes would prefer a good school with properly paid colored teachers, to forcing children into white schools which met them with injustice and discouraged their efforts to progress."[1]

Du Bois's philosophy of racial segregation was certainly true in Topeka during the 1940s. While Du Bois was theorizing about the nation's public school systems, an experiment was unfolding in Topeka public schools. A decade after the school board's enrollment policy transitioned from transient to intransigent, whites' attempt at racial containment metamorphosized into epistemological emancipation for Blacks. Historians of Black education have long established the fact that, from the period to enslavement and beyond, African Americans believed education was key to racial advancement.[2] But what constituted Black education during the Jim Crow era was as heterogeneous as Black communities and the localities in which they lived.

The chronicles of Buchanan, McKinley, Monroe, and Washington Schools diverge from mainstream storytelling about Jim Crow schools. The Topeka school board inadvertently provided Black educators with the rare opportunity to build independent educational institutions within segregated educational structures. The significance of that spatial history should not be underestimated. This chapter contextualizes Blacks against *Brown* by mapping the geographies of Topeka's four Black schools. It pushes through the material into the metaphysical to evidence Black schools' role in the performance and production of Black futurities. Black teachers consistently staged interventions on anti-Blackness by creating and disseminating situated pedagogies and knowledges. As such, they transformed Topeka's Black schools into sites of "resistance, emancipation, humanization, place-making, community building, and identity formation."[3] And yet, much of what these educators achieved would not have been possible without the unwitting assistance of the Topeka Board of Education.

A Peculiar Institution: Topeka's Jim Crow School Policy, 1929–1954

Topeka's Black teachers and administrators were in a unique position when compared to their counterparts in other parts of the country. The city with abolitionist roots spawned a peculiar institution of anti-Blackness that was accompanied by a white racial frame of benevolence. In Topeka public schools that racialist combination translated into white compliance with an unusual state law that required them to maintain "equal advantages" between Black and white schools. As a result, the Topeka school board's approach to separate schools was a departure from conventional segregationist methods in the United States. From 1918 to 1942, the city ran a tripartite educational system for whites, Blacks, and children of Mexican descent. Students assigned to the "Mexican school" were integrated in the fourth grade but subjected to educational inequities, substandard facilities, and the prejudices of inexperienced white teachers. Before legal intervention in 1941, Black students were not integrated until the ninth grade. From a policy standpoint, the school board's segregationist practices denied Black students equal educational access. And yet, by most accounts, Black students in Topeka received quality instruction from highly qualified Black educators in modern facilities.

Ironically, Black students benefitted from an ulterior frame that marked Black bodies in ways that were permanent versus permeable. That discursive racialization contributed to the Topeka school board's commitment to operationalizing the *Plessy* "separate-but-equal" standard from 1929 until 1954. Board members protected the value of whiteness through exclusion, not deprivation. So unlike students of Mexican descent in Topeka and Black students throughout the country, Buchanan, McKinley, Monroe, and Washington School students had access to equitable facilities, funding, and a shared curriculum. There were no gross disparities between Topeka's Black and white schools. When Buchanan was remodeled in 1920, Topeka's Black newspaper hailed it as "one of the most modern and complete school buildings in the Topeka school system."[4] And Monroe School was "a beautiful building" according to Linda Brown, the woman memorialized by the landmark decision.[5] Monroe alum and educator Dr. Julia Etta Parks confirmed that the district's curriculum was standardized regardless of race. "We were using the same textbooks everybody was using," she said. "The Topeka public schools then had a school district-wide adoption."[6] Carolyn Campbell graduated from McKinley Elementary School in 1954. She confirmed that "our books and other things were on the same level."[7] Even more unusual than uniform curricula and parallel facilities was the school board's policy on teachers' earnings, which were determined according to experience and education, not race.

Despite relative equity between the city's Black and white schools, a Black Topekan became the poster child for educational injustice in 1954. Because *Brown v. Board of Education* put Topeka's Black schools in the national spotlight, many Black alumni became invested in reclaiming their alma maters from the master narrative on Jim Crow schools. "My grade school education was not inferior, it was superior," Richard Ridley boasted of Monroe, the school at the center of the *Brown* case. "I never felt my school was inferior," Ridley stated. "I'm sure there were deplorable conditions in other areas."[8] Washington Elementary School alum Jack Alexander also insisted that segregated schools did not equate to a substandard education in Topeka. "The education I got was excellent," he asserted.[9]

Black Topekans' memories of segregated schools challenge conventional wisdom, but their stories are common among the alumni of America's Jim Crow schools.[10] The conflation of substandard facilities with substandard education reinscribes the "erasure and objectification of subaltern subjectivities, stories" that accompanied segregation.[11] Historical observers who focus solely on quantifiable material inequities neglect the qualitative experiences of Black students and minimize Black agency within segregated school systems. Many Black students in segregated schools benefitted from the high expectations of faculty and community, dedicated principals and teachers, and extraordinary parental involvement, despite a lack of resources. Educator and *Tampa Bay Times* columnist Bill Maxwell wrote that "three factors made the difference" for Black schoolchildren assigned to Ft. Lauderdale's Jim Crow schools. "Our parents placed nonnegotiable demands on us. Our parents had close relationships with our teachers and our principal. And our teachers were smart and tough."[12] Portsmouth,

Virginia, resident John W. Brown recalled that students at his alma mater I. C. Norcom High School had unequal facilities and secondhand course materials. However, "the caliber of teachers" was exceptional, he said. "We had dedicated teachers that went beyond the unequal requirements."[13]

The oral histories of alumni of America's Jim Crow schools disrupt dominant assumptions that separate was inherently unequal before *Brown*. However, the experiences of Black Topekans further complicate that history. Not only were their schools separate and relatively equal but they also attended integrated junior high and senior high schools. Charles Baston described that split enrollment policy as "a ridiculous situation" because it would "slam" Black students into integrated schools that had segregated extracurricular activities.[14] However, state law allowed larger cities to segregate public schools if they maintained "equal advantages." Local school boards had the power to interpret and institutionalize their definition of what constituted "equal."

Since residential boundaries were more fluid in Topeka, rigid school boundaries became critical to maintaining the property of whiteness. The Topeka school board created an 8-1-3 plan for Black students and a 6-3-3 plan for white students. Until the Kansas Supreme Court ruled that policy unconstitutional in 1941, Black students remained in elementary school until the ninth grade. The school board's spatialization of race produced dual and contradictory realities that evolved into an interest convergence. Its stratagem of white isolation was a racist violation that enabled Black insulation. From kindergarten through eighth grade, Black students were schooled in protected spaces, shielded from the racism or indifference of white teachers and administrators.

A Conflict of Interests and Conflicted Interests: Racism, Antiracism, and Topeka's Segregated Schools

Topeka's segregated schools were simultaneously spaces for racial containment and sites of racial transcendence, demonstrating the dialectical relationship between geographies of domination and "oppositional Black geographies."[15] People of African descent transformed places designed to marginalize and minoritize into what W. E. B. Du Bois called "The Colored World Within"—that is, the subterranean communities that define the Black public sphere. Much like Black churches, Black schools became gathering places for restoration, regeneration, resilience, and resistance. Whereas Black ministers created Black theologies, Black educators developed programs and practices that conscientiously engaged projections and introjections of white supremacy.

In the decades that followed the complete segregation of Topeka public schools, the city's four Black schools represented emancipatory epistemological spaces. Black educators operationalized an "affirmative refusal," or what Black Studies scholar Fred Moten called a "disruptive, invaginative preservation of the paraontological totality."[16] Like many of their counterparts throughout the country, Topeka's Black teachers were race men and women who passionately believed in a politics of racial uplift and in education's role in Black advancement. As such, they nurtured Black students' subjectivities in ways that both challenged and reflected systems of domination. Black educators embraced racial pride and self-determination, bourgeois class aspirations, and standard gendered conventions. However, unlike their peers in other parts of the country, Topeka's Black teachers were employed by a school board that was relatively disinterested in resource deprivation or the internal operations of Black schools. In an unusual turn of segregationist events, the city's Black educators had a unique opportunity to create a critical educational praxis that pivoted upon a shared epistemological standpoint: "Through education we rise."[17]

In plain speak, Black schools mattered. Black educators' mission and holistic pedagogical approach animated resistance to school integration during the 1940s and '50s. But Black demands for Black teachers in Topeka dated back to the period of Southern migration known as the Exodusters movement, even among those who desired integrated schools. For example, in December 1878 the editors of the local *Colored Citizen* simultaneously campaigned against segregated schools and insisted upon "Colored Teachers for Colored Schools." "We believe it is an outrage upon the civilization of the age, to carry on the caste schools, yet if they must be forced upon us, then we shall insist upon it that our educated sons and daughters are placed in them as teachers."[18] Six months later, the paper applauded the St. Louis school board's decision to only employ Black teachers in its segregated schools. "A very sensible thing indeed. If *race* schools are to be maintained, then by all means should persons interested in the progress of the race be put at their head."[19] Black Topekans continued to push back against the employment of white teachers in the city's segregated schools during the 1880s, leading superintendent D. C. Tillotson to address Black residents' concerns in his 1886–87 annual report. Tillotson blamed a lack of employable Black teachers for the lack of Black teachers employed. "Six years ago, with two exceptions, all the teachers in our colored schools were white; now

Third and fourth graders at Monroe School in 1892 (Brown v. Board of Education National Historical Park, National Park Service)

all teachers before this would have been transferred to white schools if capable colored teachers could have been found."[20]

A collective cognitive dissonance haunted generations of Black Topekans who opposed Jim Crow policies but valued racially separated learning environments. In 1902, when Black parents in the Lowman Hill school district discovered a plan to segregate their neighborhood school, they immediately began contacting members of the board. Gross inequities between the newly constructed white school and an older refurbished Black school resulted in *Reynolds v. Board of Education* in 1903. During the case, superintendent William Davidson testified that Black parents sought his assurance, not his interference. "It was school accommodations in their immediate vicinity that they desired and not a mixing of schools."[21] Although Davidson had a vested interest in *Reynolds*'s outcome and, thus, a motivation to mislead, his testimony was not wholly inaccurate. Some Black parents preferred Black schools because they trusted Black teachers, and none were under the delusion that those teachers would be welcomed in white schools.

Black residents' critical disengagement with the privileging of whiteness in Topeka public schools was manifest in multiple, simultaneous, nonlinear ways. Before 1929, some parents sent their children to Black schools while others sent their children to neighborhood schools. The transition to absolute segregation instigated litigation, but Black civil rights advocates consistently affirmed the quality of Black schools. "No contention is made that the Buchanan school is not as good a school and as well equipped in every way as is the Randolph school," the plaintiff's attorneys argued in *Wright v. Board of Education* (1930). In *Graham v. Board of Education* (1941), attorneys for the Graham family made a distinction between their civil rights claims and their confidence in Black education. "Plaintiff makes no claim nor does the evidence show that the teachers of Buchanan school were in any way incompetent as grade-school teachers, nor that the school was not a well-conducted grade school."[22] While desegregationists were careful not to contribute to discursive forms of anti-Blackness, the local NAACP publicly opposed *Graham* with the assistance of a well-known Black civil rights attorney. Black supporters of Black schools lost that battle, but not without overwhelming and widespread community support. Then-members of the NAACP saw no incongruity between a condemnation of segregation in public accommodations and a defense of segregation in public schools.

In retrospect, *Brown* plaintiffs also went on record to defend Topeka's four Black schools. "I had no quarrel about [Monroe] school or the education I received there," Linda Brown explained.[23] Her mother Leola Brown Montgomery also asserted that the local dispute in the historic case was not about the caliber of education Black students received in Topeka's segregated schools. Oliver Brown's widow waxed poetic about her family's alma mater Monroe over forty-five years after the case that bore her family's name. "I loved it! I loved it! The teachers were fantastic. More like an extended family, like mothers 'cause they took an interest in you."[24] And in 1992 *Brown* plaintiff Zelma Henderson felt compelled to explain that she signed on to the case because of institutional racism, not inferior instruction. "I never fought the quality of the teachers. It was just the segregation part."[25] She reaffirmed the interior and exterior value of her children's grade school during the fiftieth anniversary commemorations of *Brown*. "McKinley was a fairly nice school, and it had beautiful teaching," she said.[26]

An Ethos of Care: Black Educators and the Culture of Topeka's Black Schools

Because Black students were segregated until junior high school, most of their educational years were spent in supportive, nurturing learning environments cultivated by Black faculty, staff, and administrators. Black educators used that time and their epistemic privilege to develop and strengthen Black children's racial subjectivities. As a veteran educator and a father, Washington School principal Ezekiel Ridley bore witness to the collective racial trauma that Black children experienced in integrated schools. His daughters went to a mixed school right outside of Topeka during the 1900s. It "proved to be an unhappy experience" for the Ridley sisters, who endured "racial slurs and epithets" from white peers and the utter disregard of white teachers.[27]

Black teachers understood this racial reality and prepared their students for impending integration through instruction in reading, writing, and racial resistance. Leola Brown Montgomery remembered Monroe School teachers telling students to "always put your best foot forward, do the best you could" because white teachers "were going to be looking at you differently."[28] The messaging remained consistent through the late 1940s and early 1950s, when Alice Lee attended Monroe. "All of our teachers really expected you to do a good job. I remember being told when we were going to be going to junior high to do our best because we were going to be going to school with whites and behave yourself," she said.[29] Black faculty knew that Black student performance, curricular and otherwise, could reflect upon the capabilities of Black teachers. "They told us, 'You are going to a mixed school and we don't want you to embarrass us,'" recalled Richard Ridley.[30]

Oral histories may be complicated by nostalgia and the complexities of memory-making, but stories about the internal workings of Topeka's segregated schools are remarkably consistent, even across the Black political divide. Since anti-Blackness is intimately tied to Black intellect, Black desegregationists were careful to differentiate unequal schooling from inferior education. Through their narrative performances, the alumni of Black schools disrupted historical observers' racial imaginaries of white superiority and Black inferiority. Time and time again, they did so by emphasizing the competence and conscientiousness of Black educators. Even Lena Burnett, the widow of *Brown* architect and local NAACP president McKinley Burnett, insisted that the teachers in segregated schools "were very fine."[31]

One of Black teachers' most important interventions into Black students' experiences with anti-Blackness was through an ethos of care. Carolyn Campbell described McKinley School as her "home away from home." There, she said, "we were educated, nurtured, and valued."[32] Julia Etta Parks, Leola Brown Montgomery, and Joseph Douglas Jr. attended Monroe Elementary School during the 1930s. Their oral histories typify descriptions of the culture and climate of Topeka's four all-Black schools. "There was a definite closeness among people that I shall always cherish because I felt they had my personal development really at heart and a great interest in me," recalled Parks.[33] Leola Brown Montgomery graduated from Monroe in 1934. "I just think most of the children really loved all of the teachers, because they were a positive influence on our life," she said. "Not only did they teach you, but . . . they were kind of [like] a mother" to each student.[34]

The use of familial terms for Black educators was not limited to school or restricted by gender. Jack Alexander was a student at Washington from the mid-1930s to the early 1940s. He memorialized his school principal Ezekiel Ridley not only as an administrator but also as a patriarch. According to Alexander, Ridley was hands on, affectionate, and playful. He projected "a father image," Alexander said, adding he was a "solid disciplinarian, but a warm person."[35] The consensus among Black alumni of Topeka's segregated schools was summed up by Joe Douglas Jr. Douglas had "very warm feelings" about his grade school experience because "the teachers were excellent . . . they related to us in most instances like we were their own children, rather than like we were charges or wards that they were in charge of."[36]

Douglas's mother Imogene died when he was five, and Monroe's teachers provided him with a much-needed maternal presence. "There was a lot of mothering in their handling of us," he stated. The connection between Black teachers and their students influenced Joseph Douglas Sr.'s decision to embrace the school board's segregationist enrollment policy. "He was convinced that we got a better start and a better education at the schools we were attending," claimed Joseph Douglas Jr. Douglas's father was born around 1900 in Eskridge, Kansas, a small town forty miles southwest of Topeka. He was the fifth of nine children born to Tennessee migrants James and Sally Douglas, but he was their first native-born Kansan. Because state law only allowed segregated schools in larger cities, Douglas went to integrated schools with white teachers and predominantly white classmates. Those childhood experiences shaped his conviction about sending his children to all-Black schools in Topeka. My father "realized the importance of teachers who could relate to you as a human being," Joseph Douglas Jr. explained.[37]

Black professionals' career limitations proved advantageous for Black students in Topeka. Although one of the nation's leading Black educators lamented the "inadequate education" and "lack of professionalization" of Black teachers, a significant number of teachers in Topeka were overqualified for their positions.[38] Monroe "had outstanding" teachers because "the Black intelligentsia could only teach school," concluded alum Richard Ridley.[39] Many college-educated African Americans gravitated toward segregated schools during the Jim Crow era because racism circumscribed their employment opportunities. In fact, the teaching profession claimed at least half of all Black college graduates in 1910 and 1940.[40] "Many of the Black lawyers graduating at those days went to work at the post office," Ridley said.[41] In Topeka, the school board provided economic incentives for teachers to pursue postbaccalaureate studies. Irrespective of race, teachers' salaries were determined by years of experience and preparation as well as level of educational attainment. Consequently, many Black teachers had master's degrees. In fact, Washington Elementary was rumored to have more teachers with master's degrees than any other school in Topeka.[42]

Mamie Luella Williams and the Immortality of Influence, 1918–1959

One of those teachers was Mamie Luella Williams. "She was a brilliant woman, a staunch old-time teacher who really made you apply yourself," recalled former student Linda (Brown) Thompson. "I respected her a great deal."[43] Williams was a forty-one-year veteran of Topeka public schools. She started her teaching career at Lane College in Jackson, Tennessee, in 1915, but moved back to Topeka in 1918 for a higher salary. Williams taught at Buchanan School for twenty-five years and served as the principal of both Monroe and Washington Schools. She was an ardent educator who took great pride in her profession as well as in the fact that she had taught multiple generations within some families—including Oliver and Linda Brown. Ironically, Williams's career was a casualty of *Brown v. Board*. She was forced to retire in 1959 after the school board closed Buchanan to comply with the Supreme Court ruling. Nevertheless, Williams always believed that her compensation would extend beyond her years in the classroom. Her "reward," she wrote of an autobiographical character, "will be the immortality of influence."[44]

Williams was born in Greenwood, South Carolina, in 1896. The oldest of Blueford and Anna Williams's four children, she was three when her parents left South Carolina for Kansas in "search of better opportunities."[45] Upon moving to Topeka, the Williams family settled on Quincy Street in Ritchie's Addition, a neighborhood just southwest of downtown Topeka. The area was named after landowner and former radical abolitionist John Ritchie. Ritchie welcomed the settlement of Black newcomers and working-class whites who experienced discrimination in other parts of town. Consequently, Williams's neighborhood had a significant population of Black

Mamie Williams with students at Buchanan School before it was remodeled during the early 1920s (Kansas State Historical Society, Topeka)

residents who were not native Kansans. That racial geography influenced her racial formation. Reflecting on her childhood after retirement, Williams recalled feeling indebted to and inspired by those Southern Black migrants. She wrote that she and her peers had access to "better educational advantages than had been enjoyed by those who had moved here from several Southern states," so it was their duty to "learn all you can."[46]

As a child in Greenwood, Williams's mother attended Brewer Normal School, a boarding school for girls founded by the American Missionary Association. Mamie and her sister Ethel would continue their mother's educational legacy with accomplished academic and teaching careers. Although the Williams sisters both became teachers and principals with advanced degrees, Mamie's reputation eclipsed that of her sister. Mamie graduated from Topeka High School at the age of sixteen and received her bachelor's degree three years later from Washburn College, where she earned departmental honors in mathematics and German. She got a master's from Columbia University in 1924 after taking summer courses at Teachers College with educational innovators like William Heard Kilpatrick and

Mamie Luella Williams, 1944 (Kansas State Historical Society, Topeka)

W. C. Bagley.[47] "Mamie Williams was an intellectual. She had a great education," remembered Black resident Thayer Brown Phillips.[48]

Among Black Topekans, Williams had a reputation for being both smart and staid, in part because she maintained a carefully curated life. In 1970, Richard Kluger remarked upon her exceptional level of self-control, describing the then seventy-four-year-old Williams as a "tall, straight, unbelievably well-preserved and alert old lady."[49] Williams's lived experience and literary production exemplify the archival body, in this case, historical evidence of the traumatic embodiment of white supremacy and heteropatriarchy. Williams's performance of elevated and cultured Black womanhood was not only informed by the discursive anti-Black violence of whites but also the horizontal hostilities of Blacks.

Descriptions of Williams's physicality in interviews and oral histories project a certain gender queerness, a nonconformity that was relative to her height, skin color, and hair length and texture. When former school nurse Ida Norman reminisced about her friendship with Williams, who was also her neighbor and coworker, her portrayal was equal parts compliment and criticism. Williams never married, she said, but her teaching was "outstanding. Hair that long but man, brain."[50] Norman's contradistinction of Williams's brains and body speaks to the limitations imposed upon Black women from within, particularly the tension between social desirability and professional desires. Histories of enslavement created an elasticity around gender and work in Black communities. So Black femmes occupied a liminal gendered space where it was socially acceptable to pursue higher education and a career in the public sphere. But they were also bound to heteropatriarchal standards around coupling, and Williams's choice to remain unmarried branded her a "questionable woman."[51]

The archival silence concerning Williams's sexuality invites speculation. Some female teachers chose career over family because the Topeka school board would not employ married women until the late 1940s. Former Black educator El Dorothy Scott reflected upon the heteronormative school board policy with compassion for "many of the older teachers that were denied a family."[52] Others simply delayed marrying. "These women got married in their fifties because teachers [c]ould not be married, which was insane," recalled Richard Ridley.[53] Marriage was not Williams's destiny. Her protofeminist abstention was an example of what Saidiya Hartman called a "revolution in a minor key."[54] Some Black residents like Norman may have perceived Williams's improvised life as a deficit, but it was a subversion of expectations about a woman's doings, a "refusal to be governed" by a man or her community.[55] Williams spent summers living and learning in Harlem during a time when Blacks throughout the diaspora were seduced to migration by more than the explosion in Black intellectual and aesthetic production. At the risk of "writing at the limit of the unspeakable and the unknown," there is no documentation of that time in Williams's life.[56] But it is clear that she sought something more expansive than the ordinary. Upon learning of Williams's 1956 excursion to Europe, Kluger dubbed her a "cosmopolitan lady."[57] She was fifty-nine years old.

Despite Williams's global experiences and scholarly expertise, Black Topekans like Norman assessed her legacy using measures of embodied femininity. In a community that conferred social connections through complexion, Williams could not escape the evaluation of phenotypical signification. No level of professional accomplishment or personal comportment would penetrate Black spaces whose constituencies were contingent upon or constituted by proximities to corporeal whiteness. Black claims to epidermal intimacies with whiteness were often conjoined with social distancing from Blackness. "If you think segregation is bad outside the race, wait till you get inside the race. That's where the real segregation was," recalled Richard Ridley. Colorism created fragmentation and "internal strife" among Black Topekans, he said. "We had dark Negroes feeling inferior to light Negroes, and light Negroes feeling superior because they were closer to the white man."[58]

These intra-racial formations contributed to Black geographies that pivoted upon class and color. Residential neighborhoods, school enrollment, church memberships, social clubs, and political affiliations became signifiers of intra-racial hierarchies. Joseph Thompson became an active member of the NAACP after the Kansas Supreme Court integrated junior high schools in *Graham v. Board*. He was also a lifelong member of St. Simon's Episcopal Church, a "blue-vein church" that reportedly turned away residents based on color. In 1956 Thompson became vicar of the church he had attended for forty-five years. Colorism was transmitted intergenerationally among Black Topekans, he said, as light-skinned children were socialized into a sense of intra-racial superiority. "There was classism, though not particularly a caste system. The light complected, straight-haired children felt they were better — or they were taught that they were better than other children."[59]

While some white-adjacent Black Topekans sought an escape from the dehumanization of anti-Blackness through the dual pursuit of intra-racial privileges and interracial rights, Williams was not afforded the illusion of inclusion. She was highly critical of Black elitism. Williams chastised Black professionals whose "bread and butter" was dependent on those with whom they refused to socialize because she believed that social work was mutually beneficial. "It is only by using his talent in community betterment that he can make a life," she insisted.[60] While her demeanor may have led some Black residents to brand her a "snob," Williams did not pursue personal empowerment through externalizing intra-racial hierarchies. Instead, she endorsed racial accountability because her educational mission pivoted upon a recognition of her generational and geographical privileges. It was the responsibility of "our college men and women [to] 'invest their lives more fully in the lives of those who form their community,'" she argued.[61]

Blackness Performed and Pathologized:
Racial Uplift Politics in Topeka's Black Schools

Racial uplift was a philosophy and practice that structured the curricular and extracurricular lives of many Black teachers during the Jim Crow era, and it certainly informed Williams's articulations and performances of Blackness. She believed that racial advancement could only be realized through collective racial elevation. "If we can lift the 'cultural level' so that in the course of time our present highest group level will be reached by the majority of our people," the "frictions" between Blacks and whites could be resolved.[62] Widespread was the belief among Black elites that their racial rights were tethered to the undereducated Black working poor, so the semiassimilationist politics of racial uplift was infused with the pathologizing of Blackness embedded in white supremacist cultures. There was a difference, she believed, between Blacks who were "cultivated" and "illumined" and those who were not.[63] Consequently, Williams admired educational innovator Booker T. Washington because he "lifted the veil of ignorance from his people and pointed the way to progress through industry and education," she wrote.[64]

Proponents of uplift politics like Williams framed their claims for racial justice with critiques of individual deficiencies rather than conditions created by institutional racism. Williams had little patience for behavior that reinforced anti-Black racial scripts and insisted that her students "act like little gentlemen and ladies."[65] Like many of her peers throughout the country, Williams propagated a politics of respectability. Topeka's Black educators set high standards of decorum for their pupils, who were not only expected to study lesson plans but also to learn about "appearance, apparel and poise."[66] Julia Etta Parks remembered that teachers at Monroe were very attentive to student comportment. "They were so concerned [that] our behavior would be proper," she said. "We learned manners and cleanliness and neatness and all those things that were extensions of what we were getting at home."[67]

The goal of Black schooling was to forge pathways to freedom, and there was widespread consensus among Black teachers that the acquisition of cultural capital was an essential part of their jobs. They considered assimilationist insemination a subversion of discursive forms of anti-Blackness, which they believed would eventually undermine structural forms of anti-Blackness. As such, they acted as "bourgeois agents of civilization" who used cocurricular instruction to regulate young Black bodies in preparation for white public spaces.[68] Through intra-racial rehearsing of interracial theater, Black educators intended to perform an alternative reality into existence.

Because teaching etiquette and enforcing self-regulation were considered as important as the core curriculum, Black educators used physical discipline as a pedagogical tool. Corporal punishment was accepted practice in America's schools throughout the twentieth century, and it had yet to be outlawed in seventeen states as of 2023. Its legality was based upon the common law doctrine "in loco parentis," or the widespread belief that educators operated as parent proxies in school settings.[69] In segregated schools, those familial expectations were coconstituted with racial responsibilities. The harsh realities of anti-Blackness and anti-Black violence amplified Black communities' concerns about how Black children took up space in public. So, Black educators in Jim Crow schools wielded corporal punishment to enforce a strict code of conduct that governed Black students' movement and morality.

Student conduct was policed in Black schools because Black educators believed "proper" behavior was vital to the successful navigation of anti-Black attitudes and institutions. "There was a pact between the school and the family. If you got into difficulty in school you better bribe somebody not to tell your parents about it," stated Richard Ridley. "If you had to go to the principal's office and got a spanking at school, you would get a lynching at home."[70] Christina Jackson corroborated Ridley's declaration when she recalled the alliance between Black educators and Black parents. "When I was going to school, the teachers were allowed to give you a spanking. Then when you got home, you got some more."[71] Black alumni's narratives of physical discipline are often framed by sentimentality because they too perceived it to be an extension of the familial relationships between Black teachers and their students. William Mitchell Jr. spoke affectionately about his Washington Elementary School second-grade teacher Katherine Barker. She was "just like a mother to me," he said. "She would tan your butt and tell you go home and tell your mother. You took that whipping and went out of there smiling because you better not tell your folks."[72]

The collateral consequences of Black educators' respectability politics demonstrated a problematic political tension. The whip continued to be a tangible inheritance of enslavement, embraced by Black communities as a form of social control against the mobility of Black bodies. As literary and scholarly authors have noted, fears of white violence begat Black violence.[73] And yet, Black caregivers' protective energies and efforts were futile. White violence was indiscriminate, anti-Blackness was intractable, and

"Black corporeality is always designed as outside the limits of the proper, con-science, and normativity."[74] Despite that fact, the hopeful transcendent racial imaginaries of elite Americans of African descent were often grounded by pathologies of Blackness. For many, the cultures of working-class Black people that overlapped with essentialized ideas about Black people were to be suppressed or abandoned, not embraced. Consequently, a persistent double consciousness haunted the emergent fugitive pedagogies of segregated schools as the interrelated ideologies of anti-Blackness and anti-anti-Blackness collided.

Despite these limitations, the mission of many Black teachers was intimately tied to racial uplift ideologies as an emancipatory political vision. "Our great concern is a way that will lead out into the American way," quoted a Black studies supplement in the mid-1940s. "The cornerstone of all self-improvement is self-help."[75] In the classroom and beyond, the city's cohort of Black teachers dared to imagine and inculcate a Blackness beyond whiteness. Their dissemination of that embodied knowledge motivated the countermovement to Black school-integrationists during the 1940s. As Mamie Williams wrote, Black schools were necessary because "those who are socially informed about people can help them best."[76] There was much at stake in safeguarding protected spaces that affirmed Black being in a nation founded upon Black nonbeing. And there was much less to lose for those attending Black schools economically supported by the Topeka school board. Yet this convergence of Blackness remains an untold story of Jim Crow schools.

The dialectic between structural anti-Blackness and the creation of pro-Black infrastructures escaped the attention of many white scholars studying Black education in the pre-*Brown* era. To be fair, the interiority of Black schools was intentionally shielded from outsider view because Black educators' race work was conscientiously underground. However, the blackout on Black schools is not only a product of historical actors but also the making of historical producers. In the aftermath of one of the most important civil rights interventions in US history, Black resistance to school integration seemed understandably anachronistic. The stories of Black residents resisting school desegregation lacked urgency and relevancy for those who sought to commemorate *Brown* as a signaling of racial progress. That historical erasure demonstrates how "Black modes of being are delimited by a series of historical permissions and prohibitions."[77]

Richard Kluger's *Simple Justice* is a primary example of white liberal silencing of alternative Black voices. And yet, his interview with Williams remains an invaluable and revelatory source. In her 1970 conversation with

Kluger, Williams defied any historical narrative that propagandized the benefits of integrated schools for Black students. Well after the *Brown* decision, she continued to proudly endorse Black schools as "best for the children." But her refusal was illegible to Kluger, and he was clearly perplexed by her investment in Black schools beyond *Brown*. Williams was "not at all apologetic for her conservative position," he wrote in his interview notes, but she had "a clear believe [*sic*] in Black is Beautiful."[78]

Kluger could not comprehend that these two values were not incongruous, but their coherence was decipherable through the praxis of Black fugitivity. That racial logic shaped Williams's participation in the public sphere and her immersion into the subterranean. Governed by strategic flexibility, her political pragmatism vacillated among refusal, resistance, and the internalization of "standards imposed from elsewhere."[79] Williams was an active member of the Republican Party because electoral politics were critical for the attainment of Blacks' civil rights. But she also opposed local civil rights activists' attempts to integrate Topeka's public schools during the 1940s. "Black enrichment," she believed, was dependent upon taking up residency within anti-Black enclosures.[80]

Ezekiel Ridley and the Spirit of Washington School, 1918–1941

Black educators' social, cultural, and scholarly possession of Black schools represented a "form of abstention" that "forges a new kind of political space, one that bypasses the state."[81] The reclamation of Black schools from white externalization was constituted by multiple and multifaceted acts of self-determination. In that mission, Mamie Williams had many coconspirators, including Washington School principal Ezekiel Ridley. Ridley was a beloved educator respected by his peers and his students. "For his great achievement in all areas and climates of school life, Mr. Ridley will ever be honored by his pupils, his co-workers and the citizens of Topeka," she wrote in a 1954 memorial.[82]

Like Mamie Williams's family, the Ridleys were Exodusters. After a late-night visit from the Ku Klux Klan in the late 1870s, the family patriarch Jackson gathered his five children and left Smyrna, Tennessee. "My destination was Kansas, where I had heard children could be educated and we would be able to get our own land," he told his grandchildren.[83] With the assistance of local Quakers, Ezekiel was enrolled in elementary school in Oakland, just outside of Topeka. Although his father encouraged him to become a minister, Ezekiel had his own calling. "I feel so good about school life, pop," he told his father. "It would make me happy if I could be a teacher. I love young people."[84] Upon graduation, Ridley moved to Topeka and began janitorial work at Washington. He quickly moved up the employment ladder and realized his professional aspiration in 1892 when he was only eighteen or nineteen years old.[85] After teaching at Washington for twenty-six years, Ridley was promoted to school principal, a position he held from 1918 to 1941.

Ridley was a race man who spent his career developing Washington School into a semiautonomous, culturally affirming educational space for Black students and their families. Like Williams, Ridley was profoundly influenced by Booker T. Washington, to whom he was introduced by their mutual acquaintance George Washington Carver. The Ridleys hosted Washington during the late 1890s when he consulted with the founders of the Kansas Industrial and Educational Institute, known as the "Western Tuskegee."[86] Washington's bootstrap philosophy fused the connection between Ridley's political and professional lives. His educational mission and civic engagement pivoted upon the motto "through education we rise."[87]

Racial uplift ideologies guided Ridley's politics and practices both at work and in the community. He established wellness programs at Washington for children who were food insecure. "The undernourished children are taught in their special classroom," he explained. "Special 'privileges' are planned to help the pupils gain weight."[88] When Washington needed a new school library, Ridley personally conducted a door-to-door fundraiser. He also created evening classes for adults, reportedly the first in the state of Kansas. But Mamie Williams noted that his legacy was not limited to his work at Washington. "In other institutions he has made a record," she wrote. "In political circles his counsel is always sought."[89]

For example, in 1901 Black residents in the city's Fifth Ward selected Ridley to represent their neighborhood in Topeka's integrated Law and Order League. These mostly segregated citizen patrol groups emerged around the turn of the century to assist law enforcement in policing deviant and disruptive public behaviors. Black investment in these leagues was motivated by intersectional concerns as Black male elites sought to protect their communities through the surveillance of undesirable conduct and against the indiscriminate stigmatizing force of Black criminalization. Blacks from Tennessee Town showed up and showed out at a 1901 electoral meeting "demanding recognition" in their city league. As a result, Ridley was promoted over two white competitors whose supporters were reportedly "very angry" at the outcome.[90]

In addition to the Law and Order League, Ridley was an active member in the NAACP and the city's segregated YMCA. He was an officer in the George

Washington Carver YMCA for over forty years. He was one of the founding members of the Topeka NAACP in 1913 and served in various leadership roles in the organization until he retired from Topeka public schools in 1941.

Ridley's passion for community development and institution building was situated by Black nationalist genealogies. As the principal of Washington, his political standpoint dovetailed well with the concurrent movement to define and disseminate Black history. As African Americanist Adam Fairclough noted, the scholarship of Carter G. Woodson and W. E. B. Du Bois "found natural constituency in Black schoolteachers" during the first three decades of the twentieth century.[91] Fairclough's conclusion was certainly true in Topeka's segregated schools, where the unofficial educational objective was to decenter whiteness in the shared school curriculum. Monroe alum Joseph Douglas recalled that all of his books had "white kids in them. There was nothing Black about anything." While one of his teachers discussed George Washington Carver in the classroom, Douglas lamented the fact that Black students were required to learn a whitewashed version of American history. "There wasn't anything about our own people and their own accomplishments," he said.

Douglas's assumption was correct. Black teachers and administrators "had little or no input at all" in the board of education's curriculum standards.[92] However, they conscientiously objected to the privileging of whiteness in school curricula. Students in the city's segregated schools consistently started their days singing the "Negro National Anthem." This was especially important to teachers like Mamie Williams, who spoke about the significance of "Lift Every Voice and Sing" in 1932. An "Anglo-Saxon friend" once asked her why Black Americans would engage in "self-imposed segregation" by singing James Weldon Johnson's song when they could unite with white Americans in a rendition of "The Star-Spangled Banner." The Negro National Anthem "has helped my people," she wrote, reciting the song's lyrics, "'True to their God, True to their native land.'"[93]

Not only did students in Topeka's Jim Crow schools start each day with "Lift Every Voice and Sing," but they were also exposed to alternatives to Black alterity in classes and in school assemblies. LaMerle McCoy attended Washington during the 1920s and remembered national figures like George Washington Carver and local professionals like lawyers, doctors, and teachers speaking at monthly or bimonthly school assemblies. "That was always a great thing that we kind of prided ourselves for," said McCoy.[94] Principal Ridley also subjected them to random historical quizzes. "He would walk through the halls and he would ask [questions] like, 'Who is Marcus Garvey?'"

recalled Christina Jackson. "You'd better answer, and if you didn't answer, you would be punished in some insignificant way. You might have to go sit in his office and read about Marcus Garvey."[95]

Ridley's cocurricular programming exemplified "a project of desedimentation," an unmooring of Blackness from whiteness that was "genealogical and deconstructive, yet neither."[96] His work as an administrator embodied the performance and production of anti-anti-Blackness that was both capable and common within Black protected spaces. "Greater love hath no man," declared a film called *The Spirit of Washington*. The propagandistic film was produced around 1940 as a tribute to a retiring principal and as a counter to an upcoming civil rights school desegregation case. As such, it provided a rare view into the day-to-day rituals of one of Topeka's segregated schools. But it also testified to histories of Black sociality and the creation of Black counterpublics that pushed past race as imposition. "We strive to do more than just conduct a school but to serve the whole community. *That is the spirit of Washington*," Ridley declared.[97]

Ridley's mission was to weaponize education against the dehumanizing forces of white supremacy. *The Spirit of Washington* captured his intention, which was to create a holistic experience for Black students. "Heart and hand have been taught, character has been shaped, health has been guarded, and through work and play, the pupil has been helped toward organization and self development." At Washington, schoolwork did not stop with school textbooks. By introducing students to antiessentialist representations of Blackness, Ridley and his cohort produced counternarratives to the dominant cultural onslaught of minstrel shows and scientific racism.

Righting the Course by Writing the Course: Studies in Negro Life, 1942–1944

During the Jim Crow era, preeminent Black scholars and educators shared a conviction that supplementing core curricula was necessary to disrupt discursive practices of anti-Blackness. In 1933 Ambrose Caliver, the US Office of Education's senior specialist in the education of Negroes, wrote of the importance of incorporating Black history for Black students. "During the period of slavery the personality of the Negro was depreciated, and race pride was discouraged," he explained. "In view of these facts, therefore, teaching Negroes something about the history and accomplishments of their race in order to engender the spirit of personal and race pride becomes a matter of great importance."[98]

Three years later, the *Journal of Negro Education* published a series of articles in which contributors debated the "Reorganization and Redirection of Negro Education." Several essayists agreed: the curriculum in Black schools needed to include a unit on Black studies. NYU School of Education's assistant dean E. George Payne wrote that Black students' "growth and self-realization" would be greatly improved with academic exposure to Black history. Payne was a prominent white sociologist and advocate for racial justice, who also believed that the curricula in white schools needed to be more inclusive. He acknowledged that racism prevented the "unbiased presentation of Negro accomplishments" but insisted that correcting this "omission" was a "fundamental need of our educational reconstruction."[99] Progressive educators were concerned not only about the cultural grounding of students but also about the "social intelligence" of the nation's Black teachers. Howard University education professor Myrtle Phillips argued that training programs for Black teachers needed to incorporate specialized knowledge about "the history of his race . . . [and] a thorough understanding of the problems of his racial group" in addition to general education requirements.[100]

This theory became praxis in Topeka public schools during the early 1940s. Around 1942, the Topeka Board of Education authorized Black educators to collaborate on an instructional unit called Studies in Negro Life. Mamie Williams recalled that then-superintendent Kenneth McFarland and his Black director of colored schools Harrison Caldwell "dreamed up the idea." But according to civil rights activist Daniel Sawyer, it was proposed by the NAACP Education Committee.[101] "We knew that there was and is a lack of knowledge regarding the Negro's contributions to the progress of America," Sawyer explained in 1948. When members of the committee scheduled a meeting with the new school superintendent in 1942, part of their agenda was to advocate for a supplement in "Negro history." A more formalized study of Black history would benefit all students, they argued. Black students would develop "a sense of pride in [their] race" and find "some examples for them to emulate" while white students would gain "a wholesome respect for Negroes."[102] McFarland approved their recommendation and issued an official statement. A more inclusive curriculum would create "good will and tolerance towards all people everywhere," he wrote.[103]

Despite this public proclamation, Black teachers suspected an ulterior motive. They knew that McFarland was recruited by the school board to protect the vestiges of its segregationist policy after the *Graham* case. Although race matters were already an integral part of Black teachers' critical educational praxis, they initially balked at McFarland's proposal of a Black studies supplement. "We were all against the idea then," disclosed Williams. "It seemed like encouraging segregation." There was an important distinction between the racial objectives of Black teachers and the racist intent of Kenneth McFarland. "It wasn't a matter of inculcating pride at that time," she explained.[104]

Despite their misgivings, Williams and her cohort seized the opportunity to fill a void in the school district's educational program. "A need was found by the teachers for the teaching of Negro History," they wrote in 1954.[105] Black educators staked a claim on their intellectual property as a preemptive strike against presumptions about the inferiority of Black schools and Black teachers. Their redemption was just as important in the aftermath of *Graham* as it was in the shadow of *Brown*. The integration of junior high schools in 1941 put Black educators on the defensive, especially after the school board fired six Black teachers in an act of racial retribution. Through developing an officially sanctioned, racially affirming curriculum, Black teachers hoped to make a case for the inherent value of Black schools for Black students. Contributors to the volume saw no contradiction in promoting racially separated schools while simultaneously advocating for integration in public accommodations, "better job opportunities, higher wages and salaries," and improved living conditions.[106]

Of Merit, Achievement and Service: Studies in Negro Life [OMAS] was completed around 1944 and dedicated to retired Monroe Elementary School principal L. S. Turner. Turner had been the head of Monroe since 1928, and his peers credited him for "pioneering the project." They wrote that he was driven by a desire to provide "inspiration and guidance" to his students.[107] "No better evidence of his faith in boys and girls, and their future and the love he had for his race, could be established than this course of study in Negro History, in which he was deeply interested," wrote McKinley School principal J. S. Hunnicutt.[108]

OMAS was the pièce de résistance of Black educators' decades-long liberatory educational praxis. The supplementary reader became the material manifestation of their pedagogical petit marronage, the "unruly environment" of Black schools that nurtured Black spatial autonomy and fugitive educational practices.[109] As previously mentioned, Black teachers and administrators informally engaged a scholarly movement among African American historians that is most notably associated with Carter G. Woodson.

Consequently, they were already in a strategic position to take advantage of McFarland's formal invitation. However, divergent interests converged regarding Black schools. Unbeknownst to McFarland, Black educators created a text that critically disengaged from the shared curriculum by centering Black histories and experiences. "The purpose of this study is to acquaint the boys and girls of America with the contribution of the Negro to his country," L. S. Turner explained in the foreword.[110] Seven study groups produced the final text, which included course materials that corresponded with each grade level. The subject matter of each chapter ranged from Indigenous Africans to American slavery, Black education, and Black creative arts and science.

Contributors set out to right the course by writing the course. "It was claimed these texts would be used in the white schools too," Mamie Williams said, but "we knew it never would be."[111] So with Black students as their target audience, the teachers' objectives were two-fold: to engender an object-to-subject racial positioning and to instill a sense of communal accountability. "Its greatest lesson as implied in the title is that merit, achievement and service transform the lives of any people," they wrote.[112] The generational inheritances of *OMAS* contributors all but guaranteed that a politics of racial uplift would be integral to its pedagogical mission.[113] Like many Black elites who came of age during the violent reclamation of white power in the post-Reconstruction era, they turned their critical lens inward and focused on that which was within Blacks' control. As such, the public articulation of Black futurities in *OMAS* centered more on self-governance and less on white governing. A consequence of that conscientious decision was that both pro-Black and anti-Black ideologies influenced Black educators' methodological framework.

Williams penned the sixth-grade reader's introductory chapters. As the "director of research" she set the text's tone, advancing the subversive and conservative racial subjectivities of the city's Black educators. After thirty years of working in Topeka public schools, Williams's commitment to a nadir-inspired educational philosophy remained unwavering. Her embodied knowledge reflected that of the Exodusters generation, the migrant children or grandchildren of the formerly enslaved. "We didn't spend a lot of time looking for signs of mistreatment and prejudice," she recalled of her childhood. "We were consciously trying to improve ourselves." Economic deprivation may have been a given for these Southern migrants, but moral degradation was not an option. "One of the sayings you would hear a lot was that Lincoln lived in a dirt house but he wasn't a dirt man," Williams remembered.[114]

That perspective informed Williams's compilation of the sixth-grade unit's introductory chapter, which comprised various excerpted articles from Black newspapers. Williams used literary ventriloquism to articulate her belief that "The Challenge" facing people of African descent in the United States was not solely the color line. In fact, only one paragraph in her eight-page essay addressed anti-Black racism, which she called the "blot on the 'scutcheon'" of American civilization.[115] Williams chose indirection over direct action as she turned Black students' attention to a matter within their immediate control, self-regulation. "I must confess that much of the time I don't know whether to say the colored man is down because the white man is holding him down or because he is holding himself down," Williams quoted.[116] As a champion for and a critic of African Americans, Williams's race loyalty was unconditional but not indiscriminate. "It is our duty as a racial group to prove that the bringing of the Negro to America need not be 'perhaps the most tragic event in the history of the United States,'" she wrote. "We must show that merit, achievement and service win recognition."[117]

Many race men and women in Williams's professional cohort politicized the personal. Like W. E. B. Du Bois in 1924, Williams stood in "utter shamelessness" and figuratively declared that she "didn't care a damn about" any performance of Blackness "that is not used for propaganda."[118] Williams enjoined Black students to bring the future into being through assimilating normative cultural standards. Reinforcing the notion that "The Challenge" before Black America was Black Americans, Williams reprinted a 1943 *Kansas City Call* editorial by C. A. Franklin. Franklin assumed the "stance of the pathologist" common among Black social critics.[119] He argued that a generation of young Black "ne'er-do-wells" were wasting unprecedented educational and employment opportunities created by wartime expansion. "Present day incompetents" failed to assume the work ethic of their grandparents' generation. Franklin admonished these "slackers" for copying "the latest extreme in dress, the wildest mannerisms, the most shocking slang." Their elders may have been illiterate, he wrote, but they were smart enough to emulate "the speech and manner of their employers." By excerpting Franklin's arguments, Williams warned Black student readers, "Negroes do not have to be uncouth."[120]

Black educators relied upon a clear distinction between elevated and essentialized Blackness, primarily because they were inextricably tied to and bound by Black alterity. Yet, their push for Black acculturation was counterbalanced, and sometimes contradicted, by a pull toward racial particularism.

The polarity between pride and prejudice in OMAS became most apparent with Black educators' attempts to explore the ontology of Blackness and the origins of African America. The learning objective of OMAS's second chapter, "Africa, the Early Home of the Negro," was to familiarize Black students with their diasporic roots. But celebrating the roots and routes of African America proved challenging for Black elites who apotheosized WASP civilization. Williams's essay was a case in point.

The "Africa" in OMAS was a product of the Western imagination, a phantasmagoric place of sensation used by Williams to situate a proper Black subject. Her text leaned heavily into static stereotyped depictions of the continent replete with savage terrain, wild animals, and barbaric natives. Since mapping heterogeneity was important to racial uplift proponents, Williams recognized the "contrasts and contradictions" of Africa as well as diversity among the Indigenous, from "the Sudan Negroes and Bantus" to "the pygmies and Hottentots."[121] She then concluded that they were all heathens. "Missionaries of all faiths have gone into Africa in an attempt to bring God to the Africans and the Africans to God," she argued. "They are a primitive people with primitive ideas of religion."[122] Africa was a troubled place of racial reclamation for the Christian civilizationist. In 1933 Williams wrote that she preferred "illumined souls [who] enjoy a practical religion which lifts them to a higher level of thinking and living" over Blacks who worshipped an "anthropomorphic God."[123] Ten years later, she held firm in her faith, concluding that the transatlantic slave trade was divine intervention for "the descendants of those Negroes who were so fortunate as to be brought to America, the land of opportunity."[124]

Williams's theological conclusion defied racial logic. However, by tapping into American mythologies she staked a claim on Black citizenship while circumventing an uncomfortable discussion about the capture and forced migration of African peoples. Williams's colleague Fannie Patton also utilized that diversionary tactic in the third chapter of OMAS, "From Africa to America." Like Williams, Patton depicted slavery as a necessary evil. Whereas Williams evaded the trauma of the Middle Passage on African captives, Patton obscured the experiences of their enslaved descendants. The twenty-year veteran of Monroe School took cues from the Phillipsian School of slave historiography and portrayed slavery as a benign institution that was mutually beneficial for Blacks and whites. "Our country was greatly in need of laborers," she explained. "Negro slaves were much desired by the planters because they were industrious, cheerful, and submissive."

Patton deliberately situated the descendants of the enslaved as both American citizens and preferred laborers with a strategic pivot from the collective deracialized "we" in "our country" to the dual subject/object "Negro slaves." Consequently, her statement simultaneously affirmed essentializing discourses about Black laborers and attests to the essential role of Black labor in American history. Patton asserts Black indispensability by claiming Africans had a natural disposition for enslavement but then wrote that they were "untrained and fitted only for the simplest kind of work. The large plantation system was most favorable to such training."[125] Patton's lesson plan was conversant with white historians like U. B. Phillips, who argued that slavery was a paternalistic economic system that civilized Africans and their descendants. However, by doing so, she curiously neglected the interventions of Black historians like Du Bois, Woodson, and others who called into question the centering of slave owners in histories of slavery.[126]

The first three chapters of OMAS advanced normative epistemologies over subjugated knowledges, but the text's theoretical framework shifts as its attention turns from Black subordination to Black achievement. As previously mentioned, Black educators' pedagogical objective was to disrupt discursive forms of anti-Blackness. They had two lines of defense, condemning Black deviance and celebrating Black deviations. The latter became the focus of the final four chapters. OMAS contributors introduced students to historical and contemporary figures who represented a range of political perspectives and productivity, including abolitionist Frederick Douglass, educators Booker T. Washington and W. E. B. Du Bois, and creatives like Paul Lawrence Dunbar and Marian Anderson. Most were descendants of enslaved Americans, but a couple had diasporic roots like classical composer R. Nathaniel Dett and inventor Jan E. Matzeliger. The text was also gender inclusive. Mary McLeod Bethune and Maudelle Brown Bousfield are named among the "Great Negro Educators," while six of the twenty featured cultural artists were women, including Marian Anderson and Lena Horne.

While there was broad recognition of Black heterogeneity in OMAS, the chosen forty-three shared one thing in common. They were racial ambassadors who reflected a set of values Mamie Williams outlined in "The Challenge." "Knowledge, wisdom, faith, ambition, determination, courage, belief in truth, hope, and a love of life and humanity have effected their integration and have won for them recognition," she wrote.[127] Black educators' bootstrap mentality pervades the curricular supplement. "From Africa to America" portrayed the Middle Passage as a pathway to progress by describing

Phyllis Wheatley's ascension from "a child of the wilderness" in Senegal to a "refined" and cultured woman in America.[128] Whereas W. E. B. Du Bois is celebrated for exemplifying both "interracial combat" and respectability politics. "Dr. DuBois is without doubt the ablest living Negro," the textbook explained. "His stalwart character, his impressive manners, his erudite and refined scholarship, his fearlessness and sincerity of purpose, his challenging command of the English language make him as one of the truly great men of modern times."[129]

There was some synchronicity of purpose between Topeka's Black educators and the social justice icon who once pronounced, "I do not care a damn, about any art that's not propaganda."[130] OMAS elevated creatives who embraced Eurocentric artistic and intellectual standards like classical composer J. Rosamond Johnson, realist painter Henry Ossawa Tanner, Shakespearean actor Ira Aldridge, and opera singer Dorothy Maynor. The text also highlighted artists who engaged in racial particularism, like Du Bois's former *Crisis* colleague and McKinley School alum Aaron Douglas and former Topeka resident and renowned composer and choral director William L. Dawson. Students learned that the Tuskegee professor "long cherished the ambition of writing a symphony in the strictly Negro idiom, the themes to be derived from Negro Folk Music."[131]

Yet *OMAS* contributors were more ideologically flexible than their paragon Du Bois, who largely held Black vernacular culture in contempt for reinforcing anti-Black tropes. Their paramount concern was to showcase Black accomplishments because the "shame of the race" was its failure to advance like other "races or groups" had in "democratic America."[132] This false equivalency simultaneously humanized Blackness in relation to other minoritized groups and reinscribed Black dehumanization by obscuring anti-Black racism. Narrowly defined measures of "success" were illusive to people of African descent by design, not deficiencies. Because Black educators were fixated on Black exceptionalism, they were forced to compromise their aesthetic. For example, a chapter titled "The Negro in Fine Arts" celebrated bluesman W. C. Handy and blackface performer Bert Williams. Another chapter praised Lena Horne's "racial loyalty" because she insisted upon roles that depicted Black women in "something beyond a calico dress." But it also applauded the conscientiously apolitical Hattie McDaniels, whose cinematic embodiment of Black female servitude peaked in 1939 with an Oscar-winning performance as "Mammy" in *Gone with the Wind*.[133]

Black educators' conflicted critical racial analysis exposed a tension inherent within racial uplift politics, a dynamic cultural theorist Fred Moten identified as the "strife between normativity and the deconstruction of norms."[134] Unfortunately but unsurprisingly, their liberatory politics pivoted upon intergenerational and intersectional racial traumas that delimited the emancipatory vision of OMAS. Black educators' strategic antiessentialism weaponized heterogeneity against those who did not or refused to adhere to respectability politics. But for Topeka's Black teachers and administrators, life and lesson were intimately related.

The Ugly Side of Uplift: Sensationalism, Sensuality, and an Attack on Black Educators, 1937–1938

During the Jim Crow era there was consensus within Black communities that "because of the power of example, teachers should be of the highest type which our civilization affords."[135] Topeka was no exception. The school board took a laissez-faire approach to Black schools, but Black residents were actively engaged in teachers' affairs both inside and outside the classroom. Black educators were expected to conform to the same bourgeois respectability politics they imposed upon their students. But an undue burden of that idealized standard fell upon Black women, who constituted most of the teaching force in the city's segregated schools. Community surveillance of Black women's bodies and behavior evolved from a particular concern with discursive and material forms of anti-Blackness that exposed Black women to racial, gender, and sexual violence. Black female teachers were under added pressure because Topeka school board policy regulated their marriage status. With children in their charge and no husband in charge of them, Black female teachers were bound by a strict moral contract defined by a heteropatriarchal collectivist ethic.

Black elites during Jim Crow went beyond performing racialized gender standards. They "actually produced African American racialized conceptions of gender."[136] Black women's embodiment of gender conventions deviated from the Victorian norm in significant ways. In the professional realm, Black female teachers violated separate spheres doctrine by working outside of the home, but they were "othermothers" within their workplace. While this role conferred social power, it also restricted their mobility. Standards created to protect also policed, making Black female teachers particularly vulnerable to public scrutiny. "A teacher had to be very, very careful about social life," recalled former Georgia schoolteacher Georgia Sutton. "If a parent saw you out [at a club] and it got back to the school board, the chances are there would be some repercussions." Predictably, punitive measures tended to be more severe for women than men. "Men usually went where they wanted and did most of the things they wanted to do, but it was the ladies that had to be careful."[137]

The externalization of sensuality was forbidden among the aspirational, as were spaces that centered Black pleasure. This private contract between Black communities and Black educators became public in late 1936–early 1937 when a local Black newspaper indicted several teachers for indecent behavior. The *Capital Plaindealer* acquired a new editor in September 1936, a notorious newspaperman with a "penchant for sensationalism" named Davis Lee.[138] Lee had a reputation as an investigative and instigative reporter, having worked in several Southern cities before moving to the capital city. As an experienced publisher, Lee understood the commercial benefits of shock journalism. Since most Black newspapers were economically unstable, editors often relied on provocative stories to boost readership and advertisement sales. Lee set his sights on the city's Black educators within months of taking over the *Capital Plaindealer*.

"There are some school teachers in Topeka whose night activities run the whole gamut of immorality," he wrote in November 1936. "They gamble, drink and indulge freely in sexual orgies. We might throw in two school principals also who are guilty of these charges."[139] Two weeks later, Lee censured three teachers for public intoxication at a nightclub and threatened to expose names if he identified repeat offenders. "Can you imagine those three teachers returning to the classroom five or six hours later to teach our little ones?"[140] Lee not only targeted teachers' off-duty behavior but also their alleged misconduct on campus. A front-page article published in February 1937 accused one McKinley teacher of physically assaulting a student, and others of "drinking beer, whiskey, and smoking" in the manual training room while school was in session.[141]

Lee's gossip-mongering gained publicity for the *Plaindealer*, but it also exemplified the "socializing function" of Black newspapers.[142] According to mass media historian Jane Rhodes, the Black press was a critical site for disseminating respectability politics to Black publics. "This was a highly gendered project," she wrote. "Women were presented as African Americans' moral standard-bearers and thus ultimately responsible for racial progress."[143] Lee knew that charging Black teachers with social and sexual transgressions was highly inflammatory, especially because of the unstated but understood gender identities of the accused. In respectability politics, self-governance was a form of racial resistance to discursive associations of Blackness and the body. The salaciousness of Lee's allegations reflected shared expectations about proper behavior while articulating gendered markers of improper behavior (unchaste versus chaste, temperance versus drunkenness, etc.). His list of carnal pleasures was created to titillate the reader and evidence teachers' failure to disembody. Those who did not forsake vice for virtue endangered their reputation and occupation.

But as a newcomer to Topeka, Lee underestimated his readers' loyalties. Black teachers immediately launched an economic boycott of the *Capital Plaindealer*. They also solicited the legal advice of civil rights attorney William Bradshaw. Bradshaw was a well-known agitator of the Topeka school board. In fact, the *Plaindealer* applauded him for his school desegregation activism in January 1937.[144] Bradshaw was an opponent of all-Black schools, but he became a proponent for Black teachers amid Lee's character assassination. Bradshaw's older sister Mattie and younger sister Maytie taught in Topeka's segregated schools. Mattie had been teaching in Topeka public schools for twenty-five years, and Maytie for ten. So Bradshaw helped his sisters and their peers stage a counteroffensive against Lee's defamation campaign.

As a result, the *Plaindealer's* portrayal of Bradshaw immediately changed. The paper that considered him a racial hero in January labeled him a "jackass" in March. An antagonized Lee turned his vitriol toward Bradshaw and Washington School principal Ezekiel Ridley. "Uncle Tom Bradshaw Leads Boycott Move: The Truth Has Not Been Told Fox Ridley Plays a Secret Role," read a March 7 headline. In addition to branding Bradshaw a race traitor, Lee accused Ridley of gross misconduct. He claimed that the veteran educator was guilty of sexually harassing female students. Lee not only attacked Ridley's character but also his credentials. Washington students were academically compromised by Ridley, Lee argued, because their school principal had not gone to college. "Our children can not go higher than our educators," Lee wrote.[145]

Public outrage ensued. The schoolteachers enlisted NAACP president Elisha Scott, a revered Black attorney and renowned social justice advocate. Scott went to the school board on March 8 and demanded it exonerate Black educators from Lee's slanderous and unsubstantiated claims. School superintendent A. J. Stout assured the collective that he had sworn affidavits that refuted the *Plaindealer's* assertions.[146] Lee's journalistic crusade backfired. In April 1937, the *Capital Plaindealer* went into a three-month hiatus. Lee moved to North Carolina, and McKinley Burnett and Rev. R. S. Jackson took over publication of the *Plaindealer*. Under new management and new direction, the *Capital Plaindealer* promised to "be constructive and not destructive."

Burnett and Jackson issued a joint statement. "It is our aim to run the paper in such a way as to reflect credit to the Colored people and the community as a whole," they wrote. "There is already too much dissension between us as a minority race and too much bitterness between the two races, without unnecessarily creating any more."[147]

From an Attack on Black Educators to an Attack on Black Schools: *Graham v. Board of Education*, 1941

The *Capital Plaindealer* controversy marked a singular but interesting historical moment. Lee's polemics created unanimity among Black residents divided over the city's segregated schools. But their convergence of interests was short-lived. Four years after Bradshaw defended Black teachers, he put them on the defensive with *Graham v. Board of Education*. The outcome of that case threatened to desegregate local junior high schools, so Elisha Scott and Ezekiel Ridley joined forces to dissuade the school board from implementing that Kansas Supreme Court decision. Civil rights activist McKinley Burnett stepped in to calm community dissension after Lee's teacher tirade in 1937, but he unapologetically stoked political tensions ten years later. Burnett became the president of the local NAACP in 1946 and immediately launched the school desegregation campaign that culminated in *Brown v. Board of Education*.

In the years following *Graham*, the Topeka NAACP conscientiously avoided addressing the school board's segregationist policy because the issue was too contentious among Black residents. From *Graham* to *Brown*, Black civil rights activists struggled to find widespread support for school integration in Black communities. Black Topekans' desire to preserve the city's segregated schools was a testimony to the liberatory work of Black educators. For over twenty years, Ezekiel Ridley, Mamie Williams, and others envisioned and enlivened emancipatory epistemological spaces in educational places that were relatively equal. Black schools were considered critical to the performance and production of Black futurities. When civil rights activists set out to dismantle segregated schools, many Black Topekans resisted their efforts, both in public and in private. "I knew there was a lot of machinations going on" during that time period, Ezekiel Ridley's nephew Richard recalled of the school integration movement, "but I always had a great allegiance to my teachers because I owe them a debt I can't repay."[148]

Ridley was not alone. During the 1940s, most Black Topekans preferred intra-racial learning environments over interracial "progress." The following chapter surveys the seismic shift in the Black subterranean triggered by *Graham v. Board of Education*. The fissure exposed political divisions between those who engaged in resistance for rights and those who disengaged in resistance as refusal. Black alumni and parents who fought on behalf of separate schools embraced a viewpoint of Black and white as a difference between "'worlds' rather than 'worldviews.'"[149] While those who challenged the school board's policy did so because it violated Black Americans' constitutional rights. Both sides of the school debate had legitimate, yet conflicting, concerns. Perhaps most importantly, they had their eyes on the prize: a quality education for Topeka's Black children.

CHAPTER FOUR

Graham v. Board and the Clash of the Black Counterpublics, 1941–1948

In January 1940 the parents of Oaland Graham went to Boswell Junior High School to enroll their seventh-grade son. Graham had just finished sixth grade at Buchanan, and if he was white, the event would have been unremarkable. But Topeka school board policy mandated Black students remain in elementary school until the ninth grade. A mundane activity for white Topekans became an act of civil disobedience for Black Topekans. The principal of Boswell Junior High denied Graham admission "on account of his race and color." In turn, the Grahams sued the principal, the superintendent of Topeka public schools, and the Topeka school board for racial discrimination. The result was *Graham v. Board of Education*.

Unbeknownst to the Graham family and its coconspirators, that lawsuit would mark the beginning of the end of Topeka's Jim Crow schools. School desegregation would remain a contentious issue in the city until the school board abolished its racial attendance policy to avoid guilt by Southern association with *Brown*. Despite their haste in 1953, school board members had actively countered civil rights lobbyists for over ten years. They were not alone. Black parents, teachers, and alumni responded to *Graham* by resuscitating the defunct Topeka chapter of the NAACP. They activated the local branch to subvert, not support, the 1941 Kansas Supreme Court case. What began in the courtroom with *Graham* evolved into a decade-long dispute between Black school desegregationists and anti-desegregationists over the education of Black students. It was a protracted battle that was only resolved through outside intervention by the national NAACP and the US Supreme Court.

This chapter documents the *Graham v. Board of Education* lawsuit. In the story of Blacks against *Brown* the historical significance of the 1941 Kansas Supreme Court case goes beyond its legal outcome. The Graham family's public refusal set off a chain of events that forced Black residents to publicly articulate their privately held divergent perspectives on race and rights in Topeka public schools.

By surveying Black Topekans' public political battle over the city's segregated schools, this chapter not only evidences the long civil rights movement but also acknowledges the heterogeneity of Black experiences with Jim Crow schools before *Brown*. The national significance of the 1954 *Brown* Supreme Court decision has eclipsed the specificity of locality in scholarly writings. But the standardization of Jim Crow narratives obscures the dynamic nature of anti-Blackness, anti-anti-Blackness, and their diverse emergences. Historical narratives skew toward the political labor of Black freedom fighters who persevered despite the violent force of white retribution. Lesser known are the stories of those who resisted the seeds of historical change, not because they feared racist reprisal but because they prioritized a collective racial well-being. The intent of segregation was to negate Blackness, but Black communities reclaimed racialized geographies as sites of refuge. Topeka's four Black schools existed as protected spaces, and in turn, they became spaces Blacks wanted to protect.

Black community disunity over Jim Crow schools became visible because the *Graham* case forced subterranean tensions into the public sphere. Black civil rights organizing may have been covert, but it is well documented through NAACP correspondence, school board minutes, state supreme court transcripts, and newspaper articles. By contrast, Black school preservationists operated on a sub-subaltern level, wielding their power of influence through interpersonal interactions in Black social spheres. Consequently, they left little historical trace. The *Graham* decision put Black school lobbyists in the unenviable position of articulating public support for anti-Black school board policies. That historical moment provides an opportunity to bear witness to the "amazing paradox" of Jim Crow schools, the cognitive dissonance experienced by Black Americans who opposed anti-Blackness but appreciated Black teachers. "Small wonder that Negro communities have been torn in sunder by deep and passionate differences of opinion arising from this pitiable dilemma," W. E. B. Du Bois wrote.[1]

No Accidental Incident: Ulysses Graham and His Civil Rights Conspirators

Topeka's "Tragedy of Jim Crow" story began twenty years after the publication of Du Bois's classic essay. Much like Rosa Parks's defiance of Montgomery's city bus policy in 1955, the Graham family's refusal to comply in 1941 was no accidental incident of spontaneous activism. Both incidents stemmed from intentional, collaborative efforts. Seven months prior to the Grahams' act of civil disobedience, an exchange between Black residents and school board members hinted at the forthcoming challenge. On June 5, 1939, a delegation of three Black Parent-Teacher Association presidents and members of a Black civic club attended a school board meeting to stake their claim. The group's opening argument was a request for a Black school matron. Their point of contention was that white female students had access to a school matron two years prior to their Black counterparts because of the school board's 8-1-3 attendance policy. The mothers and "othermothers" of the Black PTAs considered a matron a critical need because bodies and behavior were intimately tied in respectability politics. An inability to self-regulate could potentially endanger Black girls at the onset of their physical development. "At this adolescent age [girls] should have the guidance and help of a matron," the delegation insisted.

After the group's spokesperson made her case, another Black attendee interjected. Thelma Chiles Lee argued that the board's 8-1-3 plan for Black students violated their right to equal opportunity. Foreshadowing arguments made in *Graham*, she stated that segregated schools' lack of departmentalized instruction, overcrowded classrooms, and unequal facilities were evidence of Black deprivation. Black students entered high schools without "adequate training," she maintained, which put them at a disadvantage compared to white students. The school board promised to "investigate," but Judge James A. McClure concluded the discussion with a foreboding warning. Integration would probably result in the dismissal of some Black teachers.[2] The price for poaching white privilege would be exacted at Blacks' expense.

The school board's chairman of the Health and Physical Education Committee provided an update on the issue a month later. On July 5, Isabel Neiswanger reported that the dispute over a Black school matron had not been resolved because the matter of segregated junior high schools was still unresolved. By August 7, 1939, the Black delegation had withdrawn their request. Five months later, Oaland Graham's family attempted to enroll him at Boswell. The rest is civil rights history.

The surreptitious nature of Black political organizing against the Topeka school board becomes observable through tracing the sum of its parts. School board provocateur Thelma Chiles Lee was an active member of the NAACP. In fact, she was an executive committee member in 1931 when the branch successfully lobbied the Kansas Board of Review to ban *Birth of a Nation*. Lee was a natural leader. When she was a toddler in 1902, her father's newspaper the *Capital Plaindealer* editorialized that "had she been a boy" she "would have made a good politician."[3] Lee's coconspirators were also involved in the Topeka NAACP. Oaland Graham's great uncle Ulysses was named his "next friend" in the 1941 school board lawsuit. The elder Graham had been a member of the local NAACP since 1915, two years after it was cofounded by Nathaniel Sawyer, a Black teacher and outspoken opponent of segregated schools. Nathaniel's son Daniel continued his legacy as a leader within the local NAACP. Daniel Sawyer was a staunch desegregationist who staged a three-month, one-man protest against the school board's racial transportation policy in late 1937–early 1938.

The *Graham* case was argued by two highly esteemed lawyers, Tinkham Veale, the president of the Shawnee County Bar Association, and civil rights attorney William Bradshaw.[4] Bradshaw was a veteran member of the local NAACP like Lee, Graham, and Sawyer. He was also a well-known school board antagonist. Bradshaw had been actively opposing school segregation since the city's racial attendance policy shifted from optional to mandatory in 1929. That year, as the plaintiff's attorney in *Foster v. Board of Education*, Bradshaw caught the attention of the mainstream Topeka newspaper the *Daily Capital*. It reported that the state attorney general's "negro assistant" evoked the Fourteenth Amendment, an amendment that "is not heard discussed often," and argued that segregated schools violated Black students' constitutional rights. The man who declared in 1929 that Black Topekans "are no longer going to stand for inequality in school matters" did not stop his educational justice campaign with *Foster*.[5] Bradshaw was a repeat offender of the Topeka school board between *Foster* and *Graham*. From the boardroom to the courtroom, he deployed multiple strategies of resistance ranging from indirection to direct action.

Dismantling Jim Crow Schools and Emancipatory Educational Spaces: The Promise and Threat of *Graham*

William Bradshaw was a master of political stratagem against the Topeka school board, but his antisegregationist stance in 1941 was unequivocal. *Graham* directly challenged the constitutionality of the city's Jim Crow schools. It was an unprecedented legal approach for Black Topekans. Previous cases *Foster* and *Wright* involved students at Buchanan, but they focused on a lack of accessibility due to busing, not deprivation through segregation. The facilities at Buchanan were equal to white elementary schools. So in order to demonstrate that the school board violated the separate-but-equal mandate of the state, *Graham*'s attorneys needed to prove that the curriculum and instruction received by seventh and eighth graders at Buchanan School was inferior to that received by their counterparts at predominantly white junior high schools.[6]

Unfortunately, this line of argumentation could be easily appropriated and weaponized against Black educators, a dilemma that was not unique to *Graham*. Some Black Southerners also struggled with exposing inequalities in Jim Crow schools because they were wary of contributing to white supremacist narratives. Ultimately for most civil rights activists, the ends justified the means.[7] But William Bradshaw was a school desegregationist whose sisters had approximately forty-five combined years of service in Topeka public schools. When a local Black newspaperman launched a defamation campaign against the city's Black teachers in 1937, Bradshaw came to their defense. It was the first and the last time these two forces were in public accordance. Nevertheless, Bradshaw was mindful of Black educators' reputations when coconstructing a legal argument in *Graham*. Alongside Veale, he issued a disclaimer about the city's all-Black schools, a precedent that was set in *Wright*. "Plaintiff makes no claim nor does the evidence show that the teachers of Buchanan school were in any way incompetent as grade-school teachers, nor that the school was not a well-conducted grade school."[8]

When word about the desegregation lawsuit spread among Black residents, many Black parents and alumni rallied in defense of Black schools. Their collusion with white segregationists was a by-product of the school board's attention to the *Plessy* standard. Because the school board provided relatively "equal advantages" for Black students, Black residents could advocate for preserving the city's Jim Crow schools with little reservation. Alternatively, Black civil rights activists opposed the anti-Black racism inherent in school segregation. The political drama that unfolded among Black Topekans was rooted in legitimate, yet divergent, concerns about Black students and the future of Black education. Their battle over all-Black schools begs the question: What happened when those who inhabited the same world embraced different worldviews about educational justice?

As previously stated, there were three prior Kansas Supreme Court cases that challenged the Topeka school board's racial attendance policy. *Reynolds*, *Wright*, and *Foster*—unlike *Graham*—had widespread support among Black residents. In fact, Black teachers were among those who organized a 1929 NAACP informational meeting about the *Foster* case that was reportedly attended by 300 Topekans.[9] But *Reynolds*, *Wright*, and *Foster* posed no threat to Black teachers' livelihood because they focused solely on the forced racial reassignment of Black students. Whereas *Graham* questioned the constitutionality of racially segregated schools. An unintended but inevitable outcome of desegregation would be the dismissal of Black teachers. Consequently, the Grahams' gamble animated a Black backlash. The fortification of racial boundaries in Topeka public schools secured a property in whiteness, but it also solidified structures that humanized Blackness. By 1941, all Black students had been attending all-Black schools for over ten years, a circumstance that deepened Black loyalty to Black educators.

Although the legal complaint in *Graham* stressed that neither the quality of Black elementary schools nor the qualification of Black elementary school teachers was in question, the damage was done. Black teachers' professionalism was discredited. Bradshaw and Veale subpoenaed three Buchanan teachers to testify that their seventh- and eighth-grade classrooms were inferior to their white counterparts'. One of those teachers was Mamie Williams. Williams was a highly educated, widely respected teacher who had been employed by Topeka public schools since 1918. After graduating from Washburn College in 1915, she started her teaching career at Lane College in Jackson, Tennessee. *Roots* author Alex Haley's mother was one of her students. Teaching was more than a profession to Williams; it was her mission. She got her master's degree from Columbia University in 1924 after taking summer courses at Teacher's College, and she traveled south to teach students at Texas College during the summers of 1928, 1929, and 1930. At the time of the *Graham* case, Williams had been at Buchanan Elementary School for twenty-two years. But that experience and expertise did not spare her from Bradshaw's aggressive examination on the witness stand.

Neither did the fact that the veteran educator and civil rights attorney had almost forty years of family acquaintance. They grew up on the same block behind their alma mater Monroe School. They were also classmates at Topeka High School during the early 1910s. Bradshaw's older sister Mattie was Williams's colleague at Buchanan during the first six years of her professional career in Topeka. Both women and the youngest Bradshaw sibling Maytie were members of Alpha Kappa Alpha sorority. Although their social circles overlapped, William Bradshaw and Mamie Williams were diametrically opposed on the issue of all-Black schools. Bradshaw proclaimed in 1929 that "the negroes of Topeka are no longer going to stand for inequality in school matters."[10] But Williams was a firm believer that Black students needed Black teachers because in her words, "Those who are socially informed about people can help them best."[11]

Bearing Witness: Black Educators Take a Stand on *Graham*

Mamie Williams took the stand in *Graham* as a hostile witness for personal and political reasons. She believed that Black students' education should extend beyond instruction in reading and arithmetic. All Black students in Topeka experienced segregated and integrated learning environments. But as an alumni and employee of Topeka public schools, Williams recognized that white teachers did not possess the will, desire, or epistemic privilege to prepare Black students for their futures. By contrast, the performance and production of Black futurities were critical curricular concerns in Black schools. Full integration jeopardized those emancipatory spaces. Williams's righteous indignation was fueled by another professional threat. *Graham* attorneys not only denigrated Black schools, but their interrogation insulted her intelligence. It was a transgression she took very seriously.

Graham attorneys maintained that Black students at Buchanan were denied a "high quality of educational advantages" provided white students at Boswell, an argument that was undoubtedly deeply offensive to Williams. Not only was she a race woman who took great pride in her professional achievements, but she was also arguably overqualified for her position, one of the few occupations available to educated Black women. When Bradshaw asked Buchanan principal J. B. Holland the requisite qualifications for a seventh-grade teacher at his school, he responded, "I don't know the minimum requirements, I just happen to know the qualifications of the particular teacher involved. I know that the teacher involved has a Master from Columbia."[12]

During her summers at Teachers College, Williams learned that students' "interests can be built and will manifest in questions about everything 'from a toad frog on up to God.'"[13] So she developed a curriculum that incorporated thematic courses of study, including creative activities like a theater production and an art gallery. She also designed a student government project that approached the classroom like a state, complete with officers and a constitution. Bradshaw was uninterested in these pedagogical innovations. He needed Williams's testimony to expose discrepancies between Buchanan and Boswell. Williams was Buchanan's only seventh-grade teacher, so her deposition was crucial to the desegregation case.

Despite Williams's commitment to Black students, the numbers conspired against her. Oaland Graham would have been one of twenty-two seventh graders in a combined classroom with thirteen sixth graders. The student-to-teacher ratio at Buchanan was double that of Boswell. The school board assigned Buchanan one seventh-grade teacher, but Boswell had nine teachers for 148 seventh-grade students. White educators at the junior high school split instructional duties, so each one taught a maximum of two subjects. Williams was responsible for all seventh-grade curricula, ten subjects that included history, geography, English, and math.

William Bradshaw intended to prove that Black students' education at Buchanan was compromised because their teacher was overextended. He cast doubt on Williams's ability to conform to the school board's curriculum and schedule guidelines because she was the sole instructor of thirty-five sixth and seventh graders. He questioned what daily subjects she taught and how much time she allotted for those subjects according to grade level. He asked which subjects she divided by grade and which she did not. At one point Williams quipped, "We don't teach subjects Mr. Bradshaw we teach children."[14] Williams found Bradshaw's interrogation exceedingly repetitious, especially his "unnecessary questions" about her timetables, subject offerings, and lesson plans.[15] "The schedule is a guide," she rejoined. "We don't have to follow it slavishly." Bradshaw scrutinized Williams's daily routine to establish that the 8-1-3 plan for Black students deprived them equal educational access. But Williams pushed back against the presumption of inferiority. "We are allowed to use all the new modern methods of teaching."[16]

Williams's resistance to Bradshaw's line of questioning was an active form of refusal. Unlike Bradshaw, she was not invested in the educational directives of an anti-Black, all-white board of education. Black teachers and administrators understood their assignment. They also had another objective. They supplemented the mandated curriculum with emancipatory epistemic practices to develop Black students' emerging racial subjectivities. As a result, segregated schools evolved into alternatives to Black alterity. During direct examination, Williams invited detractors to "stop a story that's always been told"—that is, the belief that whites' ways were the right ways.[17] She even inferred that white seventh graders were denied educational access because they studied English but not literature. "That is where we differ from Boswell," she testified. "They don't have it in the seventh grade. We have it in the colored schools."[18] Williams matched Bradshaw's intention and intensity. She was just as determined to defend Black schools as he was to dismantle them. The third time Bradshaw asked her if she taught one subject to three classes "all in one room at the same time," Williams called attention to their shared educational roots. "Yes, just as we had when you and I went to school."[19]

The "we" in Williams's comeback was evocative of "come back." Bradshaw was familiar with the interior workings of Black schools because he and Williams were classmates in elementary school. Both Monroe School alums would become successful professionals. Whether one believed their career achievements were "because of" or "despite" segregated schools depended on one's perspective. But Williams's public reminder was a private reproach of the Black civil rights attorney. In her estimation, the signifier "we" was determined by race, not political standpoint, and Bradshaw's denunciation of Black schools was a racial violation. Bradshaw was undeterred by Williams's racial subtext.

Bradshaw and Veale also summoned Buchanan School's home economics teacher. Like Williams, Ruth Ridley had been employed by Topeka public schools since 1918, the same year her father Ezekiel became principal of Washington School. Under Ezekiel Ridley's twenty-three-year leadership, racial affirmation was standardized in the curricular and extracurricular activities of Washington. He brought the same pro-Black energy to his parenting. "I was into Black history before it became popular," recalled Ruth's sister Hortense. "I was raised that way."[20]

As an adult, Ridley embodied her father's working philosophy "through education we rise." She received her bachelor's at Kansas State Agricultural College and completed graduate work in home economics at both the University of Chicago and Columbia University. Despite her professional training, Graham's attorneys claimed that her students received inadequate instruction. But Ridley, like her colleague Mamie Williams, refused to provide Graham's attorneys with ammunition against Black schools. Not only was she raised in a household that believed in racial uplift politics, but she had also attended an integrated school just outside of the city limits. As a student, Ridley endured the racism of her white peers and the indifference of her white teachers. She was intimately aware of the value of Black schools as protected spaces from anti-Blackness.

Graham's attorneys wanted Ridley to confirm that Buchanan had inferior equipment and facilities and that students had fewer hours of instruction than their white counterparts at Boswell. Ridley's strategy of refusal involved plausible deniability. She acknowledged that her seventh graders had fewer sewing machines and less modern kitchen facilities, but she also declared that they benefitted from more individual attention. She testified that students at Buchanan were more confident in their abilities than those at Boswell because they took home economics for the entire school year. Boswell students were only required to take home economics for one semester. "I feel that the children whose work is spread out throughout the year are not quite so nervous," she informed the court. "When they are rushed they don't do the work quite so good. I think my classes are a little bit more settled because they aren't so rushed."[21]

William Bradshaw was not satisfied with Ridley's conclusions or her creative math. Boswell students were allotted 100 minutes more per week in home economics than Buchanan students. And yet, Bradshaw could not get Ridley to concede that an abbreviated schedule disadvantaged her students. He asked, If a Black seventh grader at Buchanan Elementary and white seventh grader at Boswell Junior High quit school at the same time, would they have equal training? Since Bradshaw had previously objected to her use of conjecture, Ridley strategically avoided answering the question. "You wouldn't let me say what I thought [before], I can't go on what you think now." Bradshaw continued his probe. If white students were assigned more minutes per week in their home economics classroom, wouldn't they have the advantage over the Buchanan students? "According to you," Ridley countered. "What about you?" Bradshaw queried. "I don't know," she retorted. "You told me only to say what I know."[22]

The city's home economics supervisor corroborated Ridley's claim that Buchanan students received an equitable educational experience. Graham's attorneys deposed other white educators who also praised the quality of instruction at Buchanan. They verified under oath that Black ninth graders entered Boswell well prepared in English, history, Latin, math, and music. White teachers and administrators' assessments may have been accurate, but their testimonies also upheld the property of whiteness. By attesting to Black student readiness, they validated the racial attendance policy and protected the racial demographic of the city's predominantly white junior high schools.

Black and white educators who were called to testify in *Graham* had a similar stake in the case's outcome. As employees of the Topeka Board of Education, they not only had an economic incentive to side with the defendants, but they also shared a racial desire to maintain racial separation in elementary schools. The only Black Topekan to testify on behalf of the plaintiff was Daniel Sawyer. Sawyer was resolute. He did not share other Black residents' concerns about the fate of Black teachers. His focus was on his nine-year-old daughter, who was a student at Buchanan Elementary. "I don't care about the teachers," he asserted.[23]

It was a bold statement. Sawyer grew up in the house next door to Mamie Williams and on the same block as William Bradshaw. Sawyer's sister Annabel had been teaching in Topeka public schools for almost twenty years. During that time, she worked with Ezekiel Ridley at Washington, with childhood neighbors Mamie Williams and Mattie Bradshaw at Buchanan, and with William's sister Ethel at McKinley. Despite his history and connections, Daniel Sawyer vehemently opposed segregated schools.

Graham's lawyers cast Sawyer as an expert witness, a title the defense rejected. Sawyer's accomplice William Bradshaw countered and argued that Sawyer was qualified because he was the parent of two Buchanan students and a member of the Buchanan PTA. Bradshaw added that Sawyer was a registered voter and that he had conducted a private investigation of Buchanan and Boswell.[24] Despite the best efforts of Graham's attorneys, most of Sawyer's testimony was struck down as hearsay. Sawyer acknowledged that he had only been to Boswell a couple of times, but he claimed that it had a better student-to-teacher ratio, superior facilities, and more modern equipment than Buchanan. Sawyer was not an educator or an authority in educational policy. But he concluded that Black students were "getting cheated" by the Topeka school board because the 6-3-3 attendance policy and departmentalized instruction were widely recognized "as an advanced plan."[25]

Rallying to Respond: A White School Board United against Black Topekans Divided

With the *Graham* lawsuit pending, school board members debated the racial state of Topeka public schools. The board's attorney John H. Hunt clarified that "mere segregation is not discrimination" if "both races have equal facilities and opportunities." James McClure insisted that seventh and eighth grades in segregated schools were "substantially the same" as those in junior high schools, except for the latter's departmentalized instruction. He also pointed to the fact that white seventh and eighth graders at Gage and Branner had only recently been transferred to the city's junior high schools.[26] McClure's "disingenuous disavowal of racist intent" provided some insight into the relational situatedness of whiteness vis-à-vis nonwhiteness.[27] The school board's initial exclusion of Gage and Branner students from the protected class of whites indicated a pattern of racial nonrecognition. The school board rejected a request by working-class whites to expel Black students from integrated Gage Elementary in 1924, even though it had granted a similar petition for white parents in the affluent Potwin neighborhood in 1921. Meanwhile, the working-class and poor whites whose children who were assigned to Branner Elementary were also denied a property in whiteness and placed in racial-spatial proximity to students of Mexican descent at Branner Annex in 1918.

As school board members rehearsed their narrative defense in 1940, the school superintendent took advantage of his racial conservatorship and launched his own counterstrike. A. J. Stout's racial retaliation was aimed at the most vulnerable targets. In February 1940 he considered sending a truancy officer after twelve-year-old Oaland, whose family withdrew him from school due to the upcoming Kansas Supreme Court case.[28] Six months later, Stout sent a letter to Black teachers while arguments in *Graham* were being presented. Their contracts would not be renewed until the case had been decided, he wrote.

Stout's dissimulating attempt to cite the Graham family in racial contempt incited Black desegregationists to action. A group of twelve "prominent Negro citizens" calling themselves the "Topeka Council of Parents" issued a statement against the Topeka school board in June 1940. Signatories included Daniel Sawyer and two former NAACP associates of Ulysses Graham. "The schools exist for the benefit of the children and not for the teachers," they prefaced, but "the action of the Board of Education in withholding the contracts of colored teachers is unwarranted and designed to prejudice the case of *Oaland Graham v. the Board of Education.*" They insisted that Black teachers should be given the same consideration as their white peers. When the school board closed white schools, white teachers were reassigned, not released. If the *Graham* ruling integrated Black seventh and eighth graders, their teachers should either follow them into integrated schools or get transferred to "congested" segregated schools, the group concluded.

For the Topeka Council of Parents, the matter of Black teachers' contracts redirected attention from the issue that mattered most, integrating Black students. Their intention was not to advocate on behalf of Black teachers, it was to expose the school board's political chicanery. The school board's threats against Black teachers would not derail the movement to desegregate the city's schools, they argued. "This is now and has been the usual method employed to coerce and intimidate Negroes, when they attempt to obtain and better conditions for themselves and their posterity." The civil rights group concluded that the board's dishonorable conduct not only emboldened them, but it also had the potential to attract white allies. "Such action has stimulated rather than caused us to relax the vigor with which we shall prosecute this case, and we do believe that the better element of the white people in this community will not be in sympathy with this flagrant of intimidation and retaliation, when they are apprised of the facts."[29]

The civil rights activists were fighting on dual fronts, in the court of law and in the court of public opinion. They had to contend with the Topeka school board, which had the structural advantage, and Black school advocates, who had community support. Meanwhile Black teachers were caught in the crossfire between their Black adversaries and their white employer. A. J. Stout was unflinching. There was no shame in his segregationist game. As school superintendent, Stout was bound by an unspoken, but undeniable, public contract. An integral part of his job was to protect the boundaries of whiteness in Topeka public schools, and Black teachers were collateral damage. During the 1940–41 academic year, the board gave Black educators two half-year contracts, one in August and the other in January.

Although the city's Black educators were fodder in white segregationists and Black integrationists' battle over the city's schools, they did not publicly engage in the intercourse. Black teachers were in a precarious situation with their employers. Their interests may have converged, but they had divergent racial rationales. Black teachers and administrators had more than an economic investment in the city's four Black schools. Over the previous decade, segregated schools had become critical sites of Black fugitivity because of their pedagogical petit marronage. And yet, the *Graham* lawsuit exposed the limits of Black educators' agency. Despite a vested interest in its outcome, their voices were conspicuously absent from the public discussion surrounding *Graham*.

As conscious objectors, Black teachers and administrators deployed a covert mission. They circumvented the legal narrative by creating a cinematic response to *Graham*. Two months after receiving notice of their short-term winter contract, Black educators and their allies surreptitiously scheduled a school board viewing of a documentary called *Spirit of Washington, Washington School, Topeka, Kansas*. Black resident Joe Thompson introduced the silent film to the school board on behalf of Black school preservationists. Thompson was the county's first Black probation officer and city's only Black Boy Scout leader. But perhaps more importantly for this historical moment, he was the husband of Tracy Thompson, a Black substitute teacher assigned to both Washington and Buchanan.[30]

Spirit of Washington campaigned for segregated schools without mentioning the controversy swirling around them. The propagandistic film defended segregated schools from legal allegations of inferiority. It afforded viewers the opportunity to witness Black sociality beyond white prerogative. It highlighted not only the day-to-day activities of Washington's elementary program but also its night-school program for adults, which filmmakers claimed was the first in the state of Kansas. White school board members may not have recognized Black educators' politics of refusal, but the filmmakers were staking a claim to Black freedom-making within anti-Black structures. The captions read, "We strive to do more than just conduct a school but to serve the whole community. That is the spirit of Washington."[31]

Despite Black educators' attempt to demonstrate their allegiance with the school board, Stout cast a shadow of doubt on their continued employment as the school year ended. In May 1941, he announced that Black teachers' contracts for the following year would be delayed "due to the mandamus suit still pending in the Supreme Court."[32] Stout's use of passive racial aggression sidestepped accountability. Black teachers' job insecurity was not caused by the Grahams or the *Graham* case but by a segregationist school board that was unwilling to assign Black teachers to predominantly white schools. Instead of speaking truth to white power, the superintendent blamed Black change agents.

The school board's machinations did not affect the outcome in *Graham*. In June 1941 the Kansas Supreme Court ruled that the city's racial attendance policy violated the civil rights of Black seventh and eighth graders. The court cited differences in curricula, methods of instruction, facilities, and extracurricular activities. The *Graham* decision did not mandate a change in attendance policy, but it created a radical racial possibility in Topeka public schools. The Black press praised the Kansas Supreme Court for "repudiating the discriminatory practice of the Board of Education of Topeka against Negro children."[33] But Black residents were divided. The city's Black newspaper summarized the debate in a lengthy front-page headline: "Equal Education Decision Causes Uproar in Topeka; Jobs Are at Stake. Topeka Citizens Divided on Equal School Verdict: Some Prefer Equal Schools While Others Claim Equal Education More Vital than a Few Teachers' Jobs."

Black teachers had prepared for judgment day. When a local Black newspaper reported that "the case is being watched with much interest by citizens all over Kansas," no one was more anxious than the city's thirty-six teachers.[34] When Black civil rights activists began challenging the school board's racist enrollment policy in 1939, Black teachers, administrators, and their allies took possession of the local NAACP. These preservationists began mobilizing a counterstrategy to support Black schools against the Black attack and launched the production of *Spirit of Washington*.

The Topeka NAACP and the Compromise of Cohabitating Conflicting Counterpublics, 1930–1939

This moment in Topeka NAACP history evidences the stability and motility of Black geographies. After the *Wright* and *Foster* cases in 1930, the local chapter largely avoided the issue of segregated schools. It successfully opposed racial covenants, segregated parks, and the showing of *Birth of a Nation*, but it did not openly challenge the school board's racist enrollment policy. Segregated schools were contested grounds. The NAACP membership rolls included school desegregationists and anti-desegregationists. Daniel Sawyer, William Bradshaw, and Ulysses Graham were members in the 1920s and '30s alongside Ezekiel Ridley, Annabel Sawyer, and Maytie and Mattie Bradshaw. Due to a lack of consensus, there was no official NAACP campaign against the city's Jim Crow schools. The NAACP members who confronted the segregationist school board in the 1930s did so as individual citizens or alternately named collectives.

A rare breach of silence on the subject in 1933 provides some insight into the organization's challenges regarding the city's Black schools. NAACP field secretary William Pickens was preparing a state tour and requested information from each chapter about the "local issues and problems affecting the colored people in your vicinity."[35] Topeka's branch secretary Galena French responded with a letter that took inventory of the city's racial violations. Her list included segregated schools but with the caveat that their conditions were "good" as a result of "colored people asking for them." French's disclaimer was a subtle recognition of the political complexities created by the peculiar institution of anti-Black racism in Topeka, particularly when it came to the city's public schools. "The lack of cooperation among the colored people themselves and the various groups working against the things that made for solidarity and the best interest of the race as a whole has been the thing that has prevented the colored people of Topeka from making much progress in securing all rights of citizenship," she concluded.[36] But French's statement gesticulates without articulation. The "lack of cooperation" among Black residents was due to conflicting political standpoints on "the best interest of the race" regarding Topeka public schools. Civil rights activists contested schools designed with discriminatory intent, regardless of condition. Black school advocates embraced the relatively parallel dual education system because it inadvertently created sites that nurtured racial alternatives to Black alterity.

When the desegregationist contingent breached the uneasy compromise between the two factions, the NAACP imploded. According to official records, the Topeka chapter was inactive from 1939 to 1941. The national organization revoked its charter in 1939 because of a significant decline in membership. But the NAACP archive is misleading. Members of the Topeka NAACP were locked in a political struggle over the city's public schools. Withdrawal from formal affiliation was an unspoken solution to cohabitating, conflicting counterpublics. While the surreptitious activities of longtime NAACP members like Thelma Chiles Lee, Daniel Sawyer, and William Bradshaw were unbeknownst to the school board, their plans could not be secreted from others who shared the same subaltern spaces. So Black school advocates unofficially reinstated the local NAACP and solicited the help of then-president Elisha Scott.

Elisha Scott was a renowned civil rights attorney. He was a theatrical litigator whose clients ranged from sex brokers to Black bankers. Scott was notorious for his demonstrative courtroom performances; one Black resident described him as a "clown."[37] But Scott's courtroom presence itself was a public attraction. Scott was a space invader. A Black lawyer in white courts was a spectacle regardless of case or client. In fact, Scott was so well known throughout the Midwest that the Topeka post office received mail simply addressed to the "Colored Lawyer. Topeka."[38]

Scott's personal story is a tale of two cities. His parents were Exodusters who escaped Southern terrorism in 1879 only to find that Topeka was no "Promised Land." The Scott family and many of their neighbors in Tennessee Town experienced extreme levels of poverty. Scott's father died five months after he was born, so the family's economic survival depended on his mother's service work and the financial assistance of congregational minister Charles M. Sheldon. Sheldon became an influential presence during Scott's formative years. Scott attended the Tennessee Town kindergarten that Sheldon had founded in 1892. And Sheldon supplemented Scott's tuition payments when he attended the Kansas Industrial and Educational Institute, a Black vocational school also known as the "Western Tuskegee."

Elisha Scott's road to racial resistance began in high school. It is where he met his mentor, a prominent Black attorney named James H. Guy who served on the Kansas Industrial and Educational Institute's Board of Managers. Members of the Black elite like Guy were invested in the leadership and direction of the institute because it was a paragon of racial uplift. Guy was driven by a sense of racial exceptionalism. Upon arriving in Topeka from Ohio in 1884, he established St. Simon's Episcopal Church, a "blue-vein" church widely known for its colorism. He valued class and corporeal proximities to whiteness, but he was not an assimilationist. Guy was both a founding member of the Topeka NAACP and an outspoken advocate for separate educational spaces. He believed that Black futures necessitated protecting Blacks' political rights and cultural rites. "Every colored man of sense and ambition" preferred Black schools, he told a local Black newspaper in 1892. "Why do you want to push yourself into places where you are not wanted? We should recognize our differences and need to establish race pride and confidence."[39]

Elisha Scott worked in Guy's law offices while he was in high school and gained professional guidance and inspiration. He went on to become the third Black person to get a degree from Washburn Law School. Like Guy,

Scott spent his career as a freedom fighter. He pushed for antilynching legislation after representing the families of victims in Duluth, Minnesota, in 1920 and the Tulsa race massacre in 1921. He fought to integrate public accommodations. He even successfully represented the plaintiffs in *Thurman-Watts v. The Board of Education of Coffeyville*, a 1924 case that integrated junior high schools in Coffeyville, Kansas. Fifteen years later, Scott exercised the dexterity of his high school mentor. With another desegregation case looming on the horizon, the Topeka NAACP president was called to action. Only this time, it was not to challenge an anti-Black policy, it was to preserve one.

The Clash of Black Counterpublics: The NAACP v. Black Civil Rights Activists

Although the Kansas Supreme Court ruled in favor of the plaintiff in *Graham*, it reinscribed the defendant's power to determine the fate of Black students. Because integration became the Topeka school board's prerogative, Black lobbyists immediately descended upon its members to negotiate their desired outcome. School board minutes record an unprecedented baring of the subterranean conflict unfolding among Black residents over segregated schools. It is apparent that Black residents' rationale for and against integration pivoted upon an us-versus-them orientation toward all-Black schools. Civil rights activists resisted the spatialization of Black dispossession produced by the racialized attendance policy. For Black school desegregationists, racially separated schools served a white "them." But Black school preservationists rejected the sociospatial impositions of whiteness. Black educators had reclaimed segregated schools as "ours," reenvisioned them as geographies of Blackness, and affirmed Black being within structures designed to coconstruct Black nonbeing.

Two weeks after the *Graham* decision, the school board president called a special meeting to hear the concerns of a group "composed of many colored people." Black parents, alumni, and educators were prepared to defend their schools—and Black teachers' jobs. The anti-integration lobby acknowledged that the Kansas Supreme Court had found discrepancies between Buchanan and Boswell Schools. But it did not deter Black residents from petitioning for Black schools. They wanted "the same books, the same facilities, but their own teachers. They want the Board to let them alone."[40]

Washington School principal Ezekiel Ridley was among the group's representatives. Ridley had just retired after forty-nine years at Washington School. During his twenty-three years as a principal, Ridley's racial rallying cry was "through education we rise," and he was extremely intentional with his anti-anti-Blackness. With the assistance of Washington's faculty and staff, Ridley developed the segregated school into a culturally affirming educational space for Black students and their families. His presence at the June 23 meeting was critical for Black school preservationists.

That day was Ridley's first appearance before the board even though he had one of the longest service records in the city. The well-respected veteran Black administrator understood his assignment. He weaponized dissemblance. Ridley's opening statement expressed gratitude for the board's "many kindnesses." Many white Kansans were highly invested in an imagined inheritance of white liberalism and racial benevolence. Ridley appealed to school board members' racial egos to disarm any defensive former defendants. He was not there to accuse them of racism, he assured. "There is not a member of the present Board, the Superintendent, nor members of Boards in the past years who have intentionally discriminated against any colored child in the city of Topeka," he carefully stated.

Ridley also deployed storytelling to allay white fears of a Black attack. He shared a conversation he had had with Booker T. Washington. At the turn of the century, Ridley hosted Washington during a consulting visit to the Kansas Industrial and Educational Institute. According to Ridley, Washington praised the city for its lack of racial discord. He "had been all over the country," and no place in the United States had a spirit of interracialism "as cordial as it is in Topeka." Ridley's strategy was politically savvy. Washington's philosophy of separate racial spheres aligned with the beliefs of the Black delegation and the segregationist school board. Ridley concluded that the board should maintain its current attendance policy despite the Supreme Court ruling in *Graham*. "The majority of the colored people are satisfied with the schools as they are," he said.[41]

NAACP president Elisha Scott agreed. The confusion over Black schools was caused by a small minority of Black residents, he asserted. "No one can charge the Board of Education with discrimination because they have never been guilty of it." The school board should not be compelled to change its current policy because of a few Black opponents, he contended. The civil rights crusader's presence at the meeting had the potential to incite white dis-ease, but on that day he stood before the school board and endorsed its segregationist policy. "The time is not ripe yet to make a change and have [Black] children attend schools where the majority is white," he proclaimed.

Unbeknownst to school board members, Scott presided over an unsanctioned NAACP branch activated by anti-desegregationists. But that didn't matter. The NAACP president was a political shapeshifter. In 1924, he successfully argued that Coffeyville's racial attendance policies disadvantaged Black junior high school students. Seventeen years later, he claimed that Topeka's segregationist policies advantaged Black junior high school students. His position on Jim Crow schools proved situational and contextual. The Coffeyville school board had reneged on its promise to integrate the city's newly constructed junior high school in 1923. Not only did it betray Black residents, but it also deprived Black students of equal access. The city's segregated Cleveland School was overcrowded and undermaintained by school board members with alleged Ku Klux Klan involvement.[42]

By contrast, Topeka school board members' performance and production of whiteness did not include overt articulations of anti-Black racism or divestment from segregated schools. So Black Topekans felt more comfortable asking the board "to detour around the law" by keeping its racial attendance policy intact. "It is the consensus of opinion and wishes of the majority of the colored people that the Board retain the teachers under the present system and not violate the decision in the *Graham* case," Scott affirmed. While civil rights activists like Daniel Sawyer "didn't care" about Black teachers, Scott balanced their concerns with those of Black students. Scott urged school board members to prioritize the best interests of Black schoolchildren before the legal interventions of Black integrationists. "Colored teachers know the psychology of the colored children better than a white teacher could," he rationalized. Because Black students benefitted from Black teachers' epistemic privilege and ethos of care, Scott declared that "the Board cannot secure better teachers for the colored people than they have now."

Scott's definition of educational justice on June 23 pivoted on his representation, not his reputation. In fact, he provided the Topeka school board with multiple strategies of white resistance. He advised the board to "confer with the 85 percent to 90 percent" of Black parents who preferred all-Black schools. With Black parents' consent, the school board could keep its current policy and "not violate the law." He also suggested that board members could sidestep the Kansas Supreme Court ruling in *Graham* if the state legislature passed a special act. In his final proposal, the civil rights attorney suggested the erection of a segregated junior high school. The racial justice champion reasoned that an all-Black junior high school would provide job security for Black teachers and social security for Black students because "a colored teacher would do for colored children [what] a white teacher would not do."[43]

Boy Scout leader Joe Thompson's contribution to Black residents' testimonies also focused on the mental health and emotional well-being of Black schoolchildren. Three months earlier he had indirectly showed his support for Black schools with the documentary *Spirit of Washington*. This time, Thompson was more outspoken. Many Black Topekans were unaware of *Graham*, he said. But once word spread about the Supreme Court ruling and its implications, he was certain Black residents would support segregated schools because Black students were "proud of their own schools." Thompson's appeal for Black schools ironically foreshadowed the plaintiffs' arguments in *Brown*. Attending predominantly white schools was "not so pleasant for colored children," he said, and he was concerned that integration "would give the colored students an 'inferiority complex.'" The probation officer warned that negative experiences could lead to high dropout rates, "which might lead them into trouble of various kinds."[44]

The meeting left school board members conflicted over their next course of action. The legal setback posed an imminent threat to their property in whiteness. But the state's most notorious civil rights attorney ensured them that the current plan could continue with "peace, harmony and happiness" if they provided "documentary evidence" of Black support.[45] So, board members decided to test his theory. They deliberated and settled on a plan to conduct a survey of those who would be directly impacted by the *Graham* ruling. The board would ask the parents of approximately 200 Black seventh- and eighth-grade students if they preferred segregated elementary schools, integrated junior high schools, or possibly, a segregated junior high school. The board also considered the legality of departmentalizing seventh and eighth grades in Black elementary schools.

But board members' anticipation of a peaceful return to racist routine was quickly interrupted. While Black school preservationists were canvassing Black neighborhoods, Black civil rights activists prepared to "wage an 'unrelenting fight in behalf of the children.'"[46] They mobilized a media campaign that targeted the Topeka school board and its coconspirators and set their sights on recapturing the local NAACP. At the forefront of this counter-counteroffensive was Raymond J. Reynolds.

Reynolds was a militant opponent of Topeka's anti-Black racism. In 1936 editors at the *Capitol Plaindealer* celebrated him as "one of the most outspoken young men of his race" and dubbed him "Topeka's fighting attorney."[47] Considering the city's closely related active cohort of Black civil rights litigators, the *Capitol Plaindealer*'s accolades were significant. The grandson of an Exoduster, Raymond Reynolds's uncle William initiated the first legal challenge against the city's segregated schools in *Reynolds v. Board of Education 1903*. His older brother Earl argued *Foster v. Board of Education* alongside

William Bradshaw. And Raymond preceded his Kappa Alpha Psi fraternity brother Elisha Scott as the NAACP chapter president during the early 1930s. Under Reynolds's leadership, the branch targeted racial covenants, segregated city parks, and the discriminatory employment practices of private contractors working on public projects.

After a short hiatus from public-facing activism, Reynolds returned with a political vengeance in 1941. He criticized the school board's consideration of an optional attendance policy, but his righteous indignation was not reserved for the board. In a July 4 *Plaindealer* article he said that permitting Black seventh and eighth graders to remain in segregated learning environments was "tantamount to allowing the colored children and their parents the right to prefer inferior education." Reynolds condemned Black school lobbyists and accused them of political impersonation. "While [the previous] delegation pretended to be arguing for the best interest of the colored students," he impugned in the press, "it in fact offered a plan primarily designed to save a few colored teachers their jobs at a sacrifice of the rights assured to the children under the court's decision." The rights of Black students should be prioritized over the jobs of Black teachers, he insisted. If the school board kept seventh and eighth graders in segregated schools, it would "subject the students to an unscrupulous campaign of misrepresentation on the part of the colored teachers to save their jobs together with their designing friends."[48]

NAACP émigrés like Reynolds and Sawyer were outraged by their opponents' invocation of the civil rights organization to support segregation. So, they staged a takeover. They put pressure on Elisha Scott to conform to organizational norms. In a July 5 letter to the national office, Scott wrote of the chapter's intent to reinstate its official charter. Daniel Sawyer was among the newly paid members.

Two days later, the Jim Crow abolitionist and thirty-eight other Black residents attended a regularly scheduled school board meeting and demanded compliance with the *Graham* ruling. Reynolds led the group of Black dissidents who criticized the school board's poll. There was an inherent conflict of interest when highly respected educators like Ezekiel Ridley canvassed Black neighborhoods, he argued. "It did not give a true picture of the sentiment of the colored people," Reynolds maintained. "It was unfair and taken by persons prejudiced in favor of the existing system."

Daniel Sawyer also contested the community survey. He warned board members that they "would be circumventing the law as interpreted by the Supreme Court" if they gave Black parents a choice between segregated elementary schools or integrated junior high schools. Sawyer could not tolerate a racial evasion of a long-awaited legal intervention. The *Graham* ruling had already established the unconstitutionality of the school board's segregationist junior high school policy, he argued. So Black preservationists' data collection was immaterial, even if "99 percent of Black parents" wanted to keep their seventh and eighth graders in segregated schools.

Elisha Scott made a repeat appearance before the board to retract his previous defense of the defendants. In the presence of his incontrovertible peers, he pivoted slightly from his previous position. Scott clarified that he opposed anti-Black discrimination, but he supported the school board's racial enrollment policy "for the present at least, with equal facilities and accommodations."[49]

Disclaimers aside, the NAACP president's perspective was the prevalent viewpoint among Black Topekans. Most Black parents polled by the school board agreed with the anti-desegregation delegation. Sixty-five percent of those surveyed preferred all-Black schools over integrated junior high schools because Black schools subverted the structural and metaphysical violence of anti-Blackness.

Resignation and Resentment: The School Board's Reluctant and Retributive Response to *Graham*

The reasoning behind the poll was less important than the result to James McClure. McClure was a proven segregationist who joined the Topeka school board the year the city began to enforce its racial enrollment policy. From 1929 forward, McClure was the school board's great white hope, consistently and openly advocating for white privilege through Black exclusion. In 1938, it was McClure who exposed the integrationist intentionality of Daniel Sawyer's protests about the school board's revised bus policy. The following year, when Black lobbyists broached the subject of desegregating the city's junior high schools, it was McClure who subtly threatened teacher firings. He did so again in June 1941 as *Graham* was still being argued. But McClure's racial resistance was never more explicit than on July 11, 1941.

After the findings of the school board poll were announced, McClure told board members that he was "very strongly in favor of segregation as far as we can go" because "it is the best thing for the white children and far better for the colored children." The constitutional rights of Black students were of less concern to the Shawnee County District Court judge than preserving whiteness as property. Black and white students "have been segregated for years and it has been very satisfactory," he contended. McClure warned his colleagues that if integration was a failed experiment, Black seventh and eighth graders could not be reintroduced to their former schools. McClure also deployed paternalism. Black students may get accustomed to attending predominantly white schools, he said, and not want to return to segregated schools "although it might be better for them."[50] His recommendation was that the board wait a year to avoid a potentially regrettable, unretractable decision. Black parents should be allowed to decide for themselves, he conveniently concluded.

Isabel Neiswanger was the only school board member who flouted her peers' racial expectations and questioned the legitimacy of the poll's findings. Like Raymond Reynolds, Neiswanger was troubled by the possibility that Black parents had been unduly influenced by Ezekiel Ridley and his cohort of Black school preservationists. She speculated that the results may have been skewed by an overemphasis on Black teachers' retention. Neiswanger's assessment may have been accurate, but so were the apprehensions of Black educators. Because at the July 11 meeting, Stout suggested that the contracts of all Black teachers be withheld until the matter of the city's junior high schools was resolved.

Despite school board members' almost unanimous support for segregation, they decided to integrate Topeka junior high schools on August 4, 1941. Their racial self-restraint may have been unusual for white Americans but not uncommon for white Topekans. After 1929, the Topeka school board consistently, albeit begrudgingly, accommodated Black parents' grievances over racial discrepancies if those discrepancies could be confirmed with certainty. White school board members instituted changes not because they were altruistic toward Black students but to sustain racially homogenous schools for white students. Consequently, school board members continued to express reservations about integration immediately after voting to desegregate the city's junior high schools. Recently elected school board member Marlin S. Casey told his new colleagues that he felt coerced into supporting integration by a personal visit from Daniel Sawyer and Raymond Reynolds.[51]

Casey articulated the racial resentment of those who remained uncomfortable with their decision to formally recognize the constitutional rights of Black seventh and eighth graders. Other board members used paternalism as projection and voiced hollow concerns about civil rights activists exerting pressure on Black parents who did not want to enroll their students at integrated schools. But nowhere was the Topeka school board's passive aggression more evident than in their personnel decisions. As predicted, justice for Black students did not translate into fair play for Black teachers. The repercussions were swift. Six women were fired or forced to retire, which was significant considering there were only thirty-six Black educators. Emma Cooper was one of those teachers. The daughter of an Exoduster, Cooper was fired after teaching in Topeka public schools for thirty years and just two years after she received her bachelor's degree in education from Emporia State University. Isabel Neiswanger conveyed her condolences about the contract terminations. She was "very sorry that all of the colored teachers heretofore employed could not be offered contracts for the coming year," she said. But "the Board had no course other than making this reduction in the number of colored teachers" because of the desegregation lawsuit.[52]

Although Neiswanger was the only school board member who voted to integrate Black seventh and eighth graders, her act of contrition absolved her racial collaborators from their responsibility for the fate of Black teachers. But Neiswanger's denial could not hide the fact that the board's suspensions were clearly punitive. Black seventh- and eighth-grade teachers were spared because some were also school principals or assistant principals. School board members deliberated at length over what criteria would inform their decisions about which teachers would lose their positions. They debated whether to base their choices on teachers' qualifications, tenure with Topeka public schools, principals' recommendations and reports, or "various other reasons."

Retribution was among school board members' unspoken options. They relegated home economics teacher Ruth Ridley to part-time employment after twenty-two years of service. She was demoted even though she had advocated for separate schools when called as a plaintiff's witness by a *Graham* attorney.[53] Others suffered from guilt by association. William Bradshaw's and Daniel Sawyer's sisters were two of three teachers dismissed by the school board. At the time that they were fired, Maytie Bradshaw and Annabel Sawyer had been teaching in the city's segregated schools for seventeen and eighteen years, respectively. Annabel held her younger brother partially responsible for her expulsion. "Anne was angry about that clear up to '68 when I found out about it from her," recalled Daniel's daughter Constance.

No longer employees of Topeka public schools, both women left town in search of work at the age of forty-two. Maytie Bradshaw relocated to Denver, Colorado, leaving her sister Mattie as the sole occupant of their family home on Quincy Street. Annabel, who lived next door to the Bradshaw sisters, moved to Alexandria, Louisiana, where her sorority sisters found her a job as a United Service Organizations hostess. Performing gendered labor for segregated armed forces was not as financially or intellectually rewarding as performing racial labor in Topeka's segregated schools. According to her niece Constance, Annabel "had some very difficult, very hard times there economically." To make ends meet, Annabel rented out the Sawyer family home and was eventually forced to sell it. "Of course she was quite bitter about that," Constance said.[54]

Annabel was not alone. The school board's abrupt, but expected, termination of Black teachers troubled their colleagues. The "reprisals affected the morale of the colored teachers and caused some feeling of bitterness generally," Daniel Sawyer later confirmed.[55] The interconnectedness of the city's Black educators cannot be underestimated. Emma Cooper, Maytie Bradshaw, Annabel Sawyer, and Hester Hardeman were four of the six teachers released by the Topeka school board. Cooper, Bradshaw, and Hardeman had been teaching since the 1910s, at times in the same schools. But they also shared spaces of sociality that extended beyond the workplace. For example, all four women were members of Alpha Kappa Alpha sorority. In fact, more than half of the Black women who taught in Topeka from 1930 to 1954 were AKAs, including Mamie Williams. In addition to being sorors, Williams, Sawyer, and Bradshaw had been next-door neighbors on the 1500 block of Quincy Street for forty years. Since female teachers were not allowed to marry, those who were native Topekans lived in their childhood homes through adulthood. These intimate connections forged a communal interdependence among Black women that transcended their shared occupation.

The Reclamation and Redirection of the Topeka NAACP, 1941–1948

With the *Graham* case resolved, civil rights activists set their sights on Black educators' local movement center.[56] A month after the junior high schools were integrated, Raymond Reynolds began corresponding with the national NAACP to oust school preservationists from the unsanctioned Topeka branch. In a September 1941 letter to assistant secretary Roy Wilkins, Reynolds contextualized the situational commandeering of the local organization by Black teachers and their allies. A group of NAACP members had convened a meeting without "proper notice," and it "was packed for a definite purpose," he explained. The continued leadership of chapter president Elisha Scott was "not agreeable to those most interested in its rehabilitation" because Scott had been pressured into the role by members with an expressed agenda. "We were then involved in quite a school fight and they packed the said election to hold him selfishly at the head of the branch for their particular purposes," Reynolds wrote. "They were defeated, however, by the subsequent decision of the Board of Education, so I doubt now that they have further interest in the matter."[57]

Reynolds's assessment was correct. The teachers and their allies surrendered their stronghold. Reynolds was elected president of the formally reconstituted Topeka NAACP in December 1941. With the teachers' exodus, the chapter's political lens readjusted and focused on civil rights initiatives more closely aligned to the national organization. Some members discussed launching a direct challenge to school segregation after the *Graham* win. Daniel Sawyer even attempted to enroll his daughter Grace in their neighborhood school Lowman Hill at the beginning of the 1942 school year. But ultimately, Black teachers were granted a temporary reprieve. For the next seven years, war-torn and battle-weary members turned their energies from segregated public schools and toward segregated public accommodations. From an organizational standpoint, this programmatic shift was productive. Within six months the Topeka NAACP had 163 new members, a record recruitment for the local branch. In June 1942, Reynolds reported that the chapter had over 300 members.

Between 1941 and 1948, the local chapter only breached the ceasefire between school desegregationists and preservationists once. When superintendent A. J. Stout announced his retirement in 1942, Daniel Sawyer and members of the NAACP Education Committee scheduled a meeting with his successor Kenneth McFarland. According to Sawyer, the civil rights group wanted to "remedy the situation" *Graham* had created among themselves, the school board, and Black educators. The hire of a new superintendent provided them with an opportunity to rehabilitate their relationship with the board and a chance to make amends with Black teachers. The committee had a singular aim, Sawyer wrote, and that was to promote "a better understanding between the races through the medium of education."

The only archival evidence of that July 1942 event is a September 1948 letter that Sawyer addressed to the Topeka Board of Education. As such, it is more of a historical marker of the emergent school desegregation challenge in 1948 than an account of the interchange between the NAACP and the new superintendent in 1942. The committee's intentions were not as magnanimous as Sawyer described. The meeting with McFarland was not an act of reconciliation; it was a calculated confrontation. Sawyer had proven to be a politically agile opponent of the school board. He deployed circumvention with the school board in 1938, legal intervention with the Kansas Supreme Court in 1941, and dissemblance with the new superintendent in 1942. His approach was adaptable, but his objective remained consistent. From his one-man school bus protest in 1938 to his death in 1950, Sawyer's priority had always been school integration.

Sawyer's political motives may have compromised his account of the NAACP's interaction with McFarland, but his 1948 letter provides some insight into the NAACP's order of business. The education committee had several talking points for addressing the de jure segregation of elementary schools and the de facto segregation of Topeka High School. Since segregation was "an accepted fact" in Topeka public schools, the group petitioned for racial self-determination in the city's Jim Crow schools. They wanted "colored supervisors and a colored director of colored schools." This modification in structural accountability would empower Black administrators and enhearten Black educators, they asserted, because the "old setup offered no incentive or opportunity for advancement for the colored teachers."

NAACP representatives also lobbied for more gender equity in the selection of "principalships." Most Black teachers were women, but all Black principals were men. This ask was less of a feminist intervention for female teachers than it was an extension of patriarchal protections for Black children. The man who had testified "I don't care about the teachers" the previous year in *Graham* did not shift his perspective. He changed his strategy. The committee believed that Black children suffered the consequences for Black women's career limitations. "The lack of opportunity for advancement cause[s] a general feeling of apathy" among Black teachers, "which was reflected in the preparation of colored children for secondary education."

With the students at the forefront of the committee's concerns, members turned their attention to the city's "mixed" junior and senior high schools. They called for the school board to desegregate the teaching force and hire Black faculty for integrated schools. In addition, they objected to segregated extracurricular activities at Topeka High School. The NAACP representatives put particular emphasis on the high school's segregated athletic teams, which they insisted should be determined by "merit," not race. Finally, the education committee proposed the inclusion of a "Negro history" course at Topeka High School.[58]

The new school superintendent made a few, albeit significant, adjustments after meeting with Daniel Sawyer and his NAACP associates. Like Stout, McFarland would not entertain the prospect of integrating Black teachers without legal intervention. But he approved the education committee's request for a Black history supplement. Black educators completed *Of Merit, Achievement and Service: Studies in Negro Life* around 1944. The school board integrated high school athletics except for the swimming pool and the Ramblers basketball team. McFarland made two personnel decisions to accommodate the NAACP's requests. He promoted Mamie Williams to assistant principal at Washington Elementary School in 1943 to satisfy their gender concerns. He also appointed a director of colored schools. Unbeknownst to all parties involved, that decision would alter the course of local and national history.

The NAACP Education Committee's appeal for a colored supervisor was to create an official liaison between Black residents and the white school board. They wanted the superintendent to recruit "a man who would be sensitive to the aims and aspirations of the Negro parents and teachers."[59] Instead, McFarland appointed Harrison Caldwell. Caldwell quickly gained a villainous reputation among Black Topekans on both sides of the Black school issue. The colored supervisor enforced segregation with tyrannical intensity and managed Black educators and students through a system of patronage. After six years of his dictatorial reign of power, NAACP members decided it was time to effect change.

Caldwell was a key historical actor in the civil rights drama that unfolded in Topeka public schools during the 1940s. In fact, Todd cited him as a catalyst for the 1948 school desegregation campaign that evolved into *Brown*. But Caldwell's role as the Black antagonist in the *Brown* story has been largely underexplored. He is a looming figure in Black residents' oral histories but relatively absent in historical narratives. Richard Kluger (1977) and Jean Van Delinder (2008) confer dishonorable mentions, but they subordinate Caldwell to McFarland and the school board when identifying the source of Black discord with and within the city's Black schools.[60] This conclusion contradicts the testimonies of Black teachers, students, and civil rights activists who identify Caldwell as more than an accessory to white crime. The colored supervisor may not have possessed the empowered whiteness of the superintendent, but Harrison Caldwell was no subplot.

The following chapter unveils Caldwell as the Black antihero of *Brown*. The director of colored schools did not mitigate white power; he wielded it by proxy. Fully integrating the colored director into the Black backstory provides an opportunity to explore and expose uncomfortable truths about Black collusion with white domination. In addition, telling the tale of Harrison Caldwell speaks to the diversity of racial experiences, political perspectives, and personal motivations that produced competing interests within Topeka's Black communities during the 1940s.

CHAPTER FIVE

Harrison Caldwell

The Unsung Black Antihero of Brown

The year 1948 was a turning point for Topeka's Jim Crow schools. Civil rights activists breached their six-year moratorium with Black school preservationists and launched a public crusade against the Topeka Board of Education. For many historical observers the origin story of *Brown v. Board of Education* in Topeka begins when NAACP president McKinley Burnett demanded full integration of Black students and teachers at an April 23 meeting. It is a logical conclusion, but one that tethers Black resistance to school board policy. Archival evidence points to an additional, equally important source of conflict for NAACP members. Although white segregationists earned center stage as the antagonists of the landmark desegregation case, there was a lesser-known pivotal Black character in the *Brown* story.

The Topeka school board received warning of the emergent insurgency in the months that immediately followed. NAACP members circulated a petition after a local club refused to admit Black students into a Topeka High School graduation party that May. Many extracurricular activities were segregated at Topeka High, but the orchestrator of this racist event was not white. The director of colored schools Harrison Caldwell staged an intervention once he discovered that the student mixer would be racially mixed. He contacted the venue's management and urged them to prohibit Black student attendance. They complied, and Black students were denied entrance despite the inclusive intentions of their white peers.

Caldwell's public humiliation of Black students inflamed NAACP members, who mobilized under the moniker the "Citizens Committee on Civil Rights." They drafted a flyer that fixated on Caldwell's complicity with white segregationism rather than on the segregationist superintendent and school board. The citizens committee indicted the colored director for embracing "the ANTI-NEGRO PHILOSOPHY" that supported Jim Crow policies and practices in Topeka public schools. "He himself a Negro" is "a traitor to his group," they insisted. "He is Kenneth McFarland's stooge."[1] It wasn't the first time Caldwell committed "a Jim Crow outrage" or used "NAZI-LIKE INTIMIDATION," but civil rights activists hoped it would be the last. Because this time, as their petition warned, "The People Fight Back."[2]

130

Brown architects McKinley Burnett, Daniel Sawyer, and Lucinda Todd all identified Harrison Caldwell as the instigator of the breakthrough civil rights moment of the late 1940s. Caldwell's oppressive and excessive collusion with whiteness was a critical complaint in a May 24, 1948, letter Burnett wrote to national NAACP president Walter White and in a September 13, 1948, letter Sawyer penned to the Topeka school board. Todd and Caldwell were classmates at Kansas State Teachers College during the 1920s but political adversaries during the 1940s. She credited the director of colored schools with being the spark that lit the local chapter's fuse. "More than anything else, Caldwell set us on fire," she told a *Los Angeles Times* journalist in 1974. "We always knew segregation was bad, but he really focused it for us. At first, our case was just to get rid of this colored supervisor. But after we realized he was the product of an evil system, we decided to challenge the state law."[3]

This chapter interrogates how a Black man became the blackguard in Topeka public schools at the beginning of the end of the Jim Crow era. His egregious behavior was a focal point of local NAACP grievances, but his name is rarely mentioned in the scholarly literature on *Brown*. This gap between historical memories and historical writings begs the question: Why has a person at the epicenter of the *Brown* backstory been virtually absented in the narrativizing of the *Brown* backstory?

From Benevolent to Malevolent Whiteness: The Segregationist Superintendent and His Colored Supervisor

The Caldwell chronicles began in 1942. The Kansas Supreme Court decision in *Graham v. Board* caused a seismic shift in Topeka public schools that reverberated beyond the city's junior high schools. Although school superintendent A. J. Stout deployed various machinations to protect the city's racist enrollment policy, his best efforts were not good enough for local Klan members. Some held him responsible for the school board's decision to integrate junior high school students and burned a cross on his front lawn. Stout resigned in early 1942.[4] With Stout's imminent departure and the agony of the *Graham* defeat, the school board made a critical decision to revamp its culture of whiteness. After years of defending the property of whiteness through liberal racism, the school board decided to go in a different direction and hired Coffeyville school superintendent Kenneth McFarland. The school board's performance and production of whiteness immediately and intentionally changed from cultivated benevolence to unrestrained despotism.

White Topekans celebrated McFarland as an educational innovator, but Black Topekans were less than impressed. When *Simple Justice* author Richard Kluger interviewed Black residents in 1970, several spoke about the school superintendent's outward anti-Blackness. "There was the theory that McFarland was brought in to curb the integration movement that followed the *Graham* case," recalled veteran Black teacher Mamie Williams. The truth of the matter may never be verified, but it was apparent to Williams that McFarland was "full of his own superiority."[5] Her colleague Merrill Ross agreed. Ross joined the Topeka teaching force in 1944 after serving as a Tuskegee Airman. He told Kluger that McFarland was "a prejudiced man who believed in keeping the races separate."[6] Civil rights activist Lucinda Todd was less restrained than Williams and Ross in her assessment of the school superintendent. McFarland, she said, was "a regular Hitler."[7]

Despite Todd's contempt for the segregationist superintendent and the "patronizing" and "insulting" school board, she cited neither as inciters of the local NAACP. In multiple interviews over the course of forty years, Todd bestowed that claim to fame upon the white superintendent's Black confederate Harrison Caldwell. Todd's recollection is substantiated by a September 1948 letter written by Daniel Sawyer. Three weeks after NAACP members confronted the school board about its segregationist policy, Sawyer provided context for the NAACP's growing sense of unrest. The crisis of confidence in the McFarland administration dated back to a 1942 meeting between the NAACP Education Committee and the then-incoming school superintendent. NAACP members hoped to establish a more favorable working relationship with McFarland than they had with his predecessor Stout. They lobbied for a liaison between the Black community and the white board, a "colored director of colored schools." If Black students were to remain in segregated schools, the civil rights advocates wanted the board to recruit "a man who would be sensitive to the aims and aspirations of the Negro parents and teachers."[8]

In an ironic twist of fate, the director of colored schools position was created at the behest of the NAACP Education Committee. But McFarland had his own agenda for the city's Black schools. He hired an overseer instead of an advocate. According to Todd, McFarland's stance on Jim Crow schools became clear with Caldwell as his executioner: Topekans were not ready for integration.[9] McFarland's betrayal and Caldwell's treason were key points of contention in Sawyer's September 1948 letter to the school board and in the flyer circulated by NAACP members during the summer of 1948. The superintendent and his colored director "started their 'DIVIDE — AND RULE

OFFENSIVE'" as soon as they arrived in Topeka, despite the NAACP's good-will meeting.[10]

McFarland's performance of anti-Blackness was a sharp divergence from that of his predecessors. But the early years of his oppressive regime coincided with the NAACP's moratorium over the city's racist enrollment policy after *Graham*. Black educators' social capital among Black Topekans was affirmed before, during, and after *Graham*. Black school preservationists lost the courtroom battle, but they won in the court of public opinion. And while McFarland and Caldwell engaged in surveillance and punishment to protect racial boundaries in the schools, their objective aligned with that of most Black residents. Both parties wanted to maintain separate schools. The unsettling and unofficial alliance between white segregationists and Black preservationists was marked by a mutual distrust and a palpable power differential. But against their common opponent, they engaged in an obstruction of justice that involved intra-racial retribution.

Black residents' dispute over segregated schools in the decade before *Brown* involved a political triumvirate with often colliding and sometimes convergent interests. Black school preservationists shared an objective and an adversary with the Topeka school board. Although their racial motivations diverged, both groups desired separate schools and actively countered civil rights advocates seeking a more inclusive enrollment policy. Black proponents for and against all-Black schools engaged in a subterranean battle over conflicting definitions of anti-anti-Blackness and educational justice. But Black residents who had opposing views on Black schools shared an opponent in the Black school supervisor. There was consensus among NAACP members and Black educators that "Mr. Caldwell's job was to keep the Negro 'in his place.'"[11]

As the director of colored schools, Harrison Caldwell was professionally aligned with the school board and philosophically in alignment with Black educators. But in practice, the former outweighed the latter. Caldwell enthusiastically embraced his position as a gatekeeper to whiteness-as-property and quickly established an antagonistic relationship with Black Topekans on both sides of the political fence. He deployed an autocratic style of management to intimidate and threaten Black educators and students into compliance with the school board's racist policies. He also proved to be a formidable force against the local NAACP, undermining their mobilization efforts by any means necessary. In a decade marked by intense intra-racial disunion over Topeka public schools, Black civil rights activists, educators, parents, and students held one belief in common: Harrison Caldwell was the worst offender of foul play.

The Black villain in the *Brown* story is virtually absent in historical writings, despite his recurring presence in the interviews and oral histories of Black Topekans. His active collusion with white segregationists is an uncomfortable truth that troubles standard Jim Crow narratives dependent upon Black protagonists and white antagonists. Caldwell's story arc is also complicated by the fact that he was a shapeshifter. The Black protector of white privilege opted for a change of scenery when *Brown* went before the US Supreme Court. Caldwell resigned from Topeka public schools in 1954 as the second-highest paid school administrator in the city. Being an accomplice to white supremacy paid well, but the pending desegregation case threatened his personal and professional standing in the community. So, the Caldwell family relocated to Seattle, where Caldwell "hurdled the race barrier" he had helped stabilize in Topeka. In 1956, he not only became the city's first Black principal, but he also presided over an all-white school. The following year, he was celebrated as Seattle's Citizen of the Year.[12]

Seattle's Black hero was Topeka's Black antihero. Caldwell died in 1964. Since then, tributes written by Seattleites have cited him as a contributor to Topeka's school desegregation movement.[13] He was, but not in the way they presumed. This historical error is, in part, aided by an archival silence. Although the University of Washington library has a small collection of Caldwell's papers, he left little to no documentation of his time in Topeka. Consequently, Caldwell's role as a central character in the historical political production of *Brown* is largely narrated through his Black adversaries.

Caldwell's retrospective silence makes it difficult to discern his motivations for conspiring with McFarland, particularly because he was the superintendent's right-hand Black man in Coffeyville before moving to the capital city. To comprehend Caldwell's consent and cooperation is to diagnose his dissemblance, an impossible story to tell in the absence of his storytelling. Although his racial performance bestowed upon him professional power and monetary benefits, any minimalist reading of his complicity nullifies the possibility of alternative or additional explanations. Writing about Caldwell's exploits in the void of his vocal intervention begs the question posed by historian Saidiya Hartman: "How can narrative embody life in words and at the same time respect what we cannot know?"[14]

Harrison Caldwell, 1909–1935

Caldwell was a native-born Kansan but not native to Topeka. He was the second son of George and Henrietta Caldwell, but their first born in Fort Scott.

The Caldwells migrated from Tennessee at the turn of the century, well after the first wave of Southern migrants. But like their Exoduster predecessors, it didn't take long for them to learn that Kansas was no Promised Land. "Here, for the Black man, freedom loosed one hand while custom restrained the other," famed artist Gordon Parks wrote. Caldwell and Parks were childhood contemporaries in the small town located four miles from the Missouri border. The former was born in 1909 and the latter in 1912. Parks's coming-of-age stories describe the relationship between Black being and racial geographies in Fort Scott. As such, his body of work lends some interpretive space for the interiority of a man whose visible and invisible labor significantly shaped the course of Black history.

While whites in Topeka and Fort Scott shared the benefits of exclusive public spaces, the culture of whiteness differed in significant ways. Topeka was founded as a Free State town by antislavery advocates in 1854. The ethos of dominion that emerged among the dominant class of white Topekans was defined by a code of civility. By contrast, the properties of whiteness in Fort Scott emerged from its origins as a site of white violence over Black bodies. Proslavery Southerners shaped the production and performance of anti-Blackness in the town, and violence was weaponized as a method of social control. During the post-Reconstruction era, whites in Fort Scott proved that "Redemption" was not the sole province of white Southerners. Incidents of racial terrorism stood as a reminder of white power in the "Promised Land." For example, the public spectacle whites created with the March 1879 lynching of Bill Howard served as a warning to Exodusters that they were not welcome in Fort Scott.[15] It worked. Native Missourian George Washington Carver moved to Fort Scott to pursue better educational opportunities in September 1878. He left six months later after witnessing Howard's murder. The racial trauma haunted him for over sixty years.[16]

When the Caldwell family arrived in Fort Scott at the turn of the century, whites' taste for anti-Black violence was well established. There "could be trouble, lots of it" for any Black resident who defied local customs, wrote Gordon Parks.[17] "Law was white, and issued death to Blacks with the flick of a thumb."[18] As in other places throughout Kansas, whiteness-as-property in Fort Scott was secured through segregated public spaces, including schools. Kansas law banned small towns from erecting Jim Crow schools, but Fort Scott defied state prohibition. The Kansas Supreme Court affirmed Blacks' right to educational access in 1887 in *Buford Crawford v. Ft. Scott Board of Education*. But the following year, local officials circumvented that decision by petitioning state legislators to change the city's classification, an unlawful strategy that permitted them to segregate Black schoolchildren by law.[19] Gordon Parks's critically acclaimed 1963 novel *The Learning Tree* depicted the incongruity between the de jure promises of the state and the de facto practices of the town. "Living here is like havin' a good lay with a woman you don't quite trust," the protagonist's father lamented in a conversation with the school superintendent.[20]

Parks's sexual allegory spoke to the gendered subjectivities and heteronormative vulnerabilities of Black men who experienced both the pleasure and pain of illusory civil rights in Fort Scott. The brutal battle over Black bodies in town shifted from enslavement to education at the turn of the century. "A race war is on at Fort Scott," declared Topeka's *Colored Citizen* in 1900. There is a "vast amount of trouble in this city over the race question in the schools." That year the school superintendent closed one of the town's two Jim Crow schools due to a budget crisis. Black parents protested the move, so he provided transportation for Black students who were displaced by his decision. But the superintendent's solution added insult to injury. A Black resident named Jackson told the *Colored Citizen* that the covered wagon selected by the superintendent had "hauled dogs in the wagon all summer, and 'now he wants to haul niggers.'" A public outcry ensued. Like other Black residents, the "leader of the revolt" took exception to the dehumanization of Black schoolchildren. "We ain't no dogs. They only had two children in their wagon and that was two too many."[21]

Fort Scott's dual education system had stabilized by the time Caldwell and Parks attended school during the 1910s and '20s. "We were sorta handed equality on one hand then relieved of it with the other," Parks recalled in 1950.[22] Black students were deprived equal access in elementary schools and equal opportunities in integrated high schools. Structural inequities ensured that most Black students were academically underprepared when they reached the Fort Scott High School. Their classes were integrated but extracurricular activities were segregated. "Inside those walls of meager learning, Black students had to accommodate themselves to the taste of salt," wrote Parks. In addition to the anti-Black racism of white students and teachers, Black students were subjected to high school counselors whose racial script emphasized the boundedness of Blackness. "'You were meant to be maids and porters.' College for us, they said, would be a waste of time and money."[23]

Despite those racist expectations, Black students like Parks and Caldwell excelled. Caldwell graduated from Fort Scott High at fifteen and enrolled in Kansas State Teachers College of Pittsburg. Four years later, he became the first Black student to earn a master's degree from that institution.[24] His first teaching position was at Guadalupe College, a private Baptist school in Texas, where he was often younger than the students he instructed. Caldwell was driven and spent a short stint as a dean at Swift Memorial Institute in Tennessee. But his professional trajectory shifted to secondary education in 1935 when Kenneth McFarland offered him a job opportunity in his home state of Kansas.

That year, McFarland became school superintendent in Coffeyville. Like Fort Scott, Coffeyville is located in southeast Kansas, where local whites had a history of leaning into racial terrorism as a prerogative of whiteness. As such, a newly hired McFarland inherited a school district where the enforcement of white privilege was unapologetically flagrant. During the 1920s, the Klan campaigned for segregated schools in Coffeyville, and several members were on the city's school board. Topeka's "Colored Lawyer" Elisha Scott even tried to use the board's Klan affiliation to prove their intent to deny Black students' civil rights in a 1924 Kansas Supreme Court desegregation case.[25] The Coffeyville school board lost that case, not because its members were avowed white supremacists but because state law prohibited segregated high schools. When the Coffeyville school board hired McFarland, they found a sympathizer ready to pledge allegiance to whiteness. His plan for racial order called for a Black ally. McFarland wanted a Black supervisor to compel Black residents' compliance with the board's anti-Black policies and practices. McFarland reached out to his former college classmate Harrison Caldwell. Caldwell accepted the challenge.

The Colored Director and the Power of Patronage, 1942–1954

History repeated itself seven years later when McFarland was hired by the Topeka Board of Education. As the superintendent's right-hand Black man, Caldwell was described as "very abusive." His ruthless management style was developed in localities where the wages of whiteness were safeguarded in violent and unyielding ways. But Caldwell did not acclimate his approach to accommodate the passive aggression of empowered white Topekans. He understood the assignment. His call of duty was the same whether whites deployed violence or paternalism. McFarland used Caldwell "primarily as a tool . . . to keep us in line," explained Joe Douglas, who was a Black student activist during the 1940s.[26]

Dubbed the "czar of Black schools" by *Brown* attorney John Scott, Caldwell was a masterful manipulator who established his authority by cultivating a culture of fear.[27] The timing of his arrival in Topeka was significant. Black educators were still reeling from the school board's termination of six Black teachers after *Graham*. The school board exacted retributive justice for the racial insubordination of civil rights activists, despite Black educators' widespread advocacy for separate schools. Caldwell exploited the disquiet in the Black teaching force created by the sudden loss of their colleagues. "He scared the hell out of these people," exclaimed Berdyne Scott, widow of *Brown* attorney John Scott. "The teachers were scared of him."[28]

Caldwell's notoriety was amplified by his figural and figurative Blackness. In a town where Black geographies were largely defined by class and degrees of pigmentation, the colored director lacked phenotypical proximity to whiteness. Caldwell was a "great big man" who was "very dark, very articulate," recalled Douglas.[29] Douglas, who was light-skinned, was not the only Black Topekan to take notice of Caldwell's physicality, but his color commentary was notable for how it engaged racial scripts. His foregrounding of Caldwell's corporeality and deeply melanated skin can be read as an observable fact and as a racial phantasm. And yet, he refused binary articulations of race and intelligence by situating "dark" and "articulate" in relation to one another, not in juxtaposition. Douglas's brief but expansive observation simultaneously affirmed and disrupted the discursive racialization of people of African descent.

Caldwell's command was magnified by the incarnation of darkness, for as the director of colored schools he wielded a power of patronage reminiscent of the Tuskegee Machine. "He ruled with an iron hand," former Ramblers' assistant coach Wilmer Henderson recalled. "If you were one of his people, you were treated good. But if you weren't, anything bad could happen."[30] One of the few Black residents who recalled reaping the benefits of Caldwell's favor was Jack Alexander. Alexander's father was on the custodial staff for the board of education and had a cordial relationship with Caldwell that transferred to his son. The colored supervisor took Alexander on recruiting trips for new teachers. He also secured a lifeguard job for Alexander at segregated City Park, which had a swimming pool, tennis courts, softball diamonds, and a bandstand. Caldwell was a positive role model, Alexander said. He showed young Black men, "Do your thing and you can become something." However, in retrospect, Alexander understood that his was a minority opinion. He attributed his youthful admiration of Caldwell to the special attention he received and "maybe hearing some whites at that time recognizing Mr. Caldwell for the good that he was doing."[31]

The racial nuances of Caldwell's approval rating among whites may have escaped the comprehension of a teenaged Alexander, but not Mamie

Williams. Williams had been teaching in Topeka public schools for twenty-four years when Caldwell arrived and noted a sharp shift in workplace culture. The colored supervisor was "a difficult, dictatorial man" who managed Black educators using both incentives and intimidation, she said.[32] Williams approached Caldwell about receiving compensation for assuming additional duties as a school principal during the mid-1940s. "His attitude changed toward me" after that, she told Richard Kluger.[33] Caldwell attempted to leverage conscription for compliance from former Buchanan Elementary School principal J. B. Holland. "During the war, I was advised by Caldwell that that if I saw things his way, I could be kept out of the military," he recalled. "I chose the military."[34] Holland left Topeka in 1943 and returned in 1946.

Caldwell's style of stewardship was particularly effective because the school board did not tenure teachers. Employment contracts were renewed annually. "Your performance was evaluated each year fifty percent on your teaching and fifty percent on your attitude," Williams recalled. "That was their way of keeping you in line." Black women teachers were especially susceptible to Caldwell's coercive machinations because school board policy barred the employment of married women. Black community expectations bound single women to their family homes, so relocation was not a viable option for Black female teachers. With no job security and no partner to ensure financial stability, Black women educators in Topeka were economically vulnerable to Caldwell's villainy. They just "went along," Williams explained.[35]

Destabilization was critical to maintaining racial order under McFarland's administration. When he arrived in 1942, he instituted a hiring freeze in Black schools, citing a low student-teacher ratio. Once that suspension was lifted, he deployed a divisive personnel strategy. Most of the city's Black educators at the time were longtime employees and native Topekans who were socially and professionally interconnected with intimate ties to the city's Black communities. So, McFarland sent Caldwell on recruiting trips. He believed that recently uprooted teachers would be easier to control and that their presence would disrupt any solidarity within the existing teaching force. In addition, Caldwell hired recently relocated educators into administrative positions instead of promoting locals to create dissension within the ranks.

One of those newcomers was Merrill Ross. Ross and his wife Barbara moved to the city from Fort Scott in 1944. Even though he coached Topeka High School's popular Black basketball team the Ramblers, Ross perceived a "coldness" among Black educators. He believed that his colleagues' unfriendly reception was partially due to resentment toward the "light-skinned Negro."[36] Although his suspicions were not unfounded in a community where complexion conferred connections, it was more likely that familial ties created an "awkward situation" for Ross.[37] Merrill Ross was the nephew of Caldwell's wife Valeria. "Many teachers didn't trust me in the community because of Harrison," he recalled.[38] Although Ross's peers suspected him of endorsing "Harrison's program," the two men "didn't agree on anything" and being in-laws did not spare Ross from Caldwell's wrath. In fact, Ross was reassigned to another school as retribution for their disputes.[39]

The colored supervisor had little patience and no tolerance for personal or political dissent. There was no "protected class" of groups or individuals. He meted out punishment with no regard for community renown. Caldwell's disciplinary actions against the Ramblers basketball team provide a primary example. In the fall of 1945, a group of Black students named the Colored Youth Progressive Club publicly accused McFarland and Caldwell of misappropriating money allocated for the Ramblers. The fiscal deficit was critical to the unofficial high school basketball team because it relied upon school board funds and Black community donations for uniforms, equipment, and travel. According to Mamie Williams, McFarland's "hanky-panky [was] not unknown," and he was later found guilty of purposeful financial mismanagement.[40] But the CYPC also accused the colored director of thievery. Caldwell retaliated by declaring the group's leader, Ramblers' center Richard Ridley, academically ineligible to participate in team sports. The Ramblers' coach Edward Graham defied Caldwell's directive and allowed Ridley to play under an assumed name. Graham's calculated risk resulted in his discharge not only from coaching the Ramblers but also from his principalship at Monroe School. The Ramblers were summarily suspended.

Graham protested his wrongful termination with the assistance of two well-known school board agitators. NAACP members William Bradshaw and R. J. Reynolds accompanied Graham to a February 1946 school board meeting. They argued against his dismissal on grounds that the punitive decision resulted from duties unrelated to his official employment. The civil rights attorneys also seized an opportunity to call into question the constitutionality of Topeka High's two athletic programs. "The Board's illegal practice of promoting and maintaining a segregated basketball team on the basis of race and color at public expense [is] contrary to the Laws of the State of Kansas," they insisted. Graham took his case to court and was reinstated two months later.[41]

While the Graham saga unfolded, the school board allowed the Ramblers to continue their season. The student-athletes continued to protest injustice despite the board's sanctions against Ridley and Graham. The segregated team hosted their competitors at East Topeka Junior High School, a relatively new gym with a capacity of 800 people. But the official, all-white Trojan team held their games at Topeka High School's 4,000-seat gymnasium, known as "The Dungeon." No longer satisfied playing in the smaller venue, Rambler team members petitioned Caldwell for equal access.

The Ramblers' reasonable request was equivalent to insubordination under Caldwell's authoritarian racial regime, especially so soon after their accusations of financial mishandling. Caldwell immediately convened a segregated assembly and publicly reprimanded the student-athletes. He berated them for taking their "splendid opportunity to gain an education" for granted. He accused Black students of being ungrateful and insinuated that education was a privilege, not a right. "'Go back there and get your education,'" he advised. "You're going to have to conform to the rules."[42] The colored director simultaneously impugned Black students and invalidated their concerns. It was a pivotal moment in the life of self-proclaimed "rabble-rouser" Joe Douglas, who felt that Caldwell's response "just let all the wind out of the sails of everything we had done." The Ramblers felt "crushed, like they didn't have any support for what they were doing," he said. Douglas left the assembly feeling "totally disenchanted with the public educational system." He dropped out of school soon thereafter to join the army.[43]

Caldwell was not the mentor Black students wanted, but he was the mentor he thought they needed. Racial accommodationism was becoming obsolete in the post–World War II era. The Ramblers' demands evidenced an increasing militance around anti-Black racism that was occurring throughout African America. But Caldwell's admonitions were not new to the alumni of the city's all-Black schools. Most of Topeka High's Black students attended segregated schools where respectability politics guided liberatory pedagogies. The policing of Black students' behavior was standard practice in Black schools, and those who failed to comply risked corporeal punishment. "They told us, 'You are going to a mixed school and we don't want you to embarrass us,'" Richard Ridley recalled of his Monroe School teachers.[44] Preparing Black bodies for white spaces was deemed as important as the standard curriculum in the city's Jim Crow schools. But the vision of Black futurity that cultivated Black students' racial subjectivities during the 1930s stymied their student activism in the 1940s.

Caldwell's attempt at words of wisdom were lost in intergenerational translation. He presided over what Topeka High School alum Samuel C. Jackson dubbed "good-nigger assemblies." The colored supervisor segregated Topeka High School assemblies when he arrived in Topeka in 1942. He then took advantage of these closed sessions to advise his captive audience "not to rock the boat." Attendees were instructed "to be clean and study hard and accept the status quo" so they would "be as little offensive to whites as possible." Caldwell's racial counsel reflected a phenomenology of Blackness shaped by generation and geography. It was the product of the "subtly cruel" Jim Crow education he had received in his hometown: if you want to get along, go along. In return, he assured the students, "things were getting better."[45]

Caldwell's 1942 Topeka Compromise quickly earned him a reputation for being "McFarland's nigger."[46] The combination of accommodationist messaging and tyrannical management communicated to Black Topekans that his professional allegiance lay with the segregationist superintendent and school board. "Kenneth McFarland was an autocrat and Harrison Caldwell was his lieutenant," Ridley explained.[47] Ridley's conclusion was exemplified by a dispute that occurred between Caldwell and Lucinda Todd around 1948. Todd called the director of colored schools to demand equal access after she figured out that an instrumental program was being offered exclusively to white schools. Instead of relaying her concerns to his supervisor, Caldwell dismissed them and responded that Black children "didn't want instrumental music." He trivialized her grievance about racial inequities between elementary schools even though their children were classmates at Buchanan. But he "took advantage of the program" and enrolled his son Lynn in the music program when it was introduced to Black schools the following year.[48] Caldwell's willingness to defend white privilege at the expense of Black children infuriated Todd. It was the primary reason she joined the NAACP and campaigned against segregated schools.

Caldwell's notoriety among Black residents was compounded by the fact that his appeasement pleased white Topekans. While Black civil rights advocates found Caldwell's charge objectionable, white segregationists like Milton Tabor praised him for doing a "bang-up job . . . in the colored schools of Topeka." Tabor's affirmation was no revelation because he championed white entitlement to racially exclusive spaces as the managing editor of the *Topeka Daily Capital*. Tabor saw a kindred spirit in the Black guardian of white geographies. As the NAACP began mobilizing against the colored director and the school board, he seized an opportunity to applaud Caldwell for remaining undeterred by his detractors. The colored director "holds unerringly to his goal" despite being "criticized by one group, sometimes by another," Tabor wrote. He commended Caldwell for his moral fortitude for refusing "to yield to petty community pressures." He "keeps right on battling for the youth of his race," the editor claimed. Although anti-Blackness pervaded Tabor's testimonial, it was most evident in his paternalistic depreciation of Black desegregationists. He wrote that the superintendent and school board members "have consistently refused to become involved in the various controversies which develop from time to time within the racial and minority groups of the community." For Tabor, Black residents' concerns about Caldwell were immaterial because "the board of education and school officials know of Caldwell's genuine ability as an educator, and they support him."

The timing of Tabor's editorial was auspicious and suspicious. The city's mainstream press rarely reported on events or issues relating to Black Topekans. "The papers here were no friend of [Black residents]," recalled Todd. "It was hard to get any publicity at all out of them."[49] But twelve days before NAACP president McKinley Burnett openly challenged the Topeka school board's racist enrollment policy, Tabor defended the director of colored schools against the defamation of "certain militant groups which want to do away with colored schools, colored churches, and everything that smacks of 'segregation.'"[50] This reclamation proclamation raised the ire of NAACP secretary Lucinda Todd. She took offense not only to Tabor's Caldwell commentary but also his criticism of racial justice activists. She cut his editorial out of the newspaper, wrote "the reasoning of a fascist mind" on the clipping, and immediately composed a rebuttal letter.[51]

Todd's assessment of Tabor's racist standpoint was not unfounded. Although he had held his position for over twenty years, the managing editor could no longer hold his peace as calls for civil rights animated the city's nonwhite population. His private angst was publicly articulated in a 1947 letter he wrote to US senator and *Topeka Daily Capital* publisher Arthur Capper. Tabor complained about political provocateurs like Mexican American veteran Raymond Ortega, who threatened to disrupt the racial order with "insistent demands that his people be accorded absolute equality in all things." He articulated his fear of a racial invasion and claimed that many whites objected to being "thrown together" with "the Mexicans and Negroes" in city parks, theaters, restaurants, and taverns. Tabor understood the stakes were high. Integration diminished the integrity of whiteness in a city where its value depended more upon exclusion than violence or deprivation. "Once an owner opens his place to Mexican or colored patronage, they practically take it over," he asserted.

Tabor's letter to Capper was a prime example of how whiteness-as-property was underwritten by a racial imaginary of benevolence in the capital city. He shared a self-congratulatory story about a meeting between "the leading colored folks" and the *Daily Capital*'s white editorial staff during the mid-1940s. The Black delegation took exception to the paper's habitual race-labeling of Black lawbreakers. So, Tabor and his colleagues brokered a deal. If Black leaders would "quiet down their 'Eleanor Club' women and take the knives and clubs from colored school kids," the newspaper would "quit using the word 'colored' when their folks were arrested." *Daily Capital* editors also agreed to eliminate all use of racial identifications. "This had an excellent effect and the colored folks have kept their promise," Tabor confirmed to Capper. "There is little or no trouble now." While the newspaper's racialization of criminality was problematic and predictable, Tabor's appeal for peace in the streets is noteworthy in its intersectionality. His call for Black men to gain control over "their" women and children was a gender provocation suggestive of an emasculated Black masculinity. But his invocation of the "Eleanor Club" simultaneously spoke to the fragility of white patriarchal power in the postwar era.[52]

The following year, white paranoia about Black sedition emboldened Tabor to use his platform to support Caldwell and disparage the NAACP. The transparency of his politicized whiteness did not escape Lucinda Todd. Tabor's writing was "pure unadulterated nonsense," she exclaimed in a response letter she penned the day his editorial was published. "If by wanting my child to have equal education I am being 'militant' then thank God I am militant." Tabor's article raised Todd's ire, but the infuriated NAACP secretary reserved her strongest words for Caldwell. Tabor's anti-Blackness was expected, but Caldwell's collusion was inexcusable. "He merits my contempt," she wrote. "He has betrayed his race, I scorn him. I repudiate him." Not only did she deem Caldwell a race traitor, but she also accused him of professional incompetency. "The colored teachers are doing as well as they can under such inefficient, bungling, intimidating leadership he represents."[53]

Caldwell's endorsement by proven segregationists like Tabor certified the fact that he was a consummate accommodationist. At a time when the subterranean battle over Black schools was breaching the surface, Black Topekans on both sides of the debate could agree that the director of colored schools was an enigma. Standing up to or speaking out against Caldwell came with risks before *Brown*, but several Black residents openly questioned his character and motivations after *Brown*. Many struggled to comprehend his aggressive enforcement of the school board's Jim Crow policies. "Only thing I could figure was that he wanted to keep his job," Lucinda Todd speculated.[54]

An Alternate Reading of Ulterior Motives: Harrison Caldwell's Racial Uplift Politics

Caldwell clearly had a vested interest in the city's dual education system because he was economically dependent upon the existence of all-Black schools. His Black contemporaries may have found his labor unscrupulous, but he was well compensated as the Black overseer of segregated schools. The Topeka Board of Education placed high monetary value on protecting its white schools. Caldwell received a $400 raise when he was recruited from Coffeyville in 1942. His annual earnings were $2,600. As a point of comparison, Mamie Williams earned $700 less than Caldwell even though she also had a master's degree and thirteen years more teaching experience. Caldwell's salary doubled in the following decade. When the school board eliminated his supervisory position and reassigned him to Washington School in 1952, he was the second-highest-earning administrator in Topeka public schools.[55]

The school board incentivized the safeguarding of white supremacy, but Caldwell's compensation went beyond his place of employment. Caldwell may have been a conduit for racial violence, but he was also a race man. The personal and political converged for the colored supervisor. He was the sole provider for his family, a role that racial capitalism denied most Black men. The desire to conform to heteropatriarchal gender norms was a critical component of the intersectional subjectivities defined by racial uplift politics. The philosophy and practice of racial uplift not only informed Caldwell's performance of Blackness, but it also structured his articulations of Blackness. He was one of the masterminds behind *Of Merit, Achievement and Service*, a textbook supplement written and compiled by Black educators in 1942. Although some of his peers doubted his motives, Caldwell's stated objectives hinted at Black transcendence from anti-Black racism. He wrote that white students' exposure to Black history would contribute to "increased good will and tolerance towards all peoples everywhere."[56]

Caldwell held firm to his belief in the antiracist potential of racially inclusive curricula. Eleven years after *Of Merit, Achievement and Service* was complete he designed an elementary school curriculum called "Studies in Negro Life" for a University of Kansas graduate course. He believed that multicultural education would teach students "respect for the race."[57] Caldwell's curricular proposal applied that conceptual framework and surveyed the accomplishments of "a few distinguished Negro characters." Lesson plans included units on educational innovators Booker T. Washington, George Washington Carver, and Mary McCleod Bethune and artists Marian Anderson, Paul Lawrence Dunbar, and Langston Hughes to name a few.[58] There was significant overlap between the racial ambassadors featured in *Of Merit* and "Studies in Negro Life." The similarity of selections was due to a convergence of interests. Like his peers in the city's Black schools, Caldwell's educational intention was to present alternatives to Black alterity.

Caldwell curated a list of Black history-makers to model bourgeois respectability. Because racial uplift politics focused more on self-help strategies than structural racism, self-governance was a central learning outcome of his Black studies program. Course content reinforced the desired skill set. One suggested kindergarten activity was to "stress correct health habits (cleanliness, etc.)." A short biography of Booker T. Washington described the Tuskegee Institute founder as "one of the cleanest and most polite men in the world." One of his greatest achievements was that "he helped teach other people good manners."[59] This narrow fixation on hygiene and behavior was a means to an end for the cohort of race men and women who taught in the nation's Jim Crow schools. Respectability was political, not personal. Caldwell believed that the road to rights would be paved by proving Black worthiness, not through Black agitation. "What the Negro Wants," he wrote, is to be given "the opportunity to display ourselves for our full value, then we shall feel that we have been made a part of democracy."[60]

Caldwell's message of Black political disengagement was unwavering across multiple publics. Booker T. Washington was not just a subject of study for Caldwell, he was a standard for living. Like "The Great Accommodator," the colored director advocated for interracial separation and intra-racial institution building. This political pragmatism extended beyond his work for the board of education. The visibility of Caldwell's position as a Black protector of white privilege in Topeka public schools created opportunities for speaking engagements and access to mainstream media outlets. He consistently downplayed Black civil rights when speaking to white audiences. In a talk titled "The Negro in the Postwar World" Caldwell advocated for Black economic advancement and avoided the issue of racial justice. "Equality of opportunity is all the Negro will ask of the future," he assured local Kiwanis Club members.[61] Although a defense worker in Wichita inspired the Double V Campaign, in Topeka Caldwell remained unmoved. According to

Lucinda Todd, he told white Rotary Club members in the mid-1940s that "Negroes were not ready for integration and that they were not ready for their rights as citizens."[62]

And yet, Caldwell's political opacity was situational. Around the same time that he assuaged the political anxieties of white civic groups, he wrote an editorial for a local Black newspaper that subtly critiqued white resistance to Blacks' civil rights. His 1947 "Sunday Meditation" was an invitation to introspection about the values white Americans held most sacred: God and country. "We cannot love God and hate our fellowman," he wrote using a strategic literary invocation of a communal "we." His racial erasure diffused white liability and suspended reality by imagining indiscriminate discriminators. He drew attention to anti-Blackness without calling out its white perpetrators, even though the article appeared in a Black publication. Caldwell reminded readers of biblical egalitarianism after citing the great commandments. "We love our neighbor when we do not seek special privileges at his expense," he wrote. "We love our neighbor when we extend to all men the four freedoms regardless of race, color or creed."[63]

Like Booker T. Washington, Caldwell was a complex figure. He avoided civil rights conversations in white publics and suppressed Black activism in Black publics. But he also invested in the growth and development of Black ecosystems in ways that could hardly be defined as apolitical. During the summers, Caldwell organized recreational activities for Black schoolchildren at City Park and found employment for Black high school students. He segregated the city's teachers' union in 1942 but then lobbied the Kansas State Teachers Association to welcome its first Black performer at a statewide meeting in November 1943. "This was the first time in the history of the Association that a member of our race has had this opportunity," Alpha Kappa Alpha members announced in their official magazine, the *Ivy Leaf*.[64]

Caldwell also successfully petitioned white YMCA members to recognize the segregated unit as an official branch when he became the first president of the George Washington Carver YMCA's Board of Directors. The organizational upgrade was important because it meant that Black members would have access to funding opportunities through the city's Community Chest. Additional financial support was critical to ensuring the sustainability of the Carver YMCA, which had been a center of Black sociality for over forty years. Founded in 1905 as a subsidiary of the local white chapter, the Carver YMCA thrived under the leadership of Washington School principal Ezekiel Ridley. It joined Black schools and churches as a fixed place within the Black spatial imaginary in a city where residential neighborhoods were racially fluid. The segregated Y provided meeting space for Black clubs and organizations, hosted social events like teen nights on Fridays and Saturdays, and offered educational programs for children and adults. Black educators like Ridley were attracted to the YMCA's social welfare mission because it aligned with racial uplift ideologies. In fact, the first Carver Board of Directors included Ridley, Caldwell, Buchanan Elementary School principal J. B. Holland, veteran educator Eva Montgomery, and the founder of the Kansas Colored Parent-Teacher Association Tracy Thompson.

Whereas Ridley was widely respected among his peers, his successor had mixed reviews. Nevertheless, even Caldwell's adversaries had to admit that "quite a few people admired him."[65] Some Black educators who were ambivalent about his professional position were grateful for his professional connections. When Caldwell resigned from being the president of the Carver YMCA's Board of Directors in 1949, members praised him for his "untiring, unselfish, cooperative, efficient service" and "his gracious, dynamic, inspiring leadership."[66] Although Mamie Williams found Caldwell's methods objectionable, she acknowledged the tightrope that he walked as director of colored schools. "Carrying loads too heavy for others," she waxed poetic. "Championing the cause of all men as brothers." The Topeka Council of Colored Parents and Teachers commissioned Williams to pay tribute to Caldwell in 1946. The two educators shared a political standpoint despite their antagonistic relationship. So, she invoked the National Association of Colored Women's motto in a double acrostic dedicated to the colored director. "Lifting others as he climbs," she wrote. "Elevating all who within his radius come."[67]

The Master of Machiavellianism: Harrison Caldwell, 1950–1956

As an accommodationist by profession and a race man in practice, Caldwell was a complicated and calculated person. He was a master at interracial dissemblance and intra-racial dirty work. Merrill Ross's relationship with the colored director was more intimate than most, but he was uninhibited in his assessment of his aunt's husband. According to Ross, Caldwell was "a conman [and] a bigot."[68] Machiavellianism is perhaps the character trait Caldwell shared most with Booker T. Washington. The tactical maneuverings of both men suggest a belief that "politics was the art of the possible."[69]

Caldwell's career trajectory from racial gatekeeper to racial groundbreaker evidences a political flexibility that verges on contortionism. But his final years in Topeka suggest that his professional transition was more of a revelation than a progression. The Topeka school board refashioned Caldwell's position in 1950 in response to the NAACP's dual campaign against him and segregated schools. His job title changed to "inter-racial counselor," but his modus operandi remained the same. With a local school desegregation case underway, he invited Langston University president Dr. G. L. Harrison to speak before the Colored Parent and Teacher Association Congress. Harrison advised the delegation of education advocates to avoid politics and to abstain from interfering with administrators' duties.[70] The following year, Kenneth McFarland resigned after a *Topeka Daily Capital* article exposed irregularities in the board of education's financial records.[71] The school board's culture of whiteness began shifting toward a more benevolent racial imaginary as the pending Supreme Court case prompted changes in school board membership. Three years after Caldwell deployed political ventriloquism through Harrison, he swerved from his customary accommodationist stance. In a paper he wrote for a University of Kansas graduate school course during the summer of 1953, Caldwell assumed an uncharacteristically outspoken political voice. Although he fell short of demanding full citizenship for people of African descent, he warned, "It is too late ever again to keep Negroes 'in their place.'"[72]

The following year, after the Supreme Court deemed school segregation unconstitutional, Caldwell left Topeka for an assistant principal position with Seattle public schools. In 1956, he became the first Black principal of an all-white elementary school in the city of Seattle, the state of Washington, and possibly, the nation. When a journalist for the *Seattle Times* interviewed Caldwell about that pivotal moment in American racial history, he answered, "This is democracy in action."[73]

CHAPTER SIX

Blacks against *Brown*

The Final Chapter, 1948–1954

At an April 23, 1948, school board meeting, Topeka NAACP president McKinley Burnett demanded the "full and complete integration" of Black students and teachers. "Nothing less would suffice or get the job done," he insisted.[1] It was an extraordinary moment in the history of civil rights activism in Topeka public schools. Although Black residents had staged interventions at school board meetings before, their previous approach involved more negotiation than confrontation. That day in 1948 fourteen NAACP members took the first unequivocal stance for educational justice. Not only did Burnett advocate for the integration of Black students, but he also called attention to the school board's double standard of employment. "White teachers teach Negro children and the reverse order should be acceptable," he asserted.

The school board's reaction to the NAACP's direct action was also remarkable. Throughout the 1930s and '40s, their response to individual and collective Black protests usually involved some performance of benevolent whiteness. This time, Burnett and his cohort were met with an unprecedented show of open force. School board member Charles Bennett became incensed when NAACP member Minister Edward Foust warned that the school board would be "flooded with letters" if it did not desegregate its schools. Bennett responded with a circuitously articulated veiled threat. "That would be the best way not to get anything done." The board intended to be fair to all groups, he claimed, but it would not "be high-pressured by anybody."[2] When NAACP members refused to acquiesce to white power, Bennett challenged Burnett to a fistfight. The NAACP president met the board member's crude behavior with civility. He declined Bennett's invitation and "calmly informed him that he believed in settling affairs of this nature in the courts."[3]

Despite Charles Bennett's best efforts to protect "white" schools from Black space invaders, that school board meeting was the beginning of the end of Topeka's Jim Crow schools. Among the NAACP members present that day were attorneys Charles Bledsoe and John Scott. Three years later, Bledsoe, Scott, and Scott's brother Charles argued *Brown v. Board of Education of Topeka* before the Kansas Supreme Court.

"Blacks against *Brown*: The Final Chapter" is the denouement of Black Topekans' segregated school story. The plotline of the local metadrama has escaped most *Brown* historians because scholarship on Black politics during the Jim Crow era skews toward champions of structural change. Consequently, the few historical writings that include a background story of the Topeka case spotlight the efforts of the local NAACP. This chapter does so as well, but it also situates their political mobilization in relation to white and Black resistance. The Topeka school board's 1953 capitulation before the Supreme Court decision has contributed to the false conclusion that Topeka was "the least eventful in terms of organic grassroots activism" of the five lawsuits subsumed in *Brown*.[4] But opposition to school integration in the capital city was not limited to the usual suspects.

Charles Bennett's invitation to fisticuffs at the April 1948 school board meeting was the beginning and end of white violence toward NAACP members in Topeka. White residents' passive aggression may have paled in comparison to their Southern white counterparts, but their story of resistance was not the only one that defied past or present historical expectations. Black educators, parents, and their allies staged a valiant effort to save the city's segregated schools from the NAACP's legal intervention. In fact, they were almost successful. Had it not been for the tenacity of longtime civil rights activists like Daniel Sawyer, McKinley Burnett, and Lucinda Todd, the landmark 1954 Supreme Court case may not have been called *Brown v. Board of Education*.

Although Black school preservationists were central actors in the Topeka tale, they are largely absent from historical narratives on *Brown*. This chapter surveys the private and public crusades of Black school preservationists in relation to the local NAACP school desegregation campaign. Black support of Black schools was politically complicated and rife with internal contradictions. Black school preservationists simultaneously sabotaged civil rights activists, subverted white supremacy, and colluded with white domination. But scholars' singular focus on NAACP efforts to desegregate Jim Crow schools has obscured alternative productions of Black futurities in Topeka public schools. Black school desegregationists and Black school preservationists had legitimate yet conflicting ideas on what constituted educational justice in the decades before *Brown*. The NAACP's political vision was outward facing toward dismantling racist structures for Black students, while Black school advocates turned inward toward their communities to preserve Black educational institutions for Black schoolchildren.

The Topeka NAACP's postwar acceleration of school desegregation activism affirms Jacqueline Dowd Hall's historical reframing of "The Long Civil Rights Movement." Modern civil rights movement historicizing that begins with the 1954 Supreme Court decision ironically obscures the political labor of those who mobilized the school desegregation cases in South Carolina, Delaware, Virginia, Washington, DC, and Kansas. In Kansas, the architects of *Brown* inherited a history of civil rights activism against segregated schools that dated back over twenty-five years. But that journey was complicated by the peculiar institution of anti-Black racism in the capital city.

The Topeka school board's adherence to the *Plessy* standard created a relatively parallel dual education system. The city's Jim Crow schools were modern structures, and all schools shared a standard curriculum that was not determined by racial demographics. The school board's unusual approach to segregation inadvertently facilitated the development of Black protected spaces. Black teachers and administrators refused the sociospatial marking of whiteness and reclaimed Jim Crow schools as an integral part of the city's Black geographies. Throughout the 1930s and '40s, Topeka's segregated schools became emancipatory epistemological spaces dedicated to reading, writing, and resistance.

But Black students transitioned out of segregated schools during their junior high school years. Their experience abruptly shifted from interconnected to disconnected, and anti-Blackness replaced affirmations of Blackness. For the first time, Black students encountered the microaggressions of white students and the indifference or racism of white faculty and administrators. The hostile or dispassionate classroom environments of integrated junior and senior high schools were stark juxtapositions from the nurturing and familial classrooms of segregated schools. When Black resident Richard Ridley reflected upon his experiences as a student in Topeka public schools during the 1930s and '40s, he concluded, "It wasn't the grade schools that sunk me, it was the high school."[5]

The strange career of Jim Crow in Topeka public schools animated divergent forms of Black political advocacy. School integration was not a dream deferred for most Black Topekans. Black parents desired Black schools with Black teachers because Black educators cultivated safe spaces that disrupted anti-Blackness. Black residents' preference for separate schools was not inhibited by the material deprivation endemic in Jim Crow schools throughout the country. Black school preservationists could simultaneously support the existence of racially separated learning environments and oppose segregation in public accommodations.

Save Our Schools: The Politics of Black School Preservationists

When the NAACP set their sights on the Topeka Board of Education, several Black parents, educators, and alumni fought back. Armed with an awareness of the NAACP's April 23 plans, the Topeka Council of Colored Parents and Teachers prepared a counterargument. Nine elected representatives from the four segregated parent-teacher associations convened a meeting and penned a letter of support for Black educators and separate schools on April 21. "Following an open discussion at a recent meeting, it was unanimously voted that the Council would inform you as to its views relative to our children and our schools," they wrote. The school board clerk read their position statement to the school board after NAACP members demanded school integration.

The Topeka Council of Colored Parents and Teachers established its authority to speak on behalf of Black residents by introducing itself as the "only organization which officially represents the Parents of the children in the Topeka Colored Schools." The group's charge was to promote "the welfare of the children and youth in home, school, church, and community." The council's support for the current enrollment policy was based upon a shared concern for the health and well-being of Black children. Members opposed school integration for two reasons, both of which were based upon the recognition that anti-Blackness structured Black lives. School integration limited or eliminated one of the few job sectors available to educated Black Americans due to labor market segregation. "We fail to see how children can be inspired to get an education if we continually do away with the jobs they can fill after securing their education," they wrote. The council also insisted that Black schoolchildren benefitted from separate learning environments. "We want to express our faith and confidence in the efficiency of our Colored teachers. We would not be in favor of changing our present set-up without more evidence that our children would do as well and be as happy as they are now," they asserted. In the end, the council's advocacy for Black schools simultaneously invested in and transcended state-defined anti-Blackness. "It is not good for our children's education to keep their schools under constant attack because of racial reasons."[6]

Black residents' opposing viewpoints on educational justice coexisted in the subterranean from 1929, when Topeka public schools were fully segregated, until the Kansas Supreme Court ruled against segregated junior high schools in 1941. The fallout from the *Graham v. Board* decision publicly exposed the intra-racial dispute between civil rights advocates and Black school preservationists. The conflict that emerged between the two factions before, during, and after *Graham* was so intense that local NAACP members instituted an unofficial moratorium on the city's Jim Crow school policy from 1941 until April 23, 1948.

With the *Graham* case pending, Black educators and their allies occupied the NAACP and wielded its political reputation against school integration. That was no longer an option in 1948. When local civil rights activists tapped into the political resources of the NAACP, Black school advocates seized spaces of Black sociality. This "subterranean world of political conflict" was dominated by women who were mothers and teachers.[7] Their counterresistance was often improvisational but always intentional. It also commonly and necessarily occurred outside the purview of dominant publics. The shadow work of Blacks against *Brown* has been overlooked by scholarly observers dependent upon traditional historical methods and conventional definitions of the political. The submerged networking and acts of social retribution wielded against Black civil rights activists were "nonheroic" gendered forms of racial resistance, but they were highly effective.[8] Black teachers, parents, and their allies virtually immobilized the Topeka NAACP's campaign against the Topeka school board.

The authorial voice of Black school preservationists has been muted by the nature of their organizing and the arc of civil rights history. The Black educators, parents, and alumni who advocated on behalf of Black schools left virtually no written records, and they were not sought-out subjects for interviewers seeking *Brown* background stories. However, NAACP records and Black residents' remembrances attest to the strength, vitality, and efficacy of their political provocation. So, scholars' inability to register Black school advocates' resistance cannot solely be reduced to research methods. It also evidences a larger mainstream investment in liberal racial narratives.[9] Black school preservationists' claim to Black futurities cannot be attributed to false consciousness.

From Avoidance to Activism: The Topeka NAACP and Jim Crow Schools, 1941–1949

Just as Black school preservationists' refusal should not be mistaken for consent to containment, the Topeka NAACP's silence on segregated schools should not be interpreted as an act of accommodation. As previously mentioned, local NAACP leaders made a critical decision after *Graham*. To keep the peace between warring factions, they shifted the chapter's political agenda from segregated schools to segregated public accommodations. It was an effective strategy, and the branch flourished for the next seven years.

Membership rolls peaked between 1944 and 1946 with chapter president Captain Bolivar E. Watkins. The World War I army veteran was "no firebrand" when compared to former presidents Elisha Scott and Raymond Reynolds.[10] Watkins's predecessors were both renowned civil rights attorneys with established reputations as freedom fighters. By contrast, Watkins preferred mediation to litigation, which he believed would "set us back 50 years." According to *Brown* attorney John Scott, Watkins's gradualist standpoint was summed up by his belief that "we've got to learn to crawl before we can walk."[11] So as NAACP president, Watkins concentrated his attention on expanding the local chapter. "I have no time to lose fooling with anything that cannot be made to grow," he wrote in February 1946 to NAACP membership secretary Lucille Black.[12] Watkins's efforts were successful. The Topeka chapter recorded 654 card-carrying members that year.

This growth period was short-lived. In January 1947 the local branch appointed McKinley Langford Burnett as its new president. Burnett had been a member of the Topeka NAACP's Executive Board since civil rights activists had its charter reinstated after *Graham* in 1942. He witnessed the branch's diplomatic disengagement from Jim Crow schools under Raymond Reynolds and the political prudency of Bolivar Watkins. But Burnett's leadership ushered in a radical departure for the Topeka NAACP. He stepped into his new role with a sense of urgency. According to his confederate Lucinda Todd, Burnett was "a fighter from the word 'go.'"[13]

For over twenty years the Topeka NAACP challenged segregationist practices in public and private spaces, but it largely circumvented the issue of separate schools to accommodate a divided membership. NAACP members like William Bradshaw and Daniel Sawyer publicly challenged the school board's Jim Crow policy independently of the NAACP. Burnett disrupted that pattern when he became chapter president. Under his leadership, a core group of NAACP members adopted a zero-tolerance approach toward racial segregation in the city's theaters, parks, and elementary schools. Burnett's daughter Maurita Davis attributed his uncompromising political stance to one simple motivation: "He didn't appreciate being segregated."[14]

Burnett's political subjectivity evolved from his dual reality of embodied whiteness and essentialized Blackness. His racial inheritance as the grandson of an enslaver and son of enslaved parents superseded his phenotypical signification. Born in 1897, Burnett grew up in Oskaloosa, a small town northeast of Topeka. He attended integrated schools because state law prohibited cities with populations under 15,000 from segregating schools. Among his white peers, Burnett's fair skin and straight hair did not exempt him from anti-Black associations of race with the body. Davis recalled her father sharing stories about white students' microaggressions. He felt especially resentful about being relegated to subservient roles in school plays and being pressured to dance in school programs.[15]

Burnett's experiences with anti-Blackness continued into adulthood unmediated by his ability to pass for white or the freedom from community recognition that comes with social mobility. He served in a segregated army unit during World War I and returned to a segregated job market after his tour of duty. Burnett moved to Topeka to work at Santa Fe Railroad company during the Great Railroad Strike of 1922. Due to labor market segregation, his wages were higher as a strikebreaker at the railroad than at other jobs available to Black men. And yet, African- and Mexican-descended laborers were shut out of Santa Fe's skilled jobs due to a racial agreement between the company and white unions. Burnett also encountered "plenty of bigotry" when he worked at Forbes Air Force Base and the Veterans Administration hospital in Topeka, even though he was a veteran.[16] The wages of whiteness undermined capitalist productivity at Forbes' supply depot, much like it had at Santa Fe. At Forbes, Burnett "had to read the day's orders" to his white supervisor "because he could not read."[17] Personnel policies at the VA hospital were also "very prejudiced," recalled Lena Burnett.[18] Because the hospital prohibited Black veterans from eating in the mess hall, her husband and his coworkers had to leave the building for their meal breaks.

These racist indignities and others ignited Burnett's civil rights activism. He firmly believed that "whites only change in response to Black pressure."[19] So he wrote a protest letter to a state official after the manager of a local bakery refused to hire him because he was Black. Burnett also campaigned to have Black women hired as secretaries at the Forbes supply depot. According to Lena, employment discrimination was Burnett's primary motivation for becoming an NAACP member. His involvement "grew out of his anger at seeing whites getting blatant advantages in work," she recalled.[20]

Burnett's political purview quickly expanded to segregated schools when he became the president of the Topeka NAACP. His election transformed the political direction of the city's chapter and paved the way for *Brown*. And yet, the late 1940s were a bleak period for the local organization. A month after Burnett became president, the chapter lost one of its most valuable freedom fighters with the sudden death of civil rights attorney William Bradshaw. Bradshaw was a tenacious school desegregationist who represented the plaintiffs in *Foster v. Board of Education* in 1929 and *Graham v. Board of Education* in 1941. He challenged the city's Jim Crow school policy in the courtroom and the boardroom. Bradshaw was a repeat offender of the Topeka school board. He led Black lobbyists to school board meetings throughout the 1930s and '40s seeking educational equity in staffing, sports, and facilities. Bradshaw died of a heart attack in his office on February 4, 1947.

After Bradshaw's death, his coconspirator Daniel Sawyer collaborated with a small cohort of NAACP members to continue their decades-long struggle for educational justice. But when the local branch turned its attention toward dismantling Black schools, it struggled to inspirit its membership campaign. An inability to recruit new members coupled with the exodus of current members created an organizational crisis for the Topeka NAACP. Nevertheless, Sawyer was able to recruit one of the chapter's most uncompromising school desegregationists. Lucinda Todd was arguably the most important addition to the team of civil rights advocates mobilizing against the Topeka school board. She was a practiced racial dissident whose quotidian resistance to racism ranged from her deep investment in respectability politics to her refusal to participate in anti-Black racial norms. Before joining the NAACP, Todd was escorted out of the Grand Theater at police gunpoint because she would not move from the all-white seating section. "They made me leave, but the theater gave me my money back," she later declared with pride.[21]

Todd's righteous indignation was highly informed by a sense of intra-racial entitlement that pivoted upon class and color. After moving to Topeka in 1928, she carefully cultivated a sociospatial imaginary that was intimately tied to the city's Black elite. She lived in Tennessee Town, married a fair-skinned, college-educated man, worshipped at St. John AME, joined Alpha Kappa Alpha sorority, and enrolled her daughter at Buchanan School, which she described as "'the' school" among segregated schools.[22] But the privileges of whiteness were not conferred according to intersectional Blackness. Todd's intra-racial practices may have insulated her from projections of essentialized Blackness, but they could not rescue her daughter from the structural realities of racism.

Over the course of forty years, Todd carefully curated a historical narrative about her involvement in the Topeka NAACP prior to *Brown*. She consistently cited two events for igniting her activism against the Topeka school board. The first was a newspaper announcement about a spring concert highlighting student talent from the city's eighteen white elementary schools. There was no music program in the city's four Black schools and her kindergarten-aged daughter Nancy was taking private piano and music lessons. "I hit the ceiling, I was so mad," she recalled.[23] Two years later, Nancy was nearly hit by the school bus that transported her a mile to her segregated school. "I was mad!" Lucinda Todd exclaimed. "There was a grade school just three blocks from our home here. Why did she have to stand on a corner and wait for a bus to take her to another school a long ways off?"[24] After the school bus incident, Nancy's parents immediately joined the NAACP.

Nancy and Alvin Todd became members of the local NAACP the year it ended the détente on school segregation. The state of the organization was "very poor," she remembered. "Nobody [was] in it much."[25] The Topeka chapter lost approximately 400 members within the first year of Burnett's presidency. Attendance at regular meetings was consistently low, each averaging fewer than a dozen members.[26] By August 1949 the number of registered members in the Topeka NAACP dropped from 252 to 93, even though the chapter had organized a membership drive. The drastic decline in membership prompted a stern reaction from national membership secretary Lucille Black. She expressed her "disappointment" with the branch in an October 1949 letter. "There are hundreds of people in Topeka who have not renewed their memberships this year," she scolded.[27]

Black was unaware of the local dynamics that prompted the dramatic departure of hundreds of NAACP members. The emerging campaign against segregated schools took its toll on the Topeka branch. Black residents proved to be more loyal to Black educators and Black schools than they were to the national civil rights organization. Few had forgotten the impact junior high school desegregation had had on the city's Black teaching force. The school board's dismissal of eight Black teachers "created a certain feeling of fear and insecurity among the Negro population which made our task of getting the wholehearted support of our community almost impossible," Todd explained.[28]

The "People Fight Back": The NAACP Takes on the Superintendent and His Colored Director, 1948

The Topeka NAACP not only had to contend with collective memories of the past, but it was also confronted with a persistent threat in its present. School board members during the late 1940s were more defiant in their anti-Blackness than their counterparts of the early 1940s. Charles Bennett's attempt to resolve a political conflict with physical violence at the April 23, 1948, school board meeting was a sign of the changing times. While empowered

white Topekans depended upon a performance of whiteness that was gen-
teel, Bennett's behavior was an extension of the forceful enforcement of
whiteness-as-property that became emblematic of school superintendent
Kenneth McFarland's administration.

The board of education hired McFarland in 1942. "There was the theory
that McFarland was brought in to curb the integration movement that followed the *Graham* case," recalled veteran Black teacher Mamie Williams.[29]
When the board lost its case against the Graham family in 1941, some white
Topekans blamed school superintendent A. J. Stout. He resigned after the
Ku Klux Klan burned a cross on his front lawn.[30] White supremacists found
a kindred spirit in McFarland. His unapologetic stance on segregation appealed to those who were anxious about the loss of white privilege in Topeka
public schools. The superintendent-elect had personal and professional roots
in southeastern Kansas, a part of the state where anti-Black violence was
whites' racial inheritance. There was an alignment between McFarland's performance and production of whiteness because he was not invested in an
imaginary of racial liberalism. Williams described him as "full of his own superiority," and Lucinda Todd dubbed him a "regular Hitler."[31]

While McFarland embraced his charge as the tyrannical conservator of
whiteness, much of his racist dirty work was conducted by his director of
colored schools. For over a decade, Harrison Caldwell was the school board's
racial enforcer. He not only presided over segregated spaces, but he also
intervened on previously integrated ones. When McFarland recruited
Caldwell in 1942, his first order of business was to segregate the teachers'
union and Topeka High School assemblies. Black residents across the school
divide concluded that the colored supervisor's primary purpose was "to keep
the Negro 'in his place.'"[32] He did so by instituting a patronage system, wielding intimidation for compliance, and deploying retribution in instances of
racial insubordination.

Caldwell blazed a political warpath in response to the NAACP's demands
for school integration. "When the NAACP urged the school board to end Jim
Crow in the schools, threats were made that all colored teachers would be
fired if this were done; and the teachers were intimidated into silence," a 1948
NAACP petition cited.[33] In a show of force, Caldwell segregated a graduation party hosted by Topeka High School seniors that May without their consent or knowledge. When Black invitees arrived, they were turned away at
the venue. The unnecessary orchestration of Black student humiliation further incited NAACP members, especially Todd. Todd and Caldwell were
classmates at Kansas State Teachers College during the 1920s, but they

became political adversaries during the 1940s. It was the director of colored schools who initially rejected her request for an elementary school music program in 1946, even though their children were classmates at Buchanan School. Adding insult to injury, Caldwell tapped into anti-Black epistemes by asserting that Black families did not want musical instruction and could not afford musical instruments. Todd could not suffer Caldwell's collusion with white segregationists, and she held him directly responsible for the lack of equal access in Black and white schools. The colored supervisor was "the cause of much of our trouble," she wrote in a 1953 fundraising speech for *Brown*.[34]

NAACP members immediately began their plot to expel the director of colored schools. They met at Todd's house and drafted a petition called "The People Fight Back." According to Todd, the group used the pseudonym the "Citizens Committee on Civil Rights" because "during this time we of the NAACP were treated as crackpots and radicals."[35] She never said by whom. The leaflet implicated the board of education, the school superintendent, and director of colored schools in a racist conspiracy. The "'powers that BE' brought in McFarland and Caldwell 'to do a job'" after *Graham*, it stated. The civil rights activists were convinced that the superintendent and his Black confederate were recruited with the express purpose to segregate and subordinate Black students in the public school system.

The "People Fight Back" is a postwar provocation. Its authors intentionally connect global and local versions of white supremacy by calling McFarland and Caldwell "Two Little Dictators" and charging the latter with "NAZI-LIKE INTIMIDATION." While civil rights activists cite McFarland as the primary antagonist, their narrative fixation is on Harrison Caldwell. In fact, the petition is a public indictment of the director of colored schools. Caldwell is accused of embracing "the ANTI-NEGRO PHILOSOPHY" of the white school board and publicly pronouncing that "Negroes are not ready for equality." Caldwell wielded white power by proxy, and civil rights activists denounced him for his racial disloyalty. "He himself a Negro" is "a traitor to his group," they wrote. "He is Kenneth McFarland's stooge."

The petition concludes that "democratic minded Topekans have had enough!" The cohort of civil rights activists wanted "to restore fair play and democratic freedom in Topeka Schools, regardless of cost."[36] While their goal was to dismantle the dual education system, their intermediate objective was to oust the director of colored schools. To that end, the group organized a mass meeting on July 22. Todd and Daniel's Sawyer wife Theata canvassed door-to-door that summer to mobilize community support for their efforts, and according to Todd, they were able to secure between 1,000 and 1,500 signatures.

Under the "Citizens Committee on Civil Rights" moniker, NAACP members brought their petition to a September 13 school board meeting to register a formal complaint. NAACP member and civil rights attorney Prentice A. Townsend led the delegation, which included Daniel Sawyer. Sawyer had been on a personal crusade against the city's racist attendance policy for over ten years. He protested busing to segregated schools in 1937 and 1938, testified for the plaintiffs in *Graham* in 1941, lobbied the board to desegregate junior high schools after the *Graham* decision, and attempted to enroll his daughters in their neighborhood school in 1942 and 1947. This time, he set his sights on the director of colored schools.

Sawyer provided context for the citizens committee petition by presenting a letter that historicized civil rights activists' grievances with McFarland and Caldwell. The relationship between McFarland and the NAACP dated back to a July 1942 meeting NAACP Education Committee members had convened with the then-new superintendent, he explained. Tensions were high between civil rights activists, school board members, and Black educators after the battle over junior high school desegregation, and the education committee wanted to "remedy the situation." So, they presented the new superintendent with a proposal for the city's segregated schools. NAACP members advocated for the promotion of Black women teachers to administrative roles, requested the creation of a Black studies instructional unit, and pitched for the recruitment of a "colored director of colored schools." Sawyer said the education committee was optimistic about building a collegial relationship with a new school superintendent. But their sense of hopefulness devolved into feelings of betrayal when McFarland hired Harrison Caldwell as director of colored schools.

Sawyer's letter, like the NAACP petition, focused on Caldwell with the caveat that civil rights advocates' chief complaint was "against Dr. McFarland whose willing tool he is." The director of colored schools had "utterly failed" Black Topekans due to "divers[e] acts of commission and omission," Sawyer charged. "We have lost all confidence in him." Caldwell committed multiple violations against Black students and faculty, including disuniting the teachers' union and dividing Topeka High School's extracurricular activities. "We feel him to be a stumbling block to our progress and declare that his usefulness [is] at an end." Not only had Caldwell augmented segregation in Topeka public schools, but he had also undermined the Black teaching force. According to Sawyer, Black teachers' "morale has been reduced to an all-time low" because of Caldwell's oppressive style of management. Black educators who dared to "question any of his proposals" would "incur his extreme displeasure," he wrote, and Caldwell would "invoke social and economic sanctions" upon those he deemed "a non-cooperator."[37]

The school board's response to NAACP members' passionate appeal and petition was well rehearsed. For almost twenty years, Topeka school board members had answered demands for educational justice with racial paternalism. It was a pattern that began in 1930 with Black residents' first attempt to disrupt the school board's move to segregate city schools in *Wright v. Board*. The board's attorneys argued that the defendants were "acting in the utmost good faith and for what they deemed to be the best interest of both the colored and white children have attempted to separate said races in the lower grades."[38] School board members had gotten more efficient by 1948. Segregated schools were being "conducted for the best interests of the students," they told NAACP members.[39] They didn't bother to specify which students.

Reprisals and Retribution: Caldwell Unleashes "A Reign of Terror"

White school board members most likely did not know or did not care about the clash of Black counterpublics that was on the horizon. Their primary concern was the emergent Black insurgency. However, NAACP members adopted a pseudonym to avoid a Black backlash, not a white one. And in a hint of the intra-racial conflict to come, two representatives of the Kansas Congress of Colored Parents and Teachers complicated matters for NAACP members by also attending the September 13 school board meeting. Tracy Thompson was the founder of the Kansas Colored Parent-Teacher Association and a former teacher at Buchanan and Washington Schools. Her husband Joe advocated for separate schools at two 1941 school board meetings when the board deliberated integrating junior high schools after the *Graham* decision. This time, when segregated schools came under attack, Tracy Thompson appeared with Marthella Booth. Booth served on the Carver YMCA Board of Directors under Caldwell's leadership. On September 13, much like on April 23, local Black PTA members appeared at a school board meeting to oppose NAACP members' demands for integration. This time, the Black school preservationists were most likely prompted by Harrison Caldwell, for the Black PTA representatives publicly defended the director of colored schools and commended his performance as the colored supervisor.[40]

But the defamation damage was done. With a bull's-eye on his back and his job on the line, Caldwell lived up to his reputation as "czar of Black schools."[41] According to Lucinda Todd, the "Director of Negro Schools grew to be more and more of a dictator."[42] The master of machinations sought "reprisals" against anyone involved in the petition drive, she wrote.[43] Daniel Sawyer's daughter Constance said that Caldwell "started a reign of terror" over Black faculty, administrators, and students.[44] He threatened to terminate teachers who had any association with the NAACP or its members and banned them from socializing with NAACP members. Lucinda Todd was at the top of his censured list. McKinley Burnett wrote a letter to NAACP executive secretary Walter White on May 24, 1948, a month after the first NAACP–school board confrontation. He explained that Caldwell forbid four teachers from going "to a bridge party at the house of one of our members of the Executive Committee."[45] That social dictate was aimed at Todd, who also claimed that Caldwell delayed a teacher's contract as punishment for providing her daughter Nancy with supplemental summer homework.[46]

Caldwell was both a galvanizing and a polarizing force for the Topeka NAACP. He actuated members like Lucinda Todd and Daniel Sawyer, but he also proved to be a tremendous impediment to the local organization. The "very peculiar situation" the chapter faced was the subject of Burnett's May 24, 1948, letter to Walter White. "There seems to be a heaving majority of Colored people on our side, but the Negro teachers and a few of their friends are opposing us," he explained. Burnett attributed Black teachers' discord to Harrison Caldwell, not their own volition. The colored supervisor was "employing every means at his command to defeat our plans," including harassing teachers and pressuring ministers who supported school desegregation. Caldwell "declared that he would prevent the NAACP membership drive from being a success," Burnett alleged. The director of colored schools presented the local NAACP with a moral dilemma. Its executive committee was reluctant "to attack . . . a member of our own race," Burnett wrote, but they were also "confident that our cause is a failure" if Caldwell remained in office.[47]

The fact that Caldwell was the Black villain in the *Brown* story is undeniable. "Some teachers told me that they spent a Saturday praying to get out from under this burden," alleged Lucinda Todd.[48] Loss of employment was a serious consideration for Black educators who experienced "a very real fear of economic reprisal at a time when it wasn't easy to find new work," Mamie Williams recalled.[49] As the Topeka Council of Colored Parents and Teachers noted in their April 21 defense of segregated schools, there were few professional alternatives for educated Black Topekans.

"They Wanted Their Own Schools": The Economic and Educational Concerns of Black Educators

Black educators' opposition to civil rights activism cannot be solely attributed to workplace woes. Not only did they have political agency, but they also had a racial mission. Local and national NAACP members consistently underestimated the racial logic of Black anti-desegregationists and attributed Black teachers' opposition to ignorance, complacency, or economic self-interest. National NAACP representatives failed to consider alternative definitions of educational justice because they were singularly focused on building their case against the nation's Jim Crow schools. But they also had a generic approach to community organizing that reflected a deep lack of awareness about or consideration for Topeka's racial geographies.

Director of branches Gloster B. Current's letter to Burnett provides a primary example. Although McKinley Burnett addressed his concerns about Harrison Caldwell's obstruction of justice to Walter White, it was Current who responded. Current dismissed the local NAACP's concerns about Caldwell and Black educators. "Inevitably, the fight for integration arouses antagonisms especially if the Negro teachers and administrators who will be affected feel any threat to their current positions." Current advised members to defuse Black opposition by showing how "integration will improve opportunities for Negroes." He wrote, "The facts should be placed objectively before the community." Resistant residents could be converted when informed about differences in "present facilities used by white and Negro children, e.g. building, equipment, teaching load, books, curriculars, etc."[50]

Local particularities escaped the attention of the national NAACP. Current took racial disparities for granted and underestimated Black residents' situational support of Black schools. There was no mass resistance against the Topeka school board because it inadvertently subsidized liberatory educational spaces by conforming to the *Plessy* standard. The school board's parallelism also incentivized Black educators by providing relative professional autonomy and compensation. Black teachers' remuneration may not have been identical to their white counterparts in Topeka, but it was relatively comparable. The Topeka Board of Education formulated its pay scale based on years of experience, years of preparation, and level of education. Many of Topeka's Black educators pursued master's degrees because the city's teachers could obtain raises through postbaccalaureate studies. As a result, Washington School was rumored to have more teachers with master's degrees than any other school in the city.

Since wages were not solely determined by race, Black educators found the Topeka school district an attractive employer. During the 1939–40 academic year, only sixteen dollars separated the average annual salaries of white and Black teachers at $1,571 and $1,555, respectively. The racial wage gap widened to sixty-two dollars under the McFarland administration as white teachers' salaries increased and Black teachers' remained stable. During the 1951–52 academic year, white teachers were paid an average of $1,621 per year compared to $1,559 for Black teachers.

Mamie Williams's story exemplifies how gender also factored into salary distribution. She resigned from her first job at Lane College in Mississippi and moved back to her hometown in 1918 because her earning potential in Topeka was greater than in Mississippi. It was a smart investment in her future but it was not without its complications. For example, when Harrison Caldwell was hired as director of colored schools twenty-two years later, his salary was $700 higher than Williams's even though they both had master's degrees and she had thirteen years more teaching experience. During the 1940s, Caldwell's pay doubled as other Black educators' salaries stagnated. Caldwell and Williams were both administrators in the mid-to-late 1940s, but his work as a protector of white privilege was rewarded while her labor as Washington School principal went uncompensated. When she mentioned the oversight to Caldwell, "his attitude changed toward me," she said.[51] Adding insult to injury, Caldwell took over Williams's role as Washington School principal in 1952 when the school board eliminated his colored supervisor position in response to NAACP demands. Not only did he make more money than Williams, but he also became the second-highest-earning administrator in Topeka public schools.[52]

Although the interdependent material realities of racism and heteropatriarchy informed the pay scale in Topeka public schools, the wages of whiteness were far greater in school districts throughout the nation. So, it stands to reason that "the teachers were the most vocal group" opposing local NAACP members.[53] Black teachers and administrators had little to gain from school integration in Topeka. They had job security and their salaries were proportionate. Student-teacher ratios were reasonable. But beyond these quantifiable advantages, Black educators had community. They worked in favored and favorable monoracial spaces without the surveillance or depreciation of white teachers or administrators. They had the professional autonomy to create

Topeka's Black educators, 1949. Standing left to right: Merrill Ross, Myrtle Starnes, Edna Vance, Fannie Palton, Mamie Williams, Eva Walker, Harrison Caldwell, Ethel Barbour, J. B. Holland, Ida Norman (school nurse), Althea McBrier. Seated from left to right: Katherine King, Dorothy Bradshaw, Mildred North, Geraldine Gilliam, Minerva Washington, Ada Eggleston, Barbara Ross, Dorothy Crawford, Doris Love, Julia Patterson (National Park Service).

student-centered, racially affirming liberatory pedagogies. They had personal relationships with their students and their students' families. As a former Buchanan teacher, Lucinda Todd was one of the only local NAACP members who understood that Black educators' resistance to integrated schools went beyond employment concerns: "They wanted their own schools."[54]

The benefits of integration for Black students in Topeka were more ambiguous than local and national NAACP members cared to acknowledge. But the city's Black civil rights activists had little tolerance for a nuanced racial standpoint. Monroe School alum Daniel Sawyer persisted for over twenty years despite the unpopularity of his opinion or the discord it created in his family of educators. And there was little to no conflict of interest for Topeka transplants Lucinda Todd and McKinley Burnett, who grew up in small towns with integrated school districts. Black alumni of Topeka public schools knew that anti-Blackness followed proximities to whiteness because they experienced it firsthand. The outcome of integration into Topeka's junior and senior high schools was not equal access and opportunities, it was exposure to racism.

Richard Ridley attended Monroe School from the mid-1930s to the early 1940s. In the protected space of his segregated school, academic preparation transcended standardized curriculum as Black teachers readied their students to contradict racial scripts. "They told us, 'You are going to a mixed school and we don't want you to embarrass us,'" he recalled. Going above and beyond the norm was accepted practice in the city's four Black schools, so "when we went to junior high school, obviously we rose to the top rung because we were trained." Black teachers were intentional in designing instruction that nurtured Black children's racial subjectivities, but they could not protect their students from what their future would hold. "When I was in grade school I was on top of the world," Ridley said. "When I went to Topeka High School I was put into auto mechanics."[55]

Tracking was custom at the high school, so high academic achievers like Ridley could not escape projections of essentialized Blackness. As a freshman he was enrolled in auto mechanics even though "I had been on high honors coming out of junior high school," he said. Ridley was not alone. He recalled other smart, driven Black male students who were tracked into labor-focused courses like "machine shop" and woodworking. Trade courses were integrated, but they were considered "the lower echelon" for students who were not considered "college material" by white faculty and guidance counselors, Ridley recalled.[56]

There was widespread consensus among Black parents and students that anti-Blackness was pervasive at Topeka High School. In fact, Black alumni of Topeka public schools shared a collective experience of racist harm when transitioning from segregated schools to integrated ones. Even McKinley Burnett's wife Lena described the high school's all-white teaching staff as "bigots" who "didn't care" about Black students.[57]

Black students' experiences in segregated and integrated learning environments animated resistance to the NAACP's emerging school desegregation campaign. Local NAACP members were resolute in their commitment to desegregating the city's schools despite extensive anecdotal evidence that school integration was not wholly beneficial to Black students. Their investment in dismantling structures of anti-Blackness superseded their concerns about students' susceptivity to anti-Blackness.

The Topeka NAACP Makes Its Case against Segregated Schools, 1950

Undeterred by the Black blowback, the NAACP continued to lobby the school board for a change in its racist enrollment policy. School board members generally responded by deploying two interdependent strategies of racial evasion. The first and perhaps most effective was the subterranean subterfuge of the colored supervisor. Caldwell's ruthless manipulation within the Black public sphere abetted the school board's second tactic: public-facing passive aggression. School board members often chose avoidance over antagonism. Month after month, they deployed direct inaction to dissuade civil rights activists and deliberately delayed those who attended regularly scheduled meetings. NAACP member Charles Baston recalled waiting for hours to speak because school board members "would sit around and laugh or joke about something to try to extend the time" after they completed their official agenda. School board members once deferred NAACP members until midnight because they hoped "we would become discouraged enough to leave," Baston said. "We never left."[58]

When NAACP members were allowed to present their case, school board members resorted to racial custom. "They had nothing valid or nothing of substance to say other than they felt that it [was] more appropriate for their children to attend schools where the children were more familiar with each other," remembered Charles Baston.[59] Paternalism was white men's prerogative, but it was a patriarchal standard they did not extend to the Black men standing before them. Baston was a decorated army veteran who moved to Topeka after serving in the African, European, and Pacific theaters during World War II. But that didn't matter to white school board members. For veterans like Baston, Burnett, Edward Foust, and others, fighting for democracy abroad conferred no democratic rights at home. That exclusion was a painful reminder of how racism mitigated Black men's gender privileges. Burnett betrayed a sense of emasculation in a September 1, 1950, letter to NAACP executive director Walter White. "Words will not express the humiliation, and disrespect in this matter," he wrote.[60]

The final straw for Burnett was a school board meeting he had attended the previous month. After two years of school board members' dogged ducking and dodging, Burnett appeared at an August 7, 1950, meeting to, once again, "request elimination of segregation in the lower grades."[61] The school board's response was more direct but slightly less dramatic than the first time NAACP members demanded integrated schools in 1948. One school board member deferred responsibility for Jim Crow schools and offered a flippant yet prophetic suggestion that "the group appeal to the Legislature to amend the law permitting the existence of such schools."[62] A frustrated Burnett signaled toward a pending legal battle. "You've had two years now to prepare for this," he warned. Burnett's racial insubordination aggravated one school board member. "As soon as I sat down, one of the board members jumped up and roared, 'Is that a request or is that an ultimatum?'" Burnett later recalled. "He roared so load and so quick that it rather frightened me."[63] School board members did not yield to Burnett's challenge. They resolved that the school board would "continue operation of Negro grade schools." In the end, "no action was taken."[64]

The local NAACP chapter had had enough of being stonewalled by the Topeka school board, so they began preparing a lawsuit against the Topeka Board of Education. It was opportune timing. Local NAACP members captured the attention of the national NAACP as it embarked upon an unprecedented legal challenge against the nation's Jim Crow schools. Burnett and Todd both contacted Walter White for assistance and support. Todd had hosted the executive director in her home when he traveled to Topeka for a speaking engagement on April 26, 1949. His visit provided an opportune time to share stories about the local chapter's school desegregation campaign and their struggles with the Topeka school board. "He promised to help us rid ourselves of segregated schools," Todd later wrote.[65] Holding her houseguest accountable, Todd reminded White of his political pledge in an August 29, 1950, letter. She informed him that the local chapter had been challenging the dual education system for a couple of years. "Our situation has become so unbearable that the local branch has decided to test the permissible law which we have in Kansas," she wrote.[66]

In the meantime, NAACP members set up a meeting to inform Black educators of their plan to pursue legal intervention. The four Black school principals were among the attendees, including Washington School principal Harrison Caldwell. The conference was held in the offices of civil rights attorney Elisha Scott, presumably a mutually agreed upon neutral location. Even though John and Charles Scott would represent the plaintiffs in the NAACP lawsuit, their father Elisha defended Black schools in the aftermath of *Graham*. Black school preservationist Mamie Williams was present because she had a vested interest in the arising situation. The meeting failed to de-escalate tensions between the two groups. Williams claimed that one NAACP member added insult to injury by insinuating that Black schools were substandard. She recalled someone saying, "Imagine, our children have to go by these white schools and go to Black schools and be taught by Black teachers." The NAACP's overture did little to raise Black educators' confidence in their case against segregated schools. Instead, it further provoked them. According to Williams, the civil rights activists "tried to rally our support. All it did was to draw the lines."[67]

The veteran educator was not publicly outspoken about the school board's segregationist policy because she was politically astute. Although she had defended Black schools as a witness in *Graham,* she was not a member of the anti-desegregation delegation that lobbied the school board after *Graham.* It was a shrewd strategy. After twenty-three years with Topeka public schools, she witnessed the retributive firings of six Black teachers in 1941. Two of those teachers were the sisters of civil rights activists William Bradshaw and Daniel Sawyer. Maytie Bradshaw and Annabel Sawyer were Williams's longtime colleagues and lifelong neighbors. The school board also penalized Ruth Ridley. Ridley and Williams had started teaching in Topeka in 1918. Although both women had endorsed Black schools during the *Graham* trial, the school board reduced Ridley's contract to half-time when junior high schools were integrated.

Mamie Williams survived the school board's vengeance after *Graham.* She also adeptly navigated the political minefield that followed under the McFarland administration. Williams was able to do so because she was a consummate professional and a fierce protector of all-Black schools. The civic-minded educator was never a member of the local NAACP even though she was active in the Republican Party. When school desegregationists attempted to recruit Williams to their cause, she would astutely remind them, "I work for the Board of Education."[68] She may not have vocalized her standpoint on dual education in the presence of whites, but her opinion on the matter was clear. In fact, Williams reportedly undermined NAACP efforts by weaponizing dissemblance. The Columbia University alumnus who was renowned throughout the Black community as an exceptional educator reportedly told whites that she was not qualified to teach white children.[69]

However, Williams's interest convergence with the superintendent, colored supervisor, and school board could not protect her from becoming collateral damage in the NAACP's school desegregation battle. In 1950 Williams suffered her first professional setback in thirty-two years. After Burnett threatened to file a lawsuit against the Topeka Board of Education, the school board made a strategic personnel decision. It tried to accommodate civil rights activists' demands and uphold white students' educational privileges. Without modifying Harrison Caldwell's job description, they changed his job title from "director of colored schools" to "inter-racial counselor." They also assigned Caldwell the principalship of Washington Elementary, a position Mamie Williams had held for three years. Williams was demoted and transferred to Monroe Elementary.

Blacks against *Brown*: The Black Backlash
to the Topeka NAACP, 1950–1953

As the Topeka NAACP intensified its school desegregation campaign, it struggled to convince Black Topekans of its merits. Black educators performed a labor of love in the city's Black schools and earned strong community support because of their ethos of care. "Those who sympathized with the teachers called us troublemakers," remembered Todd.[70] Many Black residents regarded Black teachers as more than classroom instructors. It was not uncommon for Black school alumni to speak of their former teachers using familial terms, including Oliver Brown's widow Leola Brown Montgomery. "The teachers were fantastic. More like an extended family, like mothers 'cause they took an interest in you," she enthused.[71] Like Montgomery, Joe Douglas Jr. attended Monroe School in the 1930s and praised their nurturance of Black students. "There was a lot of mothering in their handling of us," he recalled.[72] Not only did Black teachers gain respect for their holistic approach to education, but also several were mainstays within the parallel school system. Nine women had twenty years' experience in Topeka's segregated schools when the *Brown* case was initiated.[73] Williams had "great pride" in the fact that she taught multiple generations within some families.[74] Both Oliver and Linda Brown were Williams's pupils, the father at Buchanan and his daughter at Monroe. Consequently, community loyalty to Black schools and Black educators was tenacious.

Few Black residents believed that the civil rights crusade would bring a favorable alternative to the city's Black elementary schools. In fact, the local affiliate had difficulties trying to recruit plaintiffs for the Kansas Supreme Court case, despite their door-to-door canvassing. Eventually they succeeded in convincing thirteen parents. The case that became known as *Brown v. Board of Education of Topeka* was filed at the district court of Kansas on February 28, 1951, and the trial date was set for June 25. By necessity, the NAACP's legal approach to *Brown* did not consider the special circumstances that led to Black residents' endorsement of Black educators and Black schools. Under the advisement of NAACP Legal Defense Fund attorney Jack Greenberg, Topeka attorneys presented the counterfactual legal argument that Topeka's Black schools were inferior to their white counterparts with regard to "physical facilities, curricula, teaching, resources, student personnel services."[75] In contempt of the court of Black public opinion, *Brown* attorneys claimed that Black students "are required to attend schools where they cannot receive educational advantages and opportunities."[76]

Before the Kansas Supreme Court heard arguments in *Brown*, Kenneth McFarland resigned due to a highly publicized embezzlement scandal. His successor Wendell Godwin was elected in April of 1951 and promised "to make a mighty good school system a bit better."[77] Four months later, the Kansas Supreme Court ruled in favor of the defendants. With legal endorsement, the Topeka school board continued to conduct segregationist business as usual. When the NAACP requested a meeting with board members in January 1952, they were told to attend the next public meeting.

The school board wasn't the NAACP's only unreceptive audience. The Topeka NAACP struggled to cover its legal costs as it prepared to appeal the Kansas Supreme Court ruling. Black residents were unwilling to donate to the cause because their allegiance was with Black schools and Black teachers. News of the local NAACP's challenges was widespread. Kansas assistant attorney general Paul Wilson's Black associates "advised him that few Blacks were interested" in the *Brown* case. They told him that most Black residents "regarded the Topeka NAACP as troublemakers and did not support them."[78]

Wilson's advisors were correct. The local NAACP had little moral or financial support for its desegregation campaign. The civil rights activists could only secure $100 of the $5,000 they needed to bring *Brown* before the US Supreme Court. Attorneys John and Charles Scott involuntarily volunteered their services and had to pay for legal fees out of pocket. NAACP Legal Defense Fund attorney Robert Carter tried to intervene on behalf of the Topeka chapter in September 1951. He wrote a solicitation letter addressed to the presidents of NAACP branches throughout the state of Kansas. The Topeka NAACP had been "unsuccessful in their efforts to raise the amount necessary to defray the expenses in this case," he disclosed.[79] With Black residents rallying against the local chapter, the situation was desperate. "We couldn't really finance it," Todd recalled. But she would not capitulate her cause. "I couldn't face my child unless we made the effort."[80]

Black school preservationists matched civil rights activists' indefatigability. One month after the Topeka NAACP filed its appeal with the US Supreme Court, a delegation of concerned Black citizens made its case for McKinley Elementary School. The North Topeka school closed for the 1951–52 academic year because a historic flooding of the Kaw River caused severe damages to the building that needed to be repaired. While the closure was judicious, the pending school desegregation lawsuit made Black parents anxious. They did not want McKinley to be shut down permanently. On November 5 eighty-six "patrons" attended a school board meeting to save their school.

McKinley School was an integral part of the Sand Town community, a historic neighborhood north of the Kansas River. Sand Town was settled by Exodusters on Half-Breed Reservation land that had been donated by a teenaged Charles Curtis. Curtis was a member of the Kaw Nation who would later become the first nonwhite person elected vice president of the United States.[81] Curtis shared more than a tie to the land with McKinley School advocates. They shared standpoints on educational policies that upheld the privileging of whiteness. Curtis supported federal assimilation policy at the turn of the century, while Black residents of Sand Town supported the city's segregationist school policy. However, the latter desired cultural literacy, not cultural erasure.

So, the McKinley School lobby pressed the school board to keep the segregated school open when construction was complete. The school board's rehabilitation project caused significant inconveniences for the area's Black families, they explained. It subjected forty-one students to extensive busing and forced the reassignment of Black schoolteachers. But disruption and dislocation were not the group's only concerns. They insisted that McKinley was more than an educational facility for schoolchildren. It was a meeting site for social organizations and an extracurricular space for area teenagers. The "failure of this school to re-open will hamper and retard the rebuilding of home and community life in North Topeka," they asserted.[82]

While the McKinley delegation took its cause to the boardroom, other Black school preservationists waged their battle in the streets. "You have no idea the depths of their meanness," Lucinda Todd told Richard Kluger in 1970 when interviewed for *Simple Justice*.[83] Because of their civil rights activism, NAACP members and their families became targets for retribution within Topeka's Black communities. Twenty-five years after *Brown*, Todd reflected upon the personal price she paid for her political activism. "Not all Blacks wanted the case," she told a *Washington Post* reporter. "Since I had taught school, many of my friends were teachers, and they quit speaking to me. They wouldn't come to my club meetings."[84]

Harrison Caldwell deserved some credit for blacklisting civil rights activists, but Black educators had their own incentives. Berdyne Scott, the wife of *Brown* attorney John Scott, described the social pressure Black residents exerted on members of the NAACP. "Everybody hated you," she said. "I remember a teacher that called and said, 'Bunny, talk to your husband. You don't want to see me lose my job.'"[85] Lena Burnett recalled an unpleasant encounter with Mamie Williams, who lived across the street from the Burnett family. According to Burnett, Williams confronted her about her husband's political activism and criticized the shortsightedness of the civil rights activists. "Do you think the white people would have me teach their children?"[86]

Williams vehemently denied this social intercourse in correspondence with Richard Kluger. "I adhered strictly to a policy of not discussing the case inasmuch as I was an employee of the Board of Education," she wrote in her defense. Williams twice requested that Kluger "please delete the imaginary conversation with Lena Burnett" from his monograph. She was an intentional woman with a keen awareness of both the archive as body and the archival body. She appreciated Kluger's scholarly attention to the "people, places and situations" in Topeka, and she understood the potential historiographical impact of *Simple Justice*. As such, Williams was deeply invested in Kluger's character development. She had spent a lifetime carefully cultivating a public performance based in bourgeois respectability politics. By all accounts, "proper" behavior was conduct she modeled in the classroom and in the community. So, she took exception to the allegation of her accosting another woman in the street while using vernacular English, the latter of which she presented as proof of the conversation's fallaciousness. "'White Folks' is an expression that I do not use," she insisted.[87] Kluger kept Burnett's quote, but he made a concession and changed "white folks" to "white people" in the monograph.

Whether or not Williams approached Burnett about the case, the harassment of NAACP members escalated as Black Topekans became more aware of *Brown*. The private persecution of plaintiffs came from unusual suspects. "I didn't get anything from white folks," exclaimed Leola Brown Montgomery, Oliver Brown's widow. "I tell you here in Topeka, unlike the other places where they brought these cases . . . we didn't have any threats" from whites.[88] Black Topekans were another story, she insisted. The Brown family received "derogatory remarks" from a mother who wanted her children to stay in segregated schools. Other community members were equally concerned for Black teachers. Montgomery was confronted by a Black resident who spoke of her family's involvement in the case. "'You're just going to get all these Black teachers out of a job,'" the resident scolded. "That's about the only two things that were ugly [that I] heard from folks," Montgomery recalled.[89]

Anti-NAACP hostilities among Black residents intensified in 1953. With the US Supreme Court deliberating the racial future of Topeka public schools, Topeka school board members weaponized the one thing they had left within their white power: personnel decisions. School board members tapped into Black school preservationists' worst fears and voted in a closed meeting to dismiss six Black teachers if the US Supreme Court ruled on behalf of the plaintiffs in *Brown*.[90] In his public statement, Superintendent Godwin conveyed that "if the Supreme Court rules against the Kansas permissive statute on segregation Topeka schools will not need as many Negro teachers."[91] But his official correspondence with Black educators made it clear that the school board would prioritize white parents' anti-Blackness over Black educators' livelihood. "If the Supreme Court should rule that segregation in the elementary grades is unconstitutional our Board will proceed on the assumption that the majority of people in Topeka will not want to employ Negro teachers next year for white children," he wrote on March 13. In his preemptive strike, Godwin put the letter's recipients on notice: "It is necessary for me to notify you now that your services will not be needed for next year."[92]

Godwin took a page out of former school superintendent A. J. Stout's segregationist playbook. By using passive voice both superintendents projected responsibility for Black faculty's fate from the anti-Black school board to Black school desegregationists. However, Stout did not have to contend with the legal firepower of the national NAACP. NAACP Legal Defense Fund attorney Robert Carter responded to Godwin's scare tactics with a counterthreat. "We certainly have no intention of backing down on this," he asserted in a March 31 letter to McKinley Burnett. He urged Burnett to remind the school board that firing teachers "because of race and color is as illegal as any other type of discrimination by state officials against Negroes because of race." He also wanted Burnett to inform the letter's recipients that they had the backing of the NAACP. If the teachers want to "contest this," he wrote, they should be assured that "we in this office are greatly concerned about it and are willing to lend our full support."[93]

Robert Carter seemed unaware of tensions between the Topeka branch and Black educators, despite local members' repeated reminders. Godwin's letter confirmed and inflamed rumors of potential teacher firings running rampant throughout Black communities.[94] In August 1953, two months after the US Supreme Court adjourned with no decision in *Brown*, Lucinda Todd informed NAACP national membership secretary Lucille Black of the troubled political landscape the local chapter faced. "We have a situation here in Topeka in which the *Negro Teachers are violently opposed to our efforts to integrate the public schools*," she wrote.[95]

Contested Counterpublics: Blacks, *Brown*, and Compromised Spaces of Sociality

Dissension among Black Topekans over *Brown* compromised spaces that historically operated as movement centers, most notably Black schools, Black churches, and the NAACP. Black civil rights activists struggled to mobilize support for their school desegregation campaign because each of these sites was contested political terrain. Black schools and the NAACP were positioned in opposition, so Black ministers intentionally held space for political neutrality in churches whose members were in conflict over the existence of Black schools. The abstention of St. John AME Church as a moral force or support center for the Topeka NAACP is a primary example.

St. John's origins date back to prayer circles convened by a few free Black residents and formerly enslaved Black settlers, many of whom were from Tennessee. Before it was officially recognized as an AME church in 1877, St. John's served the social and spiritual needs of Black residents in the area that would come to be known as Tennessee Town. In fact, its reverend, Columbus M. Johnson, worked alongside Benjamin "Pap" Singleton to bring 300 formerly enslaved Blacks from Tennessee to Topeka in 1873. After the Fifteenth Amendment was ratified, Kansas legislators grappled with whether to recognize Blacks' civil rights, and St. John's became a site of Black resistance to the imposition of segregation in public schools, accommodations, and transportation.[96]

Eighty years later, the church would avoid the issue of segregation to accommodate its divided membership. By then, the culture of St. John's congregation had evolved with the demographics of the neighborhood. The residents of Tennessee Town had shifted from poor Southern Black migrants to the Black professional elite. In turn, the city's Black doctors, lawyers, and educators worshipped at St. John AME. It became one of the sites where class and color converged in Topeka's Black geographies. Members had a reputation for disassociating from "lower-class" and dark-skinned Blacks. When Zelma Henderson moved to Topeka in 1940, she was warned about the colorism at St. John's. "When I first came [people] said, 'They don't even want you there unless you're light.'"[97]

During the mid-1940s, St. John's Rev. Edward S. Foust was one of the few Topeka ministers actively involved in the local NAACP's school desegregation campaign. The militant minister arrived in Topeka around 1944 or '45. Unfamiliar with the political minefield of the city's segregated schools, Foust did not proceed with caution. St. John's became a convening space for NAACP members like Daniel Sawyer who were unwilling to disengage from the city's Jim Crow school policy, according to Sawyer's daughter Cyrene.[98] Cyrene's older sister Constance recalled that the new reverend and his wife Louise were not warmly welcomed by their congregation.[99] Consequently, Foust's stint at St. John's was short-lived. Although he was reassigned to a church in Kansas City, Missouri, in November 1947, Foust continued to be active in the city's school desegregation campaign. He returned for the NAACP's April 1948 confrontation with the Topeka school board meeting and was one of the headlining speakers at an event NAACP members organized to rally Black ministers in 1953.

In the meantime, Foust's successor Rev. Eugene H. Kelly Jr. was presented with a congregation divided. Members included *Brown* architects Daniel Sawyer and Lucinda Todd, *Brown* plaintiffs Oliver Brown and Zelma Henderson, and the family of *Brown* attorney John Scott. But these school desegregationists and others were counterbalanced by Black school preservationists. "All the teachers went to St. John's," said Lucinda Todd.[100] Todd's overstated narrative embellishment speaks to Black educators' presence and prominence at the church. Retired Washington School principal Ezekiel Ridley was a longtime member of St. John AME, as were veteran educators Emma Cooper, Hester Hardeman, and Ruth Ridley, three teachers whose employment was terminated or reduced by the school board after *Graham*.

The school desegregation campaign developed among Kelly's congregants, but if he publicly backed the NAACP, he risked facing a fate similar to that of his predecessor. Consequently, Kelly never publicly declared a position on *Brown*. He was not alone. Only three Black ministers were active supporters of the NAACP's case, E. Bernard Herd from Calvary Church, P. H. Hill from Shiloh Church, and Oliver Brown.[101] Oliver Brown's reluctance to participate in the case that bore his name is well known. He was not member of the NAACP nor did he want to become involved as a plaintiff. By most accounts, Brown was "not a fighter in manner."[102] McKinley Burnett's wife Lena believed that Brown's reticence stemmed from his duties as an assistant pastor at St. John AME. "The Methodists" steered clear of the NAACP, she said, and Brown was a new pastor at a "prosperous" church "that didn't want to get involved" in the desegregation movement.[103]

As Burnett noted, the relationship between ministers and their congregations was coconstituted. Parishioners held church leaders accountable not only for their spiritual sensibilities and moral imperatives but also to their political subjectivities. Black pastors were expected to guide and to resonate. Local NAACP organizers understood Black churches' centrality to Black sociality and that they needed Black ministers' endorsement to ensure the success of their political cause. So, members planned a banquet to pay tribute to the city's Black ministers after the US Supreme Court deferred their decision in *Brown* in June 1953. "We hope by this means to gain their support and cooperation for our program," Lucinda Todd wrote to the national office.[104] The turnout was disappointing. Only eleven of the twenty-three ministers invited attended the NAACP dinner. Two months later, Lucinda Todd penned a letter to the national membership secretary and explained the chapter's public relations problem. They could not get the blessing of local ministers without the support of Black teachers, she wrote, and they could not get Black congregations on board without the approval of Black ministers. "Some of the ministers told us if it were not for our school case they could help us much more than at present," she wrote. "So you can see that we really have our work cut out for us."[105]

The city's civil rights activists were particularly susceptible to covert forms of countermobilization because many of the key organizers were Black women. Leola Brown Montgomery confirmed "that women were more out front in the meetings, in the churches, speaking out against things."[106] While Montgomery attributed that dynamic to the legacy of enslavement, it was more likely because women's political advocacy occurred under the protection of the domestic sphere. Several women involved in the civil rights case were stay-at-home wives and mothers like Todd. Some occasionally took in laundry to supplement their husband's income. But the social lives of elite Black women converged in churches and gender-exclusive clubs and organizations whether they worked in public or private. Those sites of sociality enabled the recruitment of female plaintiffs like Zelma Henderson and Maude Lawton, but they also rendered civil rights activists vulnerable to retributive acts of political resistance.

Black teachers presented a formidable challenge to the desegregation movement as active church members, but they also wielded heavy influence through Black women's social clubs. For example, many Black schoolteachers were members of Alpha Kappa Alpha (AKA) sorority. The Alpha Iota Omega chapter was chartered in 1928 at Mamie Williams's home, and four of the five charter members were Black educators. There was a collective sense among college-educated Black women that those who were not members of the sorority were social personae non gratae. Jeanette Dandridge taught at Monroe Elementary from 1938 to 1940. She became an AKA while at Washburn University because "if you got in you were somebody, and if you didn't . . ."[107] More than half of the Black women who were employed by

Topeka public schools from 1930 to 1954 were AKAs, the sorority Lucinda Todd labeled "the cream of the colored women." Todd taught at Buchanan Elementary from 1928 to 1935. Seven of her thirteen female colleagues were AKAs, and they recruited Todd to become a member.[108] During the late 1940s to early 1950s, when Todd was mobilizing against the board of education, the list of officers for the Alpha Iota Omega chapter was made up of prominent Black female educators.[109] The president, vice president, recording secretary, corresponding secretary, dean of pledges, parliamentarian, and nine undergraduate advisors were past or present employees of Topeka public schools.[110]

Allegiance to Black schools ran high among AKAs. School board members' punitive response to civil rights desegregation campaigns reinforced sorority members' political resolve. AKAs Maytie Bradshaw, Emma Cooper, Annabel Sawyer, and Hester Hardeman, a charter member, were four of the six women fired after *Graham*. Another soror, Darla Buchanan, became one of the six teachers who had their teaching contracts revoked in 1953 as retribution for *Brown*. For some AKAs, the bond went beyond Greek-letter sisterhood. As previously mentioned, Mamie Williams, Annabel Sawyer, Maytie and Mattie Bradshaw, and Emma Cooper were not only sorors, but they were also longtime colleagues and lifelong neighbors. The Williams, Sawyer, and Bradshaw families all lived within two blocks of one another on Quincy Street, while Emma Cooper grew up less than three blocks away on Jackson Street.

Lucinda Todd suffered social reprisals for her role in *Brown* because her perceived transgression was not just political, it was personal. "I lost some friends," she recalled, "They thought I betrayed them."[111] This closing of ranks among sorority members was confirmed by Jeanette Dandridge and her daughter, archivist Deborah Dandridge, who also became an AKA. During the early-to-mid 1950s, Deborah was a Washington Elementary School student. She remembered her mother being "very supportive of her sorority sisters" during their opposition to *Brown*. In fact, her parents continued to enroll her at Washington after the Topeka school board integrated the city's schools.[112] Jeanette Dandridge later spoke of the pressure to conform to a collective standpoint. She admitted that her support of all-Black schools was based less on a commitment to a cause than her concern for "being accepted socially."[113]

Black school preservationists' political crusade often devolved into personal conflicts. Their standpoint on separate schools pivoted on more than ideology. People's livelihoods were at stake. Consequently, *Brown* opponents were not always scrupulous. Black teachers weaponized submerged networking and acts of social retribution. They also deployed verbal threats, vandalism, harassing mail, and combative phone calls. The men involved in the case may have escaped the wrath of Black female educators, but Nancy Todd Noches wrote that her mother Lucinda "had to make many sacrifices, including loss of her teacher friends, threats against her husband's job, and many threats from the community."[114] While most alumni of all-Black schools like Deborah Dandridge portrayed Black teachers as nurturing, "family-oriented" people, McKinley Burnett's daughter Maurita Davis proclaimed "that wasn't our experience."[115] Although her peers described Black teachers as "othermothers," Davis remembers them being unreceptive and antagonistic. "They weren't like family to us, they were very hostile." Because of her father's involvement in *Brown*, Black teachers "were not too cordial" to the Burnett family, and children were not spared their vengeance. Davis alleged that her cousin was bullied and physically reprimanded by a teacher at her school. "There were some intimidations," she professed.[116]

Conflict Resolution: *Brown v. Board of Education of Topeka*, 1954

Despite Black teachers' best efforts, history was not on their side. In a unanimous decision on May 17, 1954, the US Supreme Court ruled on behalf of the plaintiffs in *Brown v. Board of Education of Topeka*. Chief Justice Earl Warren delivered the majority opinion that overturned *Plessy v. Ferguson*. The court resolved that segregation "has a detrimental effect upon the colored children." With the backing of social science researchers, Warren declared that state-sanctioned segregation subjected Black children to "a sense of inferiority [that] affects the motivation of a child to learn" and has a "tendency to [retard] the educational and mental development of negro children."[117] The irony of the most important civil rights case in American history is that these conclusions did not apply to the schools indicted by *Brown v. Board of Education of Topeka*.

The 1954 US Supreme Court decision in *Brown v. Board of Education of Topeka* promised to completely transform the educational system in the United States. The NAACP's win was a defeat for the nation's Black teachers. In both the short- and long-term, Black students in Topeka suffered a significant loss, not because they were integrated into predominantly white schools but because Black teachers were not. The city's Black school preservationists' worst nightmare became a reality. Black educators, and arguably Black education, became collateral damage in one of most important civil rights lawsuits in American history.

Conclusion

If there is a lesson to learn from the story of Blacks against *Brown* it is this: minoritized students' subjectivities need to be at the center of educational institution building and antiracist policymaking in the nation's public and private schools. Dismantling structural barriers is absolutely necessary, but not necessarily absolute. Before *Brown*, Black schoolchildren in Topeka and elsewhere thrived in segregated elementary schools under the tutelage and care of Black teachers. These stories operate as common sense within Black communities, but they are overshadowed in mainstream histories of segregated schools. The standardization of historical narratives about Jim Crow schools secrets the mutability of anti-Blackness, obscuring its diverse emergences and, in turn, the divergent antiracism strategies of Black communities. The Topeka school board inadvertently facilitated the advancement of Black counterpublics by maintaining a semiparallel education system for Black students. Black communities reclaimed places created with racist intent as social centers, and Black educators affirmed Black being within a school system designed to enforce Black nonbeing.

A Spectacle Unseen: Racism and Refusal in Topeka's Segregated Schools

LIFE magazine's 1953 *Brown v. Board* photographic essay evidenced the co-existence of racist politics and racial pleasure in the city's Jim Crow schools. As the nation prepared for an epochal racial moment, the magazine's editors sent twenty-nine-year-old photographer Hikaru "Carl" Iwasaki to observe the daily school rituals of Linda Brown and her younger sister Terry Lynn. The creative result was a nuanced commentary on American crises of citizenship. Iwasaki shadowed the Browns from their family home to their classroom at Monroe School. One of the more iconic moments occurred during the girls' commute to their school bus. The famed photo features the two well-dressed, pigtailed sisters as they walked with quiet composure along the railroad tracks through the Rock Island Interchange yard. The stark black-and-white picture conveyed a clear, yet subtle, provocation: Black civility persists amid white incivility.

181

Linda and Terry Lynn Brown walk through the Rock Island Interchange yard, March 1953 (Carl Iwasaki/The Chronicle Collection via Getty Images)

Iwasaki was an experienced disrupter of the white racial imaginary. Less than ten years before the *Brown* photoshoot, the Nisei San Jose native was an incarceree at Heart Mountain in Park County, Wyoming. Then-attorney general of California Earl Warren was a critical proponent of the forced relocation and incarceration of Japanese Americans like the Iwasaki family. War Relocation Authority representatives at Heart Mountain recruited the budding photographer to document the lives of imprisoned Americans of Japanese descent. So Iwasaki was already well-versed in using composition as a form of refusal when *LIFE* assigned him to the *Brown* project. Through his lens, Iwasaki bore witness to shared phenomenologies of racial containment and the dispossession of nonwhite citizens. The subtle exchange between the Japanese American photographer and his African American subjects becomes perceptible when "listening to images."

Black Topekans cocreated the published narrative by staging visual resistance to Black dehumanization. The image of the Brown sisters in the Rock Island Exchange yard was a racial invocation. The girls' trip to the "other side of the tracks" tapped into collective understandings about geographic lines of racial demarcation. But looks were deceiving. Residential segregation was not enforced in Topeka. The Brown sisters left their home in one integrated neighborhood to attend their segregated school in another integrated neighborhood. "Curiously," a *New York Times* reporter wrote in 1961, the Browns "lived next door to a white family, and for most of her life Linda had played with white children without concern or wonder."[1] The girls walked six blocks to get to their school bus, which was provided by the Topeka school board. In addition, they traversed a far less distance than their counterparts in Clarendon County, South Carolina, where board chairman Roderick W. Elliott told Black parents in 1947, "We ain't got no money to buy a bus for your nigger children."[2] Unlike the defendants in *Briggs v. Elliott*, those in *Brown v. Board* maintained a whiteness as property through distance, not deprivation. So, when Iwasaki photographed Linda Brown at her Jim Crow school, she stood before a modern two-story, thirteen-room, Italian Renaissance–style brick and limestone building.

Brown brought Black Topekans into full view, and yet, they remained a spectacle unseen. Close inspection of Iwasaki's photojournalistic essay reveals not only the uncommonality of their commons but also the intimate spaces of Black sociality. Despite the staged nature of his assignment, Iwasaki captured contradistinctive moments of containment and refusal. The segregated school bus, schoolyard, and classrooms became sites of intra-racial affirmation. In one photo, Linda Brown and her classmates

Linda Brown and her sister Terry Lynn (*far right*) ride the bus to Monroe Elementary School, March 1953 (Carl Iwasaki/The Chronicle Collection via Getty Images)

Linda Brown and her sister Terry Lynn (*far right*) in front of Monroe Elementary School, March 1953 (Carl Iwasaki/The Chronicle Collection via Getty Images)

Nine-year-old Linda Brown (seated in first desk, second row from right) in Mamie Williams's Monroe School classroom, March 1953 (Carl Iwasaki/The Chronicle Collection via Getty Images)

listen to their teacher with their hands clasped and placed firmly on their desks. While the photo's documentation of the daily doings of Black students was humanizing in its ordinariness, the students' self-regulation was an exercise in respectability politics. Black educators enforced disciplined bodies and behavior in pedagogical, albeit somewhat problematic, resistance to anti-Blackness. Iwasaki's presence gave veteran Black educator Mamie Williams an opportunity to stage an intervention against the growing chorus of voices discrediting Black teachers' classroom capabilities. The body politics of racial uplift were common instructional practices in Black schools, but students' conformity was especially critical that day in March 1953. The eyes of the nation would be upon them.

Topeka's four Black schools transcended the school board's anti-Black intentions to become spaces of Black intentionality. Black educators reclaimed the city's segregated schools and conscientiously created protected spaces that nurtured Black students' racial subjectivities. Williams had been teaching in Topeka public schools for thirty-six years when the

Brown decision was announced. She took issue with the Supreme Court's conclusion that segregated schools have "a detrimental effect upon the colored children." She insisted that Black children were "not damaged by being in separate schools." Like many other Black Topekans, Williams firmly believed that the city's Black schools were "best for Black children" because of Black educators' situated pedagogies and knowledges.[3] "Those who are socially informed about people can help them best," she wrote.[4] Reading, writing, and resistance to anti-Blackness were central to the liberatory educational mission of Jim Crow schools throughout the nation. But the peculiar institution of Topeka public schools enabled educators like Williams to harbor Black sociality and unmoor Black subjectivities in exceptional ways.

The NAACP's legal intervention exposed the vulnerability of Black institutions created by and dependent upon the will and whims of white policymakers. The local branch wielded a double-edged sword in its war against the city's segregated schools. Its civil rights campaign challenged the school board's racist enrollment policy and threatened the existence of schools that briefly insulated Black children from anti-Black racism. But the racial politics of their Black adversaries was also complicated. Black school preservationists colluded with white segregationists to protect anti-Black enclaves that intentionally subverted white supremacy.

The End of an Era: The Gradual Desegregation and Disappearance of Topeka's Black Educators, 1953–1963

Despite their interest convergence with the Topeka school board, Black advocates for Black schools could not withstand the tides of historical change. The board of education voted to desegregate Topeka public schools on September 3, 1953. For empowered whites, the tribulation of the trial was not practical but optical. *Brown* disrupted the not-South/not-racist relational subjectivity that defined dominant whiteness in the state. Prior to *Brown*, white Kansans would "rub shoulders" with Southern whites at education conventions and boast of their intra-racial differences, recalled Stanley Stalter, who started working as a principal for Topeka public schools in 1949. "They would say, in our schools the Black people have the new textbooks and the new buildings," he said. Their racial paternalism assuaged their white guilt. "We have treated them very well, we just don't have to associate with them."[5] It was guilt by Southern white association that prompted the Topeka school board to announce its policy change eight months before the Supreme Court ruling in *Brown*. However, superintendent Wendell Godwin clarified that Black students' space invasion would be gradual because "it is a social impossibility to terminate segregation suddenly." The timeline for desegregation would be determined by city residents, not the school board, he equivocated. Its "speed . . . depends largely on the forbearance and self-discipline of both the white and colored people."[6]

Sidestepping aside, the school board gave some Buchanan School parents an opportunity to enroll in their neighborhood schools that year. It was poetic justice. Buchanan had been the city's most contested school site for twenty-five years. The school was in Tennessee Town, a community that was home to an elite class of Black Topekans who touted Buchanan as "'the' school" among segregated schools in Topeka.[7] But the school board did not care that some Buchanan families considered themselves to be among "the better class of colored people."[8] The privileges of class and color that Black elites experienced in intra-racial spaces did not mitigate anti-Blackness in interracial ones. Black children who lived within or outside the western border of Tennessee Town were denied access to Lowman Hill, an all-white school located one-half mile from Buchanan. So, Buchanan parents may have been vocal about the school's prestige, but they were also at the forefront of political resistance to segregated schools. Before *Brown*, three out of the four Kansas Supreme Court desegregation cases originating in Topeka involved Black families assigned to Buchanan. Two of the three Black *Brown* architects were the parents of Buchanan students, and seven of the twelve *Brown* plaintiffs were Buchanan students.

The school board's first phase of desegregation was a coup for Lucinda Todd. Todd became politically activated by the school board's discriminatory policies during the mid-to-late 1940s when her daughter Nancy started school at Buchanan. When the historic Supreme Court ruling was announced, Topeka NAACP members rejoiced. But they were compelled to do so in private. Linda Brown's friend Carolyn Campbell was twelve in 1954, and her family attended Rev. Oliver Brown's church St. Mark's AME. Sixty years later she discovered that in other places "there was jubilation and celebration. But here in Topeka because of the negative outcome for our educators, there was no celebration."[9]

Local NAACP members were unsettled by the defamation of Topeka's Black educators and Black schools that coincided with *Brown*. During commemorative celebrations of *Brown*, several plaintiffs seized opportunities to redeem the reputations of segregated schoolteachers. "I never fought the quality of the teachers. It was just the segregation part," Zelma Henderson asserted.[10] Henderson had two children enrolled at McKinley School when she signed on to the case in 1950. In retrospect she stated that "McKinley was a fairly nice school, and it had beautiful teaching."[11] Leola Brown Montgomery attended Monroe during the 1930s. "I loved it!" she exclaimed. "The teachers were fantastic."[12] Linda Brown also defended Monroe from public assumptions about the quality of segregated schools. "I had no quarrel about [Monroe] school or the education I received there," she attested.[13] Her former school principal J. B. Holland believed that NAACP attorneys exaggerated the psychological impact of segregated schools on Black students and asserted that "Linda was a happy child" at Monroe.[14] Despite their positive experiences, the Brown women and their alma mater were at the center of the case that would change the course of civil rights history.

The children of the *Brown* case recognized their parents' sacrifices while acknowledging their own sense of loss. In 1954, thirteen-year-old Nancy Todd was a student at Boswell Junior High. While Lucinda Todd waged a valiant effort against the city's segregated schools, her daughter was distressed about leaving her segregated school. "I knew most of my elementary teachers" at Buchanan, she recalled. "I did not feel cared for in my junior high. I was the only Black student in my classes. I did not know my teachers outside of class."[15] Like Todd, Buchanan alum Katherine Carper Sawyer described the move to junior high school as a "big change."[16] The daughter of *Brown* plaintiff Lena Mae Carper was a year younger than Todd and a witness for the US Supreme Court case at age ten in 1952. Two years later, she was one of few Black students at Capper Junior High School. It was an "incredibly lonely time," Sawyer said.[17] While Noches suffered from white teachers' benign neglect, Sawyer faced outright racial hostility. "There were teachers who didn't like us being there and didn't mind letting you know," Sawyer claimed.[18] The five-year-old daughter of *Brown* attorney Charles Scott Sr. attended Buchanan for a year before it closed in 1959. Lowman Hill was located a block from their family home but was undergoing reconstruction. Deborah Scott's kindergarten year left a lasting impression. "I think we left a part of ourselves in the segregated school," she said. "The unity was sure there."[19]

Black school alumni wax poetic about their educational experiences in Black schools, primarily because of the holistic and humanizing pedagogical approach of Black educators. But Black residents' widespread endorsement of Black educators did not factor into Topeka school board personnel decisions. As Black Kansans waited for the US Supreme Court to decide the fate of the nation's students, their concerns about a "Purge of Negro Teachers" heightened. "Anticipating the end of segregation by Supreme Court edict, school authorities are working toward the integration of pupils in the classrooms but plan to 'weed out' the Negro teacher wholesale," the *Kansas City Call* reported in April 1953.[20] School districts throughout the state quietly leaned toward Black employee attrition, and Topeka was no exception. When the school board announced its intent to eliminate Black schools in September 1953, it was silent about the reassignment of Black teachers. The school board's disinclination became even more transparent the following month. Superintendent Godwin reported that a teacher shortage was "reaching the stage of crisis," but he provided no update on or proposal for the district's Black employees.[21] The racist subtext was clear. There would be a one-way flow of integration: Black students to white schools.

The former director of colored schools Harrison Caldwell became the proverbial canary in the coal mine. The Black enforcer of school segregation resigned two days after the *Brown* decision and relocated to Seattle, Washington. There, his career trajectory abruptly shifted from racial gatekeeper to racial groundbreaker. Caldwell became the first Black principal of an all-white school in Seattle in 1956. Topeka's Black antihero was celebrated as a Black hero in the Pacific Northwest. "This is democracy in action," he declared.[22]

White Seattleites embraced the nation's historic milestone with racial tokenism, but they did little to desegregate the city's predominantly Black schools that resulted from residential segregation. Meanwhile in the Free State, the school board's reluctance to integrate Black teachers exposed the limits of their benevolent white racial imaginary. Empowered whites' desperate desire to disassociate from Southern segregationists only extended to Black schoolchildren. The introduction of Black teachers into white classrooms presented a potentially more threatening challenge to white supremacy than did Black students. It not only compelled white proximity to Black bodies, but it also subjected white students to Black minds presumed inferior by dominant discourse. In a 1956 *Topeka Capital* article, journalist Anna Mary Murphy framed the school board's Black teacher dilemma in a manner that foreshadowed conservative whites' weaponization of *Brown* attorney arguments. "The question to be resolved was: If it is psychologically damaging for Negro pupils to be segregated, as the Supreme Court ruled, is it equally damaging to have them taught by a segregated faculty?"[23]

With no easy answers or viable solutions, white Kansans stalled. When the Supreme Court announced its ruling on May 17, 1954, the beleaguered state attorney general attempted to salvage the state's reputation from *Brown's* blot. Harald R. Fatzer assured the public that the decision created "no real problem in Kansas" and then negated his statement with an equivocation. "The placement of Negro teachers in nonsegregated systems is a problem which must be solved by local school administrators."[24] Fatzer's disclaimer was a disingenuous and duplicitous deflection of white Kansans' racist resistance to Black integration. The state's relational racial problem vis-à-vis Black students was a real problem for Black schoolteachers. The school board's quick capitulation to *Brown* temporarily obscured, but did not cure, its anti-Black racism. The entrenchment of white supremacy in Topeka public schools after *Brown* was most evidenced by its deferred integration of Black teachers, not its gradual integration of Black students.

But this development came as no surprise to Black Topekans who had predicted this outcome since *Graham v. Board of Education* in 1941. The plight of Black teachers weighed heavily on the mind of ten-year-old *Brown* plaintiff Katherine Carper when she testified before the Kansas Supreme Court in 1951. "After giving my testimony, my main concern was that I had done something that would make my all-Black, female teachers at Buchanan School upset with me," she recalled. Carper felt conflicted about the lawsuit's outcome. "What if my testimony helped integration but also caused them to be out of a job?" Carper was the only student who had testified in the original *Brown* case, and she overheard Black residents express doubts about Black teachers' employability if the city's schools were desegregated. "They would never be able to get a job teaching at the white schools, it seemed, from hearing comments from some of the adults."[25]

After the NAACP won its landmark school desegregation case, it immediately launched a national campaign to save Black educators' jobs.[26] But the damage had been done. "They just wanted integration," recalled Barbara Ross. Ross taught intermittently at Washington School and was the wife of Merrill Ross, who became Washington's school principal in 1954 after Harrison Caldwell resigned. "They didn't care whether [teachers] would have a job or not," she recalled.[27] Former Monroe School principal J. B. Holland's Kappa Alpha Psi fraternity brothers John and Charles Scott represented the plaintiffs in *Brown*. Like Ross, he felt the NAACP's civil rights litigation neglected Black teachers. "If they were going to have integration, I wanted them to go the whole way—teachers as well as pupils."[28] In the years leading up to the US Supreme Court case, local and national NAACP members consistently demonstrated less consideration for Black teachers than Black students. NAACP Legal Defense Fund attorney William Ming estimated the potential fallout of *Brown* for Black schools and Black teachers and callously concluded in 1952, "There are fatalities in all social change."[29] In Topeka, *Brown* architect and longtime NAACP leader Daniel Sawyer had a track record of disregarding Black residents' support for Black educators. "I don't care about the teachers," he stated bluntly on the witness stand during the *Graham* case in 1941.[30] Although the Topeka NAACP issued a moratorium on addressing segregated schools to avoid conflict with Black educators and their supporters after *Graham*, Sawyer continued to challenge the school board's racist enrollment policy by attempting to register his daughters at Lowman Hill in 1942 and 1947.

Like Sawyer, McKinley Burnett refused to let the fate of Black teachers interfere with his provocation of the Topeka school board. However, unlike Sawyer, he advocated for Black teachers' right to inclusion before and after *Brown*. Black teachers were incorporated in his demand for "full and complete integration" in 1948, and he continued to lobby for Black teachers in 1955 and 1956. The school board had made some progress on its promise to integrate Black students by 1955, but the future of Topeka's twenty-nine Black educators had been uncertain since its formal desegregation announcement in September 1953. "Word was rampant that Black teachers were going to be kicked out in the event of integration," Monroe School principal J. B. Holland recalled.[31] Community concerns for Black educators heightened in February 1955 when the school board decided to cease operation of the city's segregated schools. The board reported that Buchanan, Monroe, and Washington would remain open until all enrolled students completed their sixth-grade year, but that McKinley would be closed permanently that summer. There was no mention of reassignment for McKinley's teachers. Dorothy Scott was teaching at Washington in 1955. She remembered feeling righteous indignation about the school board's willful neglect of Black educators. "You can't close these schools and just throw these teachers to the wolves," she said. "The fight began."[32]

NAACP president McKinley Burnett protested school board members' continued silence about Black educators' employment prospects at a March 1955 school board meeting. The NAACP had always desired "equality of opportunities for Negro teachers and students," he asserted.[33] Ten months later, the Topeka school board had still issued no formal plan for Black educators. So, Burnett attended a January 1956 meeting to demand administrative accountability. "The negro teacher had been completely left out of desegregation," he stated. He then read "excerpts from various publications on this subject" before reiterating his plea that "the negro teacher be integrated along with the other teachers and children in the Topeka schools."[34]

Despite Burnett's repeated call for action and a citywide teacher shortage, it took another nineteen months before a Black teacher was assigned to a formerly white elementary school. The Topeka school board's reluctance to integrate Black teachers was a rote racial response. As previously noted, the integration of Black teachers introduced an unprecedented dilemma for the Topeka school board, for the exchange value of Black labor was not only fixed to Black bodies but also to Black minds. In addition, the degradation of Black labor is foundational to racial capitalism, and the wages of whiteness were undermined by proximity to Black laborers. The field of education was no exception. Labor market segregation forced educated Black men and women into segregated schools. So, integration threatened the competitive edge that white teachers received due to anti-Black racism. "Most teachers at Monroe had their M.A., which was not the case at Sumner," said Monroe principal J. B. Holland.[35] And yet, Black teachers' high educational attainment did not protect them from employment precarity after *Brown*, a fact that evidences the inherent conflict between racial logics and capitalist productivity.

The school board's interim school choice policy gave the city's Black teachers a short reprieve, but those who were left would only maintain employment for as long as the city's remaining segregated schools stayed open. The school board never considered open enrollment for white students even though Buchanan, McKinley, Monroe, and Washington Elementary Schools were in predominantly white neighborhoods. Public schools were critical sites of race-making in a city where residential segregation was not enforced. White integration into Black schools threatened the property of whiteness, even if those schools were in better condition than some of their white counterparts. So, white students who lived close to one of the four well-maintained, modern, segregated school buildings had to walk past them to attend their all-white schools. The school board provided school buses for Black students, even in a limited capacity after *Brown*, but it never offered transportation for white students.

Fortunately for Black teachers, most Black parents continued to enroll their children in Buchanan, Monroe, and Washington Elementary Schools even after Black students were allowed to attend their neighborhood schools. There was no "massive exodus of Black children from the predominantly Black schools." NAACP members sacrificed Black schools for the greater good, but many Black Topekans were troubled by how integration would disable Black teachers, disrupt Black education, destabilize their communities, and possibly damage Black children's mental health and well-being. As Washington School alum Deborah Dandridge noted, Black parents "could have abandoned these four Black schools, but, of course, it did not occur."[36]

Black parents who registered their children in integrated schools had to help them negotiate the anti-Black racism of classmates and teachers. The parents of Pamela G. Hollie confronted a white female teacher at Sheldon

Elementary for deflating her grades because, "as she put it, I had to learn to accept disappointment."[37] Other parents wanted to protect their children from these experiences for as long as they could. The cost-benefit analysis of Jeanette and Milburn Dandridge led them back to Black schools. Jeanette "felt very strongly" that their daughter Deborah should remain at Washington even though Parkdale Elementary was located three blocks from their family home. "Both my parents expressed fear of my treatment at Parkdale" because of its all-white teaching staff, Deborah recalled. During an uncertain time of radical racial change in Topeka public schools, the Dandridges were unwilling to jeopardize their daughter's emotional and physical well-being. "They were not going to risk going into a setting that would be extremely volatile," she said. But the Dandridges' decision was informed not only by fear of white teachers' anti-Blackness but also by their faith in Black teachers' anti-anti-Blackness. Deborah remembers her parents "wholeheartedly" chose Washington because "the environment was stable [and] supportive." They also believed that the instruction she received there "was excellent and not something that they felt could be improved by going to a non-Black school," she recalled.[38] Jeanette's commitment to Black schools was also motivated by her loyalty to her sorority sisters, several of whom were Black educators.

Thayer Phillips sent his son Jesse to kindergarten at Monroe Elementary in the fall of 1956, a year and a half after the official termination of open enrollment in Black schools. The permitted but supposedly prohibited admission of new Black students into segregated schools spoke as much to the school board's commitment to preserving white schools as it did to some Black parents' commitment to preserving Black schools. But Phillips was not invested in the political significance of space invasion. "I was indifferent related to integration," he said, but preferred Monroe over his neighborhood school because his son "got good, kind treatment" and "the teachers liked him. I couldn't think of a better school."[39] The Massey family moved to Topeka from California in 1961 and registered their nine-year-old daughter Beryl at Monroe Elementary School, which was also their neighborhood school. As an adult, Beryl New became a teacher and administrator in Topeka public schools and, after twenty-nine years with the school district, she was appointed the director of equity in 2017. Like other Black school alumni, New spoke of strict, caring teachers, or "visionaries," as she called them, who had high expectations for Black schoolchildren. "Monroe Elementary School has always been more to me than just the pivot in a court case," she said. "It was an incubator of hope, expectation, and promise for all children."[40]

By the time the Massey family relocated to Topeka, the city's Black educators had few opportunities and very little time left. In 1956, three years after the school board voted to desegregate public schools, it had only integrated three Black employees. Part-time school nurse Ida Norman and special education teacher Ercelle Collins were reassigned to predominantly white schools, and Vance Williams was hired to teach at Topeka High School. Four Black educators had resigned: Harrison Caldwell; Barbara Ross, the wife of Washington's principal; and a married couple, Arnold and Dorothy Grant. In total, the Black teaching force was down almost 20 percent, from twenty-nine to twenty-four teachers. The school board had convened a committee "to review possible future transfer of another Negro teacher" in June 1956, but members "decided not to make another assignment at this time," even though the district needed 100 additional teachers for the 1956–57 academic year.[41]

A group of Black residents registered their discontent with the school board's personnel procrastination at a February 1957 meeting. The spokesperson for the Ministerial Alliance Group conveyed community concerns about the continued employment of Black schoolteachers after the scheduled school closings. It is "not the intention to eliminate Negro teachers from this system," a school board member responded. "But this thing will iron itself out to the mutual satisfaction of all." School board members' patronizing assurances of fair exchange failed to dissuade the already dissatisfied supporters of Black teachers. It had been three and a half years since the board announced its intent to desegregate Topeka public schools and two years since it decided to discontinue segregated schools. Not only had the school board failed to reassign its existing Black teaching staff, but it had also failed to employ any new Black teachers from its mass recruiting drive. The ministers demanded answers. "Out of all the teachers hired, why have no Negro teachers been included?" Rev. C. P. Raines interrogated. "Why are Negro teachers so systematically eliminated?" School board member Mose J. Whitson dismissed Raines's accusations of anti-Blackness with the assertion that the district had adopted a race-neutral review of new jobseekers. We do "not count applications by color," and there were "no questions about race on teacher application[s]," he contended. Whitson then contradicted his claims of a colorblind screening process by divulging the district's new racist safety mechanism: each applicant had to submit a photograph. Adding racial insult to racist injury, school board members insisted that only one qualified Black person had applied for a position in the school district, and they assigned him to Topeka High School.[42]

The city's Black ministers were not the only political force applying pressure on the Topeka school board. Fred Rausch recalled being lobbied by Black residents who insisted that "white teachers wouldn't understand [Black students] as well as their former Black teachers" when he joined the school board in 1957.[43] But one of his first school board memories involved a board attorney who strongly recommended the integration of Black teachers. "So we started that process immediately," he stated. As the conflict between the logistics of anti-Blackness and the optics of white benevolence once again became transparent, the Topeka school board understood what was at stake. Under legal advisement they could not risk another public revelation, especially when Southern whites were mobilizing a massive resistance movement.

Superintendent Wendell Godwin provided a progress report on the integration of current and future Black teachers into predominantly white schools in June 1957. He had recruited Topeka High School teacher Vance Williams, NAACP president McKinley Burnett, and Rev. E. B. Hicks to provide recommendations of "well-qualified" Black teachers who could be assigned to the city's predominantly white schools. According to Godwin, the search committee only endorsed one Black educator, Jean Price. Price was subsequently hired to teach students with emotional and behavioral disorders at the Topeka State Hospital. With the addition of Price, the school board's social experiment remained largely confined to marginalized educational settings. Williams was the only Black teacher in a mainstream school. But Godwin proposed the reassignment of two Monroe School educators, principal J. B. Holland and Myrtle Starnes, for the following school year. The school board was begrudgingly "favorable to this plan" after contemplating the racial intangibles. The "complications were not legal," they concluded, "but psychological and social ones in this further step toward advancement of integration."[44]

After much deliberation and political pressure, Holland and Starnes began teaching at predominantly white schools in September 1957. That month, white resistance to school integration in Little Rock, Arkansas, captured the nation's attention. "We never saw anything like that in Topeka," recalled Nancy Jones. Jones was a fourth grader at Clay Elementary when the first Black students arrived in 1954.[45] There may have been no defiant governor who deployed the National Guard like Orval Faubus in Little Rock, but the Topeka school board also mobilized to protect the vestiges of white privilege in Topeka public schools. The two longtime Black educators were slowly introduced to predominantly white classrooms. Each taught half-days at former all-white schools, Holland at Randolph and Southwest Middle Schools, and Starnes at Central Park and Stout Elementary Schools.

In addition to its gradualist approach, the school district allowed white parents to opt out of Black-led classrooms. The same day the Arkansas National Guard blocked Black students' entry into Central High School, the principals of Central Park, Stout, Randolph, and Southwest Schools called white parents to warn them of the racial breach. "Parents should not be subject to surprise in finding the Negro teachers in these schools," Godwin explained.[46] White parents were then given the choice to claim their racial prerogative or support racial progress. "It was essential that there be two rooms of the same grade in each building in order to avoid the circumstance of coercion in assigning white children to Negro teachers," reported the local newspaper.[47]

Godwin's strategy to devise a plan that would involve "few social hazards" depended on an elitist conception of variegated whiteness.[48] White school board members and administrators' continued investment in a "good white/bad white" racial allegory was evidenced by the way they deployed class as a marker of normative and nonnormative whiteness. The school board introduced Black teachers in schools that were situated in educated, middle-class white neighborhoods because they believed "there would be a stronger feeling against integration" in "the poorer areas of the city," recalled Randolph's principal Stanley Stalter.[49] One of those schools was Southwest, which was considered an elite school in Topeka because its student demographic skewed toward the white professional class. The principals of integrating middle schools confessed to engaging in classist, class-based social engineering. "The first year I pretty much chose the children who went into [Holland's] room, certainly not blue-collar kinds of people" but "leading businessmen, who were broad minded," admitted Southwest School principal Frank Wilson.[50]

But Wilson and Stalter quickly discovered that class was not an accurate predictor of the production and performance of white supremacy. Middle-class white families were not in fact less anti-Black than working-class or poor white families. Stalter was tasked with calling white parents about classroom assignments in 1957, and he found it difficult to recruit willing participants. "Some were adamant" in their refusals, he said. One unashamedly tapped into narratives of Black sexual deviance when expressing concern about his twelve-year-old daughter being in close physical proximity to Holland, who was forty-eight. "She is beginning her menstrual period and this is not the time of her life to be put in here with a Black teacher, a male."[51] Mike

Worswick's parents were among those whose race-neutral decision was akin to white allyship. "J. B. Holland was my sixth-grade teacher for a half-day," Worswick recalled. "Having him be my teacher was a most rewarding experience for me. We had a white teacher for the other half of the day. I couldn't tell you his name. But J. B. Holland sure made an impression on me. I've never forgotten him."[52]

Within the course of that first year, Holland became such a coveted teacher at Southwest that he was given a full-time teaching assignment there the following year. Brent Green was a Southwest student during the mid-to-late 1950s. He was unaware of *Brown* or its significance for public education because it had no impact on the racial composition of his school. "There is not a single individual of color in any of my annual class photos from that time. This was 'school as usual' for my peers and me," he wrote. But Green remembered the collective excitement among his peers about the possibility of being in Holland's sixth-grade science class in 1960. Holland had "developed a celebrity status," he recalled. "Many of my peers received stimulating and inspiring lessons in life from Mr. Holland and owe his memory a debt of gratitude."[53]

Holland was adept at navigating his new all-white teaching environment because he had an acute awareness of the racial stakes. "He just oozed the milk of human kindness," recalled Southwest's principal. "He was "an outstanding individual, a marvelous teacher, and it was obvious why they chose him."[54] After years of modeling and disseminating racial uplift politics for Black students in Black schools, Holland was extremely prepared for this moment. *Simple Justice* author Richard Kluger would later describe Holland as "cagey and confident."[55] It was an astute, albeit unwitting, observation of the proverbial veil of double consciousness. Holland's white students and coworkers would never know his inner life nor would they understand that he entered unchartered racial terrain armed with a politics of respectability and a sense of intra-racial exceptionalism. The fact that Holland exceeded whites' expectations said more about their racial essentialism than it did about his capabilities. "And yet," as W. E. B. Du Bois had noted sixty years earlier, "being a problem is a strange experience" for erudite Black space invaders.[56]

It is unclear why the school board chose Holland and Starnes out of the twenty-four remaining Black educators to be the first introduced into the city's all-white schools. But the school board's deferred integration of Black educators and devaluation of their contributions to Topeka public schools "was demeaning," Barbara Ross recalled.[57] Both Holland and Starnes brought years of experience and expertise to their positions. Starnes was a thirty-year veteran of Topeka public schools and was assigned to a school named after former segregationist superintendent A. J. Stout. Holland spent seventeen years as a principal in both Buchanan and Monroe Schools. When the school board offered him an opportunity for racial advancement, the contract came with a personal sacrifice. To become a member of Southwest's teaching staff, Holland had to accept a demotion. The choice between maintaining employment or dignity was amplified both by the historical significance of the proposal and the fact that Holland's wife Flossie was also an employee of Topeka public schools. Holland's decision to relinquish his role as an administrator in Black schools to integrate a white school was common among Black principals "threatened with extinction" in the aftermath of *Brown*.[58]

When school board members discussed the "psychological and social" complications of integration, they did not center the experiences of Black students and teachers. Because racial solipsism is a critical component of white supremacy, it stands to racist reason that school board members' singular concern was about the discomfort of white parents and schoolchildren. Because they presumed proximities to whiteness wholly desirable, there is no record of any school board member ever questioning how to better situate Black students and educators in potentially hostile learning or work environments. Without the care or consideration of white school board members, Black people had to develop a "thick skin" to withstand anti-Blackness, explained Dorothy Scott. Scott was Parkdale Elementary School's first Black teacher. On her first day, Parkdale's principal told her that he had surveyed white parents that summer to "see if they minded" having a Black teacher. One family refused, he reported. "That's what I went into," Scott recalled. "Can you imagine?" Scott acknowledged the racial indignity, but she refused to be diminished by white parents or her peers. "It didn't affect me," she said. Her students were "just darling, just as dear as they could be."[59]

While the Topeka school board decided whom to integrate where, Black educators were forced to weigh their options. Few Black educators were reassigned to formerly all-white schools after *Brown*. Local school boards throughout the country simultaneously hired new white teachers and terminated Black educators. Topeka was no exception. It was a sobering reality for Oliver Brown. "'As one retires or leaves,' he says sadly, 'she is always replaced by [a] white teacher,'" a *New York Times* reporter wrote in 1961.[60] The process was gradual in the capital city because segregated schools were discontinued one by one. When the Topeka school board shut down McKinley in 1955, its two teachers were reassigned to other segregated schools. All but two members of Buchanan's teaching staff were absorbed into Monroe and Washington after it ceased operations in 1959. One of those departures was voluntary. Loyce Abbott was "a very capable, talented young woman" in her late twenties when Buchanan closed.[61] With no job security in Topeka, Abbott "went to California," recalled Merrill Ross. "She didn't tarry around here."[62]

As an elder, Mamie Williams had run out of time and options in Topeka public schools. The school board did not consider transferring her to the two remaining Black schools or to a predominantly white school, despite her forty-one years of service. Instead, Williams was forced to retire at sixty-three. Since 1918, the highly and widely respected veteran educator had dedicated her life to her career, cocreating protected spaces where Black schoolchildren were valued, nurtured, and guided. Her unceremonious dismissal in 1960 was one of the more tragic local outcomes of the national case. But that same year, in an interesting turn of events, the school board hired Lucinda Todd to teach sixth grade at Central Park Elementary School. She had not taught in Topeka's schools since 1935. Todd's new position was poetic justice for the local NAACP, but it certainly added insult to injury for those whose jobs were still in limbo in the aftermath of the *Brown* decision.

As the last Black students began matriculating into desegregating schools in 1960, Washington School principal Merrill Ross was one of the twelve Black educators left in the two remaining Black schools. Ross had been teaching in Topeka public schools for nearly twenty years and was a school principal for almost ten years. His wife Barbara taught at Washington for fourteen years before she chose to be a stay-at-home mother in 1955. Five years later, the couple had two young children and Merrill was the sole income producer in his family. Barbara recalled the "terrible strain" they were under while the school district deliberated over Black educators' futures.[63] Black educators who once had job mobility had few options for employment after *Brown*. The demand for Black teachers declined throughout the nation as local school boards grappled with school desegregation orders. Merrill Ross filled out "several applications" and was prepared to relocate to Milwaukee before school superintendent Mose Whitson contacted him in 1962. Whitson offered Ross an assignment at Parkdale Elementary School, but there was one condition. White Topekans were not "ready for a Black principal to come in and head their students," Whitson explained, so Ross would be Parkdale's new assistant principal.[64] Ross accepted the position.

The following year, the Topeka school board shut down Monroe and Washington Schools. It was the end of an era. Schools that had been crucial sites of the city's Black geographies were left in ruins. The people who enlivened those spaces were forcibly discharged. The halls would no longer echo with children's voices singing the "Negro National Anthem" before each school day. There would be no more lessons in reading, writing, and respectability politics. Twelve years after the local NAACP initiated *Brown*, the Topeka school board fully desegregated its public school system.

With Black students in predominantly white schools, Black teachers virtually disappeared. People who had been integral members of the city's Black communities were fired, retired, or dispersed to other cities. Monroe alum Richard Ridley lamented their loss. "They were outstanding, and they paid a tremendous price."[65] The political collision between school desegregationists and Black school preservationists left scars that ran deep and long in Topeka. Twenty-five years after the Supreme Court decision, Topeka's plaintiffs were invited to Washington, DC, to mark the occasion, but there "were no festivities in Topeka." The reason was "painfully obvious" to alumni of the city's four Black schools. School integration "has had a devastating effect on the Black community in Topeka," Hollie wrote. Lucinda Todd reported that many of those involved in the Black school conflict "were still on the outs" in 1979.[66] Barbara Ross remained critical of the NAACP's political campaign twelve years later. At sixty-five, she continued to hold the civil rights activists in contempt for their disregard of Black teachers' lives and livelihoods. Ross subjected local NAACP members to a higher standard of accountability than the white school board members, who had the power to determine Black teachers' employability. "When they wanted integration, they never considered the effect that it would have on the Black teacher who was very qualified," Ross chided in 1991. "Practically all of them had their masters." While Black Americans throughout the nation celebrated the NAACP's legal intervention on behalf of Black students, Ross conveyed a sense of racial betrayal because of its impact on Black educators. Local NAACP members "didn't care whether they had a job or not. Now these are their own people."[67]

The Maleficent Malleability of White Supremacy in Black, White, and *Brown*

Blacks against *Brown* flip the script on dominant historical narratives. The tale of Topeka public schools disrupts presumptions about Black desires for and definitions of educational justice during the Jim Crow era. The telling of this story is not intended as a retrospective prescriptive, and as the saying goes, hindsight is twenty-twenty. But there are some interesting prefigurations. Black school preservationists' objections before *Brown* warned of a future that came into being after *Brown*. Their misgivings about eliminating Black schools emerged from Black students' painful transition into predominantly white junior and senior high schools. Many Black school alumni struggled mentally and academically with the violent shift from affirmations of Blackness to anti-Blackness. As such, the experiences of Topeka's Black school alumni presaged the devastating toll "desegregation" exacted on the emotional well-being and educational achievements of Black students throughout the country.

Black school preservationists were not prognosticators, they were pragmatists. They were keenly aware of the maleficent malleability of white supremacy and white supremacist narratives. Since the period of statehood, empowered white Kansans simultaneously celebrated their abolitionist roots and preserved racial apartheid. That discord between the sayings and doings of whites extended from the Kansas of John Brown repute to the Kansas of *Brown v. Board* dispute. In fact, the school board's racist evasion of Black residents' civil rights prior to *Brown* foreshadowed their passive resistance to school desegregation and integration after *Brown*. School board members continued to propagandize a white imaginary of paternalistic benevolence while intentionally operationalizing anti-Blackness through decisions that protected the racial privileges of white students and teachers.

White resistance to school desegregation was always multivocal and multifaceted. But racist subterfuge would become standard practice for district courts, school districts, and private citizens seeking to protect whiteness-as-property and circumvent the historic antiracist *Brown* Supreme Court decision. White school superintendents, school board members, and school administrators in Topeka were well rehearsed in anti-Black stratagems by 1954, having inherited twenty-five years of experience in bypassing the state's civil rights law. So, when the Supreme Court ruling compelled white school board members to perform a not-South/not-racist relational version of whiteness, their predecessors had already proved that privileging whiteness in the city's public schools hinged on Black subordination, not distance or deprivation.

But the white man's burden always fell heaviest upon the dehumanized subject, and this time was no different. The façade of racial inclusion was just as damaging as racist exclusion. Ironically, it was the liminal space between segregation and integration that evoked "a sense of inferiority" that "affects the motivation of a child to learn." A broad body of literature from diverse disciplinary backgrounds and perspectives has explored and explained the reverberations of *Brown* on Black students and Black education. It wasn't segregation per se that had a "tendency to [retard] the educational and mental development of negro children"; it was Black students' intimate interface with white supremacy.[68] There was no ethos of care for Black students in schools led by white teachers, and their racial experiences shifted from Blackness as engagement to Blackness as encounter. "Linda Brown never found herself all alone in a white classroom as I did," wrote *New York Times* journalist Pamela Hollie. When Hollie moved from Buchanan to Sheldon Elementary in 1957, she was in the fifth grade. There, she learned what it felt like to be treated like a "second-class citizen," she said. "Naïvely, I didn't know I was supposed to be inferior."[69]

The story of Blacks against *Brown* exposes some uncomfortable truths about how people of African descent in the United States sometimes blurred the line between racism and antiracism. White Topekans' defense of segregated schools demonstrated the limits of white liberalism in Kansas. But Black Topekans' divergent responses to segregated schools demonstrated the limitations of Black political agendas and exemplified how white supremacist logics, if left unexamined, delimit Black freedom movements. The political standpoints of civil rights activists and Black school preservationists simultaneously resisted and reproduced forms of anti-Blackness. Black advocates for all-Black schools colluded with anti-Blackness to preserve Black schools as protected spaces within Black communities. Meanwhile, local NAACP members disregarded community concerns about Black students, educators, and communities in their push to amend the school board's racist enrollment policy. Their legal victory simultaneously ignited the modern civil rights movement and dismantled structures that affirmed Black humanity, not only for Black students but also for local Black communities that embraced Black schools as spaces of Black sociality.

Perhaps the most twisted turn of events involves the appropriation of *Brown*'s antiracist arguments to serve anti-Black political agendas. Conservative whites and their nonwhite allies quickly and continuously co-opted the concept of "color-blind constitutionalism" to obstruct racial justice. The insidious elasticity of white supremacy did not escape the attention of *Brown* attorney-turned-Supreme-Court-justice Thurgood Marshall, who wrote the dissenting opinion in the 1978 *Bakke* case. He confronted the racist effrontery of the Supreme Court's anti–affirmative action decision. The Supreme Court willfully ignored "the most ingenious and pervasive" forms of anti-Blackness for 200 years but effectively protected a white man's racial inheritance twenty-four years after *Brown*. He wrote, "It is more than a little ironic that, after several hundred years of class-based discrimination against Negroes, the Court is unwilling to hold that a class-based remedy for that discrimination is permissible."[70]

The national NAACP had no control over how its racial rhetoric would be weaponized against civil rights after *Brown*. But the dynamism of white supremacy lies in its motility and mutability. White conservatives' usurpation of liberal ideas is one example, but another is the surreptitious ways white supremacy infiltrates the performance of Black futurities. As described in chapters 2 and 3, Black elites who stood up for and against segregated schools articulated a class politics that drew lines of demarcation between themselves and other othered Blacks. Civil rights activists who publicly proclaimed themselves to be a "better class of colored people" demonstrated an introjection and projection of white supremacy. That sense of intra-racial exceptionalism, based upon classism and colorism, fueled their resistance against the Topeka school board from the late 1920s through the 1940s. The illusion of inclusion escaped Black school preservationists, who tended to be more deeply melanated than their desegregationist counterparts. And yet, Black educators also relied upon a discursive distinction between elevated and essentialized Blackness in their production of situated knowledges. As Mamie Williams once wrote, "If we can lift the 'cultural level' so that in the course of time our present highest group level will be reached by the majority of our people," the "frictions" between Blacks and whites could be resolved.[71]

In racial uplift politics, elevated Blackness was imagined as a necessary pathway to emancipated Blackness, a state of civic and civil being they believed was threatened by working-class and poor Blacks. The fact that both groups attempted to transcend the boundaries of Blackness in ways that approximated normative whiteness is a testimony to the power and pervasiveness of white supremacy. Respectability politics animated resistance to and the refusal of anti-Blackness in Topeka public schools. But it also undermined the political intentionality of Black school desegregationists and preservationists. Often the "respectability" in respectability politics signaled an idealization of whiteness as corporeality and comportment. Blackness and/or Black people were valued or devalued based on color, class, and conformity to bourgeois heteronormative gender standards. In Black classrooms that meant that the surveillance and policing of Black women and children's bodies and behavior was a critical part of extracurricular instruction. Noncompliance invited corporal punishment for children and social ostracization or unemployment for Black female educators. The widespread belief that violence was an appropriate pedagogical tool is evidenced by the consistency of Black school alumni's complaints about the lack of control white teachers had in integrated classrooms.

The alchemy of race and rights in Topeka complicated Black residents' pursuit of educational justice. Black school preservationists' race-conscious politics and Black school desegregationists' politics of race neutrality smudged the relationship between anti-Black racism and antiracism advocacy. Civil rights activists' hard-fought battle for school integration was waged on behalf of students whose racial subjectivities were endangered when introduced to structures designed for their subjugation. For Black school preservationists, the cost of that freedom was too high. As such, their interests converged with the segregationist school board, and Black school advocates lobbied to maintain the city's racist enrollment policy. Their audacious support of schools devised for racial containment was not a sign of complacency, it was the consequence of contentment. Racially exclusive educational spaces became sites of Black power, places where race men and women introduced antiracism ideologies, emphasized Black students' humanity, and prioritized Black children's personal and educational development.

Making a Way Out of No Way: The Battle for Black Schools after *Brown*, 1960s–2010s

Those invested in scholarly conversations and political debates about the subjugation of minoritized students vis-à-vis public policies and private practices may be tempted to attach contemporary meaning to a past moment when Black students thrived in Black schools with Black teachers. But that only works in abstraction. As Donna Haraway wrote in 1988, there is a "serious danger of romanticizing and/or appropriating the vision of the less powerful while claiming to see from their positions."[72] This is not a call for a return Blackward. But the oral histories of Black school alumni do provide critical lessons. Black students' success was intimately tied to educators' attentiveness to their intersectional experiences. Black educators' epistemic privilege informed their holistic approach to schooling that included wellness programs for students who were food insecure and literacy programs for their parents and grandparents. In addition to generating networks of care, Black educators developed curricular and extracurricular activities that staged interventions on anti-Blackness. Their commitment to fortifying Black students' racial subjectivities was manifest through Black studies supplements, exercises that facilitated Black pride, and assemblies that featured Black professionals in multiple fields.

The work of Black educational justice activists after *Brown* reflected a desire to provide alternatives to Black alterity in ways that are reminiscent of Topeka's Black school preservationists and other Black educators working in segregated schools prior to *Brown*. During the late 1960s and '70s, the community-control movement, the Black Panther Party's "Liberation Schools," and the proliferation of Afrocentric schools demonstrated Black Americans' continued commitment to fugitive educational practices. The political legacies of independent Black educational institutions extended through the late twentieth and early twenty-first centuries, as Black parents, educators, and their allies attempted to disengage from or strategize around the racism embedded within the nation's public education systems.

In fact, the national NAACP found itself embroiled in another intra-racial controversy about race, racism, and public schools when it declared a moratorium on the expansion of charter schools in 2016. That year, more Black parents chose to send their children to charter schools than to assigned public schools, especially those who lived in urban areas.[73] The president of an educational advocacy group named 50CAN called the NAACP's announcement "the worst kind of betrayal." For Black parents, "charters are about opportunity," Derrell Bradford insisted.[74] NAACP critics argued that the organization was on the wrong side of history and "out of step with the desires of so many parents across the country who are demanding more options and quality education for their children."[75]

There was no denying the fact that many Black parents were desperate for ways out of assigned public schools. There was collective agreement in Black communities and among Black education reform advocates that mainstream public schools were failing Black students. "Our children are brilliant," Clark Atlanta University professor Chike Akua of the Teacher Transformation Institute affirmed in 2019. "But many of them are in schools or school systems where they're seen as a problem, rather than as people."[76] Black parents who dared to imagine the possibility of invaginated spaces within racist structures embraced charter schools as a solution for underresourced, underperforming racially segregated schools. They were attracted to the promise of predominantly Black schools as protected spaces with Black educators, individualized curriculum that included Black histories, and disciplined classrooms. Elaine Wells sent her three sons to a Black-led charter in Philadelphia. "These are schools that share in the experiences that our kids share in," she said. "They know the challenges that your kids face. They know where our kids are coming from."[77]

Over sixty years after *Brown*, divergent definitions of educational justice continue to haunt Black communities trying to make a way out of no way. Both sides of the charter school debate had legitimate standpoints and similar arguments to those made by Black school preservationists and desegregationists in Topeka before *Brown*. Black advocacy for predominantly Black charter schools was an affirmative refusal, an unmooring of Blackness from anti-Black racism. The NAACP opposed the enduring and ever-evolving racism inherent in public school policy even though there were more Black parents who supported charter schools than attendance area schools. The echoes of the past are undeniable. But, as Blacks against *Brown* evidenced, there is no clear-cut path to educational justice for minoritized communities when there is mutuality and overlap between racism and antiracism.

Charter school success stories do not negate the fact that the privatization of public schools reinscribes discriminatory educational policies and practices that target at-risk minoritized students. Charter schools not only divert public funding from neighborhood schools, but they also redirect community investments. Whitefoord Elementary in Atlanta's Edgewood neighborhood and Farragut Elementary in St. Louis's the Ville are primary examples. Whitefoord and Farragut were predominantly Black schools in historic Black neighborhoods. They were symbols of pride for community residents who valued the schools, not only for their academic successes but also as sites that produced intergenerational continuity. But these "communally bonded" schools could not compete with the lure of local charter schools, even though their students performed well on standardized tests.[78] The Atlanta and St. Louis school boards cited declining student populations as the reason for shutting down Whitefoord in 2017 and Farragut in 2021.[79]

Furthermore, disparities among predominantly Black charter schools reflect dominant cultural values. Black educators founded Afrocentric schools to disrupt white supremacy. But they needed to strike a balance between disseminating emancipatory epistemologies and teaching toward externally determined, racially biased standardized tests to maintain public funding. The racial mission and curricular goals of these pro-Black schools did not weigh into local school districts' decisions on which charter schools to save if they did not meet academic yearly progress requirements. Detroit was a mecca of Afrocentric schools in the 1980s and '90s. But when the school district underwent emergency management in 1999, it drastically changed the landscape of Detroit public schools. Only three out of twenty Afrocentric schools remained in 2019, which was a loss of around 8,500 seats in twenty years, according to Paul Robeson Malcolm X Academy principal Jeffrey Robinson. The academy, which claimed to be the first in the nation of its kind, was one of the only Afrocentric schools left in Detroit in 2023.[80]

Afrocentric schools were not alone in their vulnerability to local school board cuts. Across the board, Black-led predominantly Black charter schools assumed greater risks of closure when they failed to meet benchmarks. In Philadelphia, where 60 percent of Black students attended charter schools in 2019, the African American Charter School Coalition (AACSC) of Philadelphia publicly indicted the school board for racism due to its disproportionate closing of Black-led charter schools. "Our schools have collectively dealt with racism, inequity, and biases when it comes to our schools' oversight, expansion, and renewal opportunities," argued Naomi Johnson Booker, leader of the coalition, which represented fifteen out of the seventeen Black-operated charter schools in Philadelphia. Statistics supported the AACSC's charges. Black-led or Black-founded charter schools made up only 20 percent of Philadelphia's charter schools, but they represented 80 percent of the charter schools shut down between 2010 and 2020. So, the coalition launched a "Black Schools Matter" campaign in 2020. The founder of West Philadelphia Achievement Elementary Charter School Stacy Phillips emphasized Black charter schools' importance for protecting the educational rights of Black children. "This is the first time in this country's history that Black people have been able to organize, start, operate and be able to be the major decision-makers for public schools for our children," Phillips said. "That is absolutely worth preserving and protecting."[81]

Anti/Racist Im/Possibilities in Public Education: The Moral of the *Brown* Story

Historical reverberations of the Jim Crow era cannot be ignored. How do Black parents, educators, and their allies pursue possibilities in impossible situations? NAACP Legal Defense Fund attorney Robert L. Carter argued that the NAACP had nothing to lose in its relentless pursuit of integration before *Brown*. Twenty-five years later, the US district court judge acknowledged the limitations of integration as a mechanism of education reform. "To focus on integration alone is a luxury that only the Black middle class can afford," he asserted. "They have the means to desert the public schools if dissatisfied."[82] Wealthy and middle-class Blacks became untethered from working-class and poor Blacks as the perimeters of anti-Blackness shifted after the civil rights movement. Consequently, there were tangible benefits to those whose class status afforded them proximities to whiteness, and in turn, proximities to the privileges of whiteness. Members of the Black middle class not only had more options at the turn of the twenty-first century, but they also, at times, limited poor and working-class Black parents' ability to opt in. In Philadelphia eight out of the nine school board members who shut down Black-led charter schools in 2020 were people of color. Racist structures operate with or without racist people. A *Philadelphia Inquirer* journalist recorded charter school supporter and parent Elaine Wells's frustration with a process through which outsiders' decisions outweighed insiders' desires. "People in power tell Black parents what's best for their children 'but none of those people are sending their kids to the schools that they try to tell you your kid should go to.'"[83]

Historically, the privileging of whiteness in public schools has pivoted upon a divestment in and distancing from nonwhite people and communities. The more things change, the more they stay the same. Resegregation in the late twentieth century intensified a restoration of white over nonwhite as Black and Latinx students once again were subjected to racist containment. Only instead of the separate Jim Crow and Juan Crow schools of the early-to-mid twentieth century, resegregated schools in the late twentieth and early twenty-first centuries were predominantly Black and Latinx. Although the story of Topeka public schools was unique in form, it was not unique in function. The Topeka Board of Education's material investment in its parallel school system benefitted Black schoolchildren, but that outcome was a collateral consequence of its anti-Black racism. Buchanan, McKinley, Monroe, and Washington Schools were created to protect the property of whiteness. Although Black educators reclaimed and redefined the city's segregated schools, the fact remains that anti-Blackness defined the parameters of those Black geographies for Black students and teachers. The same can be said for Black-led charter schools. But with Jim Crow schools, all Black students had access to the educational benefits of racially separate schools because all Blacks in segregated school districts attended all-Black schools. Now, most Black students lack access to well-funded, predominantly Black pro-Black private or public schools.

The moral of the *Brown* story is this. Black children should be able to learn in an environment that is free of the discursive and material violence tied to race, class, citizenship, gender, sexuality, and dis/ability. Black histories show us that Black students benefit from being in schools with institutional cultures that are defined by an ethos of care. White parents, school boards, and public officials need to be equally invested in maintaining "equal advantages" for the education of minoritized children, not in the interest of upholding white supremacy but in the interest of neutralizing and dismantling it. As the NAACP moratorium on charter schools insisted, all children deserve access to "full funding and support of high quality free public education."[84] The successes of Topeka's four Black schools prove that with structural support, educators can develop pedagogies that subvert phenomenologies of oppression, and in turn, holistically address students' well-being and academic development. As Monroe School alumni Beryl New explained, the power of Topeka's Black educators was their empowerment of Black students. "The true essence and fabric of Monroe Elementary School is embodied in the educators who cared for their charges with a fierce and tangible love," she asserted. "These were professionals who waged war on ignorance in every form and on every level. Though they taught us survival skills, their focus was not on limitations but on possibilities."[85] May their legacy be the true lesson of Blacks against *Brown*.

Notes

Introduction

1. Robert L. Carter, interviewed by Jean Van Delinder, October 5, 1992, MS 251, Brown v. Topeka Board of Education Oral History Collection, State Archives and Library, Kansas State Historical Society, Topeka (hereafter BOHC).

2. The city's junior high schools were integrated in 1941, and high schools were never segregated.

3. Robert L. Carter to Charles Bledsoe, September 18, 1950, folder 23, box 1, Mrs. Lucinda Todd Papers, State Archives and Library, Kansas State Historical Society, Topeka.

4. Peniel Joseph, "Waiting till the Midnight Hour: Constructing an Alternative Civil Rights Narrative," *Souls* 2 (Spring 2000): 8.

5. Sundiata Keita Cha-Jua and Clarence Lang, "The 'Long Movement' as Vampire: Temporal and Spatial Fallacies in Recent Black Freedom Studies," *Journal of African American History* 92, no. 2 (2007): 265–88.

6. See Quintard Taylor, "The Civil Rights Movement in the American West: Black Protest in Seattle, 1960–1970," *Journal of Negro History* 80, no.1 (1995): 1–14; and Matthew C. Whitaker, *Race Work: The Rise of Civil Rights in the Urban West* (Lincoln: University of Nebraska Press, 2005).

7. Richard Ridley, interviewed by Jean Van Delinder, January 21, 1992, MS 251, BOHC.

8. For studies on *Brown* and the civil rights movement, see James T. Patterson, Brown v. Board of Education: *A Civil Rights Milestone and Its Troubled Legacy* (New York: Oxford University Press, 2004); and Mark V. Tushnet, *The NAACP's Legal Strategy against Segregated Education* (Chapel Hill: University of North Carolina Press, 1987). For legal scholars' debates on *Brown*, see Derrick Bell, *Silent Covenants*: Brown v. Board of Education *and the Unfulfilled Hopes for Racial Reform* (New York: Oxford University Press, 2004); and Michael Klarman, *From Jim Crow to Civil Rights: The Supreme Court and the Struggle for Racial Equality* (New York: Oxford University Press, 2004). For social scientists' work on the legacy of *Brown*, see Peter Irons, *Jim Crow's Children: The Broken Promise of the* Brown *Decision* (New York: Viking, 2002); Raymond Wolters, *The Burden of Brown: Thirty Years of School Desegregation* (Knoxville: University of Tennessee Press, 1984); and Mac A. Stewart, ed. *Promise of Justice: Essays on* Brown V. Board of Education (Columbus: Ohio State University Press, 2020).

9. For monographs that discuss *Brown v. Board* and Topeka, see Richard Kluger, *Simple Justice: The History of* Brown v. Board of Education *and Black America's Struggle for Equality* (New York: Vintage Books, 1977); and Raymond Wolter's *The Burden of Brown*. For journal articles, see Mary L. Dudziak, "The Limits of Good Faith:

Desegregation in Topeka, Kansas, 1950–1956," *Law and History Review* 5, no. 2 (Autumn 1987): 351–91; Robert Beatty and Mark A. Peterson, "Covert Discrimination: Topeka—Before and After *Brown*," *Kansas History* 27, no. 3 (Autumn 2004): 146–63; and Jamie B. Lewis, "Legal Challenges to Segregated Education in Topeka, Kansas, 1903–1941," *Educational Studies* 37, no. 1 (2005): 56–76.

10. Scholars like Jacqueline Dowd Hall and Peniel Joseph problematized the strict periodization of and rigid distinctions between the civil rights and Black Power movements. Jacquelyn Dowd Hall, "The Long Civil Rights Movement and the Political Uses of the Past," *Journal of American History* 91, no. 4 (2005): 1233–63; see also Steven F. Lawson and Charles Payne, *Debating the Civil Rights Movement: 1945–1968* (Lanham, MD: Rowman & Littlefield, 1998).

11. Joseph, "Waiting till the Midnight Hour," 8.

12. Joseph, "Waiting till the Midnight Hour," 8.

13. Patterson, Brown v. Board of Education, 210; Paul Finkelman, "Racial Justice and the Public Schools," *History of Education Quarterly* 19 (Fall, 1970): 373.

14. Robert Lowe, "Simple Justice," *History of Education Quarterly* 44, no. 1 (2004): 127.

15. Mamie Williams, interviewed by Richard Kluger, in her home, October 24, 1970, transcript, folder 111, box 6, MS 759, Brown vs. Board of Education Collection, Manuscripts and Archives, Yale University Library, New Haven, CT.

16. Kluger, *Simple Justice*, 379.

17. Williams, interview.

18. Williams, interview.

19. Lowe, "Simple Justice," 131–32. Lowe interrogates Kluger's narrativizing of Black anti-Black resistance that fell outside of the parameters of the civil rights movement.

20. Williams, interview.

21. Charles M. Payne, *I've Got the Light of Freedom: The Organizing Tradition and the Mississippi Freedom Struggle* (Berkeley: University of California Press, 1995), 392.

22. James C. Scott, *Domination and the Arts of Resistance: Hidden Transcripts* (New Haven, CT: Yale University Press, 1990).

23. Jean Van Delinder, *Struggles before* Brown: *Early Civil Rights Protests and Their Significance Today* (Boulder, CO: Paradigm Publishers), 2008.

24. Van Delinder, *Struggles before* Brown, 50.

25. Jean Van Delinder, "Early Civil Rights Activism in Topeka, Kansas, Prior to the 1954 *Brown* Case," *Great Plains Quarterly* 21, no. 1 (2001): 45–61. Historian of education Vanessa Siddle Walker takes issue with this widespread assumption. Vanessa Siddle Walker, "Tolerated Tokenism, or the Injustice in Justice: Black Teacher Associations and Their Forgotten Struggle for Educational Justice, 1921–1954," *Equity & Excellence in Education* 46, no. 1 (2013): 64–80.

26. Kluger, *Simple Justice*, 393 and 380.

27. W. E. B. Du Bois, "A Philosophy of Race Segregation," ca. October 1935, p. 1A, MS 312, W. E. B. Du Bois Papers, University of Massachusetts Amherst Libraries, Special Collections and University Archives, http://credo.library.umass.edu/view/pageturn/mums312-b197-i071/#page/3/mode/1up.

28. Avaren Ipsen, *Sex Working and the Bible* (London: Taylor & Francis Group, 2014), 8.

29. Noliwe Rooks, *Cutting School: Privatization, Segregation, and the End of Public Education* (New York: New Press, 2017), 93. Rooks's work historicizes private investments in and experiments on public education that advantage rich whites but disadvantage poor Blacks.

30. See Nancy Fraser, "Rethinking the Public Sphere: A Contribution to the Critique of Actually Existing Democracy," *Social Text*, no. 25/26 (1990): 56–80; Alberto Melucci, John Keane, and Paul Mier, eds., *Nomads of the Present: Social Movements and Individual Needs in Contemporary Society* (Philadelphia: Temple University Press, 1989); Aldon D. Morris, *The Origins of the Civil Rights Movement: Black Communities Organizing for Change* (New York: Free Press, 1986); James C. Scott, *Domination and the Arts of Resistance*; C. R. Squires, "Rethinking the Black Public Sphere: An Alternative Vocabulary for Multiple Public Spheres," *Communication Theory* 12, no. 4 (2002): 446–68.

31. James C. Scott, "Infrapolitics and Mobilizations: A Response by James C. Scott," *Revue française d'études américaines* 131, no. 1 (2012): 112–17.

32. Alberto Melucci, *Nomads of the Present*, 208. See also Michael Warner, "Publics and Counterpublics," *Public Culture* 14, no. 1 (2002): 49–90.

33. Ewa Majewski, "On Weakness, Solidarity, and Non-Heroic Resistance. The Weak Avant-Garde: A Feminist Analysis Lecture by Ewa Majewska," filmed March 16, 2016, at Museum of Modern Art in Warsaw, video, 1:41:51, https://artmuseum.pl/en/doc/video-muzeum-otwarte-o-slabosci-solidarnosci-i-nie-heroicznym.

34. Morris, *Origins of the Civil Rights Movement*, 40; Clayborn Carson critiqued the romanticization of the role of Black churches in his review of Morris's book, citing how studies have ignored Black clergy's conservative resistance toward political activism. Clayborn Carson, review of *The Origins of the Civil Rights Movement: Black Communities Organizing for Change*, by Aldon D. Morris, *Constitutional Commentary* 3, 1986: 616–21.

35. Natalia Molina, *How Race Is Made in America: Immigration, Citizenship, and the Historical Power of Racial Scripts* (Berkeley: University of California Press, 2014).

36. Minutes of the school board of education, June 5, 1935.

37. Groundbreaking Black historians of education like James D. Anderson and Vanessa Siddle Walker shifted scholarly focus on segregated schools from the external to the internal. They pushed past questions of material deprivation to explore how Black teachers and communities envisioned schools as educational sites of racial uplift. See James D. Anderson, *The Education of Blacks in the South, 1860–1935* (Chapel Hill: University of North Carolina Press, 1988); Vanessa Siddle Walker, "Valued Segregated Schools for African American Children in the South, 1935–1969: A Review of Common Themes and Characteristics," *Review of Educational Research* 70, no. 3 (2000): 253–85.

38. Henry Allan Bullock, *A History of Negro Education in the South: From 1619 to the Present* (Cambridge, MA: Harvard University Press, 1967), 34.

39. Birdie Wilson Johnson, "Leadership, Struggles, and Challenges of Hortense Ridley Tate: A Twentieth Century African-American Woman's Legacy to Methodism and Community Service" (PhD diss., Drew University, 1998), 54.

40. See Vanessa Siddle Walker, "Ninth Annual *Brown* Lecture in Education Research: Black Educators as Educational Advocates in the Decades before *Brown v. Board of Education*," *Educational Researcher* 42 no. 4 (2013): 207–22. Vanessa Siddle Walker, *Their*

Highest Potential: An African American School Community in the Segregated South (Chapel Hill: University of North Carolina Press, 1996).

Chapter One

1. H. H. Robinson to Edward Arn, December 10, 1953, folder 16, box 62, Correspondence of the Governor: Arn Administration, 1951–55, Kansas State Archives, Kansas State Historical Society Collection, Topeka.

2. Historians' use Robinson's letter as an example of white Kansans' internal conflict over *Brown* and how it reflected negatively upon the racial reputation of the state. See Mary L. Dudziak, "The Limits of Good Faith: Desegregation in Topeka, Kansas, 1950-1956," *Law and History Review* 5, no. 2 (Autumn 1987): 368–69; Rusty Monhollon and Kristen Tegtmeier Oertel, "From Brown to *Brown*: A Century of Struggle for Equality in Kansas," *Kansas History* 27, no. 2 (Spring/Summer 2004): 132.

3. For exceptions, see Peter Jackson, "Constructions of 'Whiteness' in the Geographical Imagination," *Area* 30, no. 2 (1998): 99–106; Alastair Bonnett, "Geography, 'Race' and Whiteness: Invisible Traditions and Current Challenges," *Area* 29, no. 3 (1997): 193–99; Owen J. Dwyer and John Paul Jones, "White Socio-Spatial Epistemology," *Social & Cultural Geography* 1, no. 2 (2000): 209–22; Laura Pulido, "Rethinking Environmental Racism: White Privilege and Urban Development in Southern California," *Annals of the Association of American Geographers* 90, no. 1 (2000): 12–40; and Laura Pulido, "Geographies of Race and Ethnicity 1: White Supremacy vs White Privilege in Environmental Racism Research," *Progress in Human Geography* 39, no. 6 (December 2015): 809–17.

4. Dwyer and Jones, "White Socio-Spatial Epistemology," 211.

5. A. Bower Sageser, "*The Battle Cry of Freedom: The New England Emigrant Aid Company in the Kansas Crusade* (Review)," *Civil War History* 2, no. 2 (1956): 96–97.

6. Sara Ahmed, "A Phenomenology of Whiteness," *Feminist Theory* 8, no. 2 (2007): 149–68.

7. Brent M. S. Campney, *This Is Not Dixie* (Urbana: University of Illinois Press, 2015), 13.

8. Kristen Tegtmeier Oertel, "What Makes a Man in Bleeding Kansas?" *Kansas History: A Journal of the Central Plains* 25 (Autumn 2002): 179.

9. Ahmed, "Phenomenology of Whiteness," 155.

10. Robinson to Arn, December 10, 1953.

11. "'Why Kansas?' Asks an Editor," *Topeka Daily Capital*, December 20, 1953, www.kshs.org/km/items/view/211810.

12. F. J. Cloud to Harold Fatzer, July 8, 1954, folder 2, box 1, p. 63, Board v. Board Files, Records of the Attorney General's Office, State Archives and Library, Kansas State Historical Society Collection, Topeka.

13. Nicole Etcheson, *Bleeding Kansas: Contested Liberty in the Civil War Era* (Lawrence: University Press of Kansas, 2004); Kristin Tegtmeier Oertel, *Bleeding Borders: Race, Gender, and Violence in Pre–Civil War Kansas* (Baton Rouge: Louisiana State University Press, 2009); and Campney, *This Is Not Dixie*.

14. The work of Gunja SenGupta, Nicole Etcheson, and Kristin Tegtmeier Oertel examined the variant politics of white supremacy among pro- and antislavery settlers in

territorial Kansas. Gunja SenGupta, *For God and Mammon: Evangelicals and Entrepreneurs, Masters and Slaves in Territorial Kansas, 1854–1860* (Athens: University of Georgia Press, 1996).

15. While not the originators of exclusion laws, Ohio (1804 and 1807) and Oregon (1849) had among the most stringent anti-Black exclusion laws in the Northwest and Oregon Territories. Oregon was the first state admitted into the Union with an exclusion law.

16. *White Cloud Kansas Chief*, November 28, 1861.

17. Claude Emerson, interview by Jean Van Delinder, Oct. 25, 1991, MS 251, Brown v. Topeka Board of Education Oral History Collection, State Archives and Library, Kansas State Historical Society, Topeka (hereafter BOHC).

18. Quakers, Presbyterians, and Congregationalists were among those settlers who believed civil rights should be extended to Blacks. Randall B. Woods, "Integration, Exclusion, or Segregation? The 'Color Line' in Kansas, 1878–1900," *Western Historical Quarterly* 14, no. 2 (April 1983): 196.

19. C. F. W. Dassler, *General Statutes of Kansas: Being a Compilation of All the Laws of a General Nature, Based Upon the General Statues of 1868*, 1 (St. Louis, MO, 1876): 330.

20. Paul E. Wilson, *A Time to Lose: Representing Kansas in* Brown v. Board of Education (Lawrence: University of Kansas, 1995), 37.

21. Ella Myers, "Beyond the Wages of Whiteness: Du Bois on the Irrationality of Anti-Black Racism," Items: Insights from the Social Sciences, March 21, 2017, https://items.ssrc.org/reading-racial-conflict/beyond-the-wages-of-whiteness-du-bois-on-the-irrationality-of-antiblack-racism/.

22. George Lipsitz, *The Possessive Investment in Whiteness: How White People Profit from Identity Politics* (Philadelphia: Temple University Press, 2018).

23. For more on how white settlers negotiated whiteness in relation to Blacks and Indigenous peoples, see Kristen Tegtmeier Oertel, *Bleeding Borders*, and Kim Cary Warren, *The Quest for Citizenship* (Chapel Hill: University of North Carolina Press, 2010).

24. Robert Oppenheimer, "Acculturation or Assimilation: Mexican Immigrants in Kansas, 1900 to World War II," *Western Historical Quarterly* 16, no. 4 (1985): 431.

25. Approximately 1,500 Mexican and Mexican American residents were deported from Topeka and 800 from Kansas City. Oppenheimer, "Acculturation or Assimilation," 443.

26. Dionicio Nodin Valdés, *Barrios Norteños: St. Paul and Midwestern Mexican Communities in the Twentieth Century* (Austin: University of Texas Press, 2000), 89. Senator Allen supported the Harris Bill in 1930 that would have added Mexico to the restrictive quota system created by the 1924 Immigration Act.

27. Diana Fuss, *Essentially Speaking: Feminism, Nature & Difference* (New York: Routledge, 1989), xi–xii. Kristin Tegtmeier argues that abolitionist articulations of manhood shifted toward militance as the conflict between pro- and antislavery forces escalated. See Kristen Oertel Tegtmeier, "'The Free Sons of the North' versus 'the Myrmidons of Border Ruffianism': What Makes a Man in Bleeding Kansas?" *Kansas History: A Journal of the Central Plains* (Autumn 2002): 174–89.

28. Gordon Parks, *Voices in the Mirror: An Autobiography* (New York: Doubleday, 1990), 1. Parks wrote about racial dynamics in Ft. Scott, Kansas, during the 1910s and early '20s.

29. "The Colored Emigrants," *Colored Citizen*, March 29, 1879. Editors argued that racial anxieties were less about public health and more about a potential for Black political power.

30. Brent M. S. Campney, "'Ever Since the Hanging of Oliphant,' Lynching and the Suppression of Mob Violence in Topeka, Kansas," *Great Plains Quarterly* 33, no. 2 (2013): 72.

31. Campney, "'Ever Since the Hanging of Oliphant,'" 75.

32. Campney, "'Ever Since the Hanging of Oliphant,'" 84.

33. "Mayor Says Negroes Not Barred from Parks," *Daily Capital*, June 18, 1933.

34. "May Close City Parks to Avert Race Trouble Com. Snyder Says Negroes Threaten to Invade All Parks," *Topeka Daily Capital*, June 17, 1933.

35. One white resident told the local newspaper that park commissioner Harry Snyder "ran anybody and everybody out of the park if you but looked at him cross-eyed." "Gage Park Memories," *Topeka Capital-Journal*, June 22, 2003.

36. "Mayor Says Negroes Not Barred."

37. Roy Wilkins to *Topeka Capital Journal*, June 23, 1933, NAACP Topeka Branch Office Files, Kansas State Historical Society, Topeka.

38. Chris Hansen, interviewed by Jean Van Delinder, October 5, 1992, MS 251, BOHC.

39. Anonymous, interview by author, Topeka, KS, December 27, 2008.

40. Gordon Parks, *The Learning Tree* (New York: Random House, 1963), 20.

41. W. E. B. Du Bois, "Dark Water: Voices from Within the Veil," Project Gutenberg, 2005, www.gutenberg.org/files/15210/15210-h/15210-h.htm.

42. Lena Burnett, interviewed by Richard Kluger, in her home, 1970, transcript, folder 13, box 1, MS 759, Brown vs. Board of Education Collection, Manuscripts and Archives, Yale University Library, New Haven, CT.

43. William Mitchell Jr., interviewed by Ralph Crowder, November 20, 1991, MS 251, BOHC.

44. Bryan Wagner, *Disturbing the Peace* (Cambridge, MA: Harvard University Press, 2010), 2.

45. Orlando Patterson, *Slavery & Social Death: A Comparative Study* (Cambridge, MA: Harvard University Press, 1985).

46. Burnett, interview.

47. John Hanna, "McKinley Burnett Forgotten, but Played Key Role in Brown Case," *Los Angeles Sentinel*, June 19, 1997.

48. Maurita Davis, interviewed by Jean Van Delinder, July 15, 1994, MS 251, BOHC.

49. Mitchell, interview.

50. Barbara Gibson, interviewed by Cheryl Brown Henderson, September 25, 1992, MS 251, BOHC.

51. Richard Ridley, interviewed by Jean Van Delinder, Jan. 21, 1992, MS 251, BOHC.

52. Throughout the twentieth century, people of Mexican descent were called "Mexican" in mainstream newspapers, public records, and the oral histories of white and Black Kansans, regardless of citizenship.

53. Jan Biles, "Ties That Bind: Roots Were in Mexico, but Jobs Were in Topeka," *Topeka Capital-Journal*, July 13, 2003.

54. Emerson, interview. Claude Emerson was a native Topekan born in 1942.

55. Davis, interview.

56. See Jean Van Delinder, *Struggles before* Brown: *Early Civil Rights Protests and Their Significance Today* (London: Routledge, 2016).

57. David Long, "Topekan Meets with Carter," Topeka newspaper unknown, May 29, 1977, Lucinda Todd Papers, Kansas State Historical Society, Topeka.

58. Davis, interview. Maurita defied her father's command to steer clear of the city's movie theaters because she "was young and dating."

59. James C. Scott, "Infrapolitics and Mobilizations: A Response by James C. Scott," *Revue française d'études américaines* 131, no. 1 (2012): 112–17.

60. Tina Marie Campt, "Black Visuality and the Practice of Refusal," *Women & Performance* 29, no. 1 (2019): 80.

61. Anonymous, interviewed by Jean Van Delinder, February 7, 1992, MS 251, BOHC.

62. Deborah Dandridge, interviewed by Jean Van Delinder, July 26, 1994, MS 251, BOHC.

63. Emerson, interview.

64. Lance Murphy, interview by author, tape recording, Topeka, KS, December 26, 2008.

65. Davis, interview.

66. David Lloyd, "The Social Life of Black Things: Fred Moten's Consent Not to Be a Single Being," *Radical Philosophy* 2, no. 7 (Spring 2020): 81.

67. Jack Alexander, interviewed by Ralph Crowder, 1991, MS 251, BOHC.

68. Steve Fry, "Black and White: Topeka High Basketball in '49: A Game of Race," *Topeka Capital-Journal*, October 11, 2009.

69. Fry, "Black and White."

70. Merrill Ross, interviewed by Richard Kluger in his home, folder 13, box 1, p. 1, MS 759, Brown vs. Board of Education Collection, Manuscripts and Archives, Yale University Library, New Haven, CT. Ross didn't start with Topeka public schools until 1946 because he was drafted in 1944.

71. Alexander, interview.

72. Johanna Hall, "The African American Community in Topeka, Kansas, 1940–1951: Crucial Years Before Brown" (master's thesis, University of Kansas, 1993), 33.

73. Fry, "Black and White."

74. Alexander, interview.

75. Fry, "Black and White."

76. Charles Baston, interview by Jean Van Delinder, May 14, 1992, MS 251, BOHC. Baston also spoke of racially biased loan practices at Capital Federal Savings and Loan during the mid-1950s.

77. Ridley, interview.

78. Raymond J. Reynolds to Walter White, April 23 1932, NAACP Topeka Branch Office Files, Kansas State Historical Society, Topeka.

79. Ridley, interview.

80. Hall, "African American Community in Topeka," 45–46.

81. Barbara Ross, interviewed by Jean Van Delinder, Nov. 13, 1991, MS 251, BOHC.

82. Ross, interview.

83. Matthew Frye Jacobson historicized the process by which immigrants from southern and eastern Europe, "probationary whites" deemed inferior by native-born whites of Anglo-Saxon descent, became included in the privileged category of whiteness. Matthew Frye Jacobson, *Whiteness of a Different Color: European Immigrants and the Alchemy of Race* (Cambridge, MA: Harvard University Press, 1998).

84. Norman E. Saul, "The Migration of the Russian-Germans to Kansas," *Kansas Collection: Kansas Historical Quarterlies* 40, no. 1 (Spring 1974): 38–62, www.kshs.org/p /the-migration-of-the-russian-germans-to-kansas/13242.

85. Saul, "Migration of the Russian-Germans."

86. Saul, "Migration of the Russian-Germans."

87. Tom Rodriguez, "Growing Up in 'The Bottoms' of Topeka, Kansas," *Somos en escrito: The Latino Literary Online Magazine* (January 2013), www.somosenescrito.com /2013/01/growing-up-in-bottoms-of-topeka-kansas.html.

88. Berdyne Scott interviewed by Ralph Crowder, Nov. 24, 1991, MS 251, BOHC. Scott, born in Topeka in 1918, was the wife of John Scott, original attorney for the plaintiffs in *Brown v. Board of Education*.

89. According to historian Robert Oppenheimer, most of these Mexicans immigrated from Silao, Guanajuato. Oppenheimer, "Acculturation or Assimilation," 435.

90. Jan Biles, "Ties That Bind."

91. Biles, "Ties That Bind."

92. Scott, interview.

93. Joseph Douglas interviewed by Ralph Crowder, October 24, 1991, MS 251, BOHC; Mitchell, interview.

94. Maurice J. Lang, interviewed by Jean Van Delinder, January 20, 1992, MS 251, BOHC. Lang served as the assistant pastor of St. Mark's AME under Rev. Oliver Brown during the late 1950s. He went on to become the first white pastor of an AME church in Manhattan, Kansas.

95. Art Schaaf, "Topeka White vs. Brown," *Topeka Capital-Journal*, May 13, 1979.

96. Emerson, interview. Emerson recalled asking his white playmates, "What did you learn in school today?" to determine if there were racial disparities in school curricula. His mother Marguerite was a *Brown* plaintiff.

97. Deborah L. Scott, interviewed by Jean Van Delinder, November 15, 1991, MS 251, BOHC.

98. E. B. Hicks, interviewed by Jean Van Delinder, November 22, 1991, MS 251, BOHC.

99. Lang, interview.

100. Lupe Perez, "Legacy of Brown: Separate but Equal Also Affected Mexican-Americans," *Topeka Capital-Journal*, May 9, 2014.

Chapter Two

1. George Mack, "State to Defend School Statute on Segregation," *Daily Capital*, December 5, 1952.

2. In her classic 1978 article "Disloyal to Civilization: Feminism, Racism, Gynephobia," feminist scholar Adrienne Rich wrote of white solipsism as "a tunnel-vision which simply does not see nonwhite experience or existence as precious or significant." Adrienne Rich, *On Lies, Secrets, and Silence: Selected Prose, 1966-1978* (New York: W. W. Norton, 1979), 306.

3. Mary L. Dudziak "The Limits of Good Faith: Desegregation in Topeka, Kansas, 1950–1956," *Law and History Review* 5, no. 2 (1987): 351–91.

4. Dudziak, "Limits of Good Faith," 52.

5. Charles Bledsoe to Robert L. Carter, November 24, 1950, p. 454, folder 124, MS 759, Brown vs. Board of Education Collection, Manuscripts and Archives, Yale University Library, New Haven, CT.

6. Even Missourians bought into the Free State narrative, as the Missouri press described the case as a "paradox" and asked, "Why Kansas?"

7. "Case Is a Paradox," *Kansas City Star*, May 17, 1954.

8. Sue Shore, "Destabilising or Recuperating Whiteness? (Un)mapping 'the Self' of Agentic Learning Discourses," in *Whitening Race: Essays in Social and Cultural Criticism*, ed. Aileen Moreton-Robinson (Canberra: Aboriginal Studies Press, 2004), 99.

9. George Lipsitz, *The Possessive Investment in Whiteness: How White People Profit from Identity Politics* (Philadelphia: Temple University Press, 2006), 215.

10. Lucinda Todd, "For the Negro Press Suit Hits Separate Schools in Kansas," 1951, p. 359, folder 124, MS 759, Brown vs. Board of Education Collection, Manuscripts and Archives, Yale University Library, New Haven, CT.

11. Lupe Perez, "Legacy of *Brown*: Separate-but-Equal Also Affected Mexican-Americans," *Topeka Capital-Journal*, May 9, 2014. Perez went to junior high school before they were desegregated in 1941.

12. Founded as the United States Indian Industrial Training School, the school was renamed Haskell Institute in 1887.

13. Kim Cary Warren writes extensively about the convergence and divergence of early white interests in nonwhite education in Kansas during the post-Reconstruction period. Kim Cary Warren, *The Quest for Citizenship: African American and Native American Education in Kansas, 1880-1935* (Chapel Hill: University of North Carolina Press, 2010).

14. General Laws of the State of Kansas, Passed at the Third Session of the Legislature, Commenced at the Capital, January 13, 1863 (Lawrence, KS: 1863), 93.

15. Thomas C. Cox, *Blacks in Topeka, Kansas, 1865-1915: A Social History* (Baton Rouge: Louisiana State University Press, 1982), 27–28.

16. "The Colored Schools, Pupils and Teachers," *A Centennial History of the Topeka Schools, Compiled by Retired Teachers of the School System, 1954*, 3, Kansas Collection, Center for Historical Research, Kansas State Historical Society, Topeka.

17. Cox, *Blacks in Topeka*, 28.

18. C. F. W. Dassler, Compiled Laws of Kansas, 1879: Being a Compilation of All the Laws of a General Nature Based Upon the General Statutes of 1868 (St. Louis, MO: 1879), 843.

19. Minutes of the school board of education, October 6, 1924.

20. The Topeka school board desegregated the city's junior high schools after the 1941 Kansas Supreme Court decision in *Graham v. Board of Education of Topeka*.

21. In 1905 white residents demanded separate high schools after a racial incident led to the shooting death of a white high school student. The state legislature appeased white racial anxieties by passing a special act that exempted the city from state law prohibiting racial segregation in high schools.

22. Perez, "Legacy of *Brown*."

23. Dennis Nodín Valdés, *Barrios norteños: St. Paul and Midwestern Mexican Communities in the Twentieth Century* (Austin: University of Texas Press, 2000), 32.

24. "The Race Problem," *Republic* (Kansas City), November 30, 1917, p. 4, quoted in Robert Martin Cleary, "The Education of Mexican-Americans in Kansas City, Kansas, 1916–1951" (master's thesis, University of Missouri, 2002), 39.

25. Cleary, "Education of Mexican-Americans," 39.

26. Cleary, "Education of Mexican-Americans," 55–56.

27. For more on how students of Mexican descent were treated in multiple Kansas cities, see Rubén Donato and Jarrod Hanson, "In These Towns, Mexicans Are Classified as Negroes," *American Educational Research Journal* 54, no. 1 (2017): 53S–74S.

28. Allen Ecord, "A Principal Looks at Urban Renewal," *Research Department, Menninger Foundation* (Topeka, KS: April 1967), 3, quoted in Marian Frances Braun, "A Survey of the American-Mexicans in Topeka, Kansas" (master's thesis, Kansas State Teachers College, Emporia, 1970), 13.

29. Perez, "Legacy of *Brown*."

30. Celia Llopis-Jepsen, "Historian: Topeka's Hispanic Segregation Often Forgotten," *Topeka Capital-Journal*, May 8, 2014.

31. Natalia Molina, *How Race Is Made in America: Immigration, Citizenship, and the Historical Power of Racial Scripts* (Berkeley: University of California Press, 2014).

32. Jeff Wiltse historicizes swimming pools as sites that marked race, class, and gender distinctions through discrimination. Jeff Wiltse, *Contested Waters: A Social History of Swimming Pools in America* (Chapel Hill: University of North Carolina Press, 2007).

33. Minutes of the school board of education, May 7, 1942.

34. Historian Lynn Hudson opens her book *West of Jim Crow* with a story of a Black woman who moved from Kansas to California during the Great Depression to escape anti-Blackness, only to discover that the pools in Pasadena restricted Black swimmers to "Negro Day." Lynn Hudson, *West of Jim Crow: The Fight against California's Color Line* (Urbana: University of Illinois Press, 2020).

35. Athena D. Mutua, "Shifting Bottoms and Rotating Centers: Reflections on LatCrit III and the Black/White Paradigm," *University of Miami Law Review* 53 (1999): 1177.

36. Jan Biles, "Memories Remain of School Where Hispanics Attended," *Topeka Capital-Journal*, July 13, 2003.

37. Ecord, "A Principal Looks," 13.

38. Ecord, "A Principal Looks," 13.

39. Perez, "Legacy of *Brown*."

40. Biles, "Memories."

41. Donato and Hanson, "In These Towns," 66S.

42. Jan Biles, "Ties That Bind: Roots Were in Mexico, but Jobs Were in Topeka," *Topeka Capital-Journal*, July 13, 2003.

43. Minutes of the school board of education, August 3, 1942.

44. Dennis Nodín Valdés attributes the Topeka school board's policy change to interest convergence in *Barrios Norteños*. The civil rights lobbying of Mexican and Mexican American residents coincided with a request by the "armed forces" to use the building, he concluded.

45. There is one "unspecified" complaint brought by a "colored delegation" in 1900 about teachers' salaries. Minutes of the school board of education, April 2, 1900, p. 156. However in 1898 and 1899 most teachers, regardless of race, made $55 a year. There was more variation in principals' salaries, which appeared to be based on how many years a principal served in that position and the number of rooms in a principal's school building.

46. Glouster Current to Dr. Porter Davis, September 15, 1948, Kansas State Conference Files, NAACP Papers, Microfilm Division, Kansas State Historical Society Collection, Topeka.

47. The *Graham* case is the subject matter of chapter 4, so it will not be discussed here.

48. William Reynolds v. Board of Education of Topeka, depositions, September 6, 1902, Kansas Memory, Kansas Historical Society, 64, www.kshs.org/km/items/view/209523.

49. Minutes of the school board of education, March 3, 1902.

50. *Reynolds*, depositions, 17 and 31.

51. *Reynolds*, depositions, 84.

52. Owen J. Dwyer and John Paul Jones, "White Socio-Spatial Epistemology," *Social & Cultural Geography* 1, no. 2 (2000): 210.

53. *Reynolds*, depositions, 107.

54. *Reynolds*, depositions, 107.

55. Jamie B. Lewis, "Legal Challenges to Segregated Education in Topeka, Kansas, 1903–1941," *Educational Studies (Ames)* 37, no. 1 (2005): 59.

56. William Reynolds v. Board of Education of Topeka, mandamuses, March 1903, Kansas Memory, Kansas Historical Society, www.kshs.org/index.php?url=km/items/view/209565.

57. George Lipsitz, *The Possessive Investment in Whiteness: How White People Profit from Identity Politics* (Philadelphia: Temple University Press, 2006), 215.

58. "Brief for the Plaintiff," Reynolds v. Board of Education of Topeka, 66 Kans. 672–37 (1903): 2.

59. "Brief for the Plaintiff," Reynolds v. Board, 6.

60. "Brief for the Plaintiff," Reynolds v. Board, 8.

61. "Brief for the Plaintiff," Reynolds v. Board, 13.

62. "Brief for the Plaintiff," Reynolds v. Board, 12–13.

63. *Reynolds*, mandamuses, 16.

64. *Colored Citizen*, September 20, 1878.

65. "Out They Go: Trouble at Lincoln School Comes to a Head," *Topeka State Journal*, September 24, 1908.

66. "The Strike Spreads: Thirty-Two Children in Garfield School Walk Out," *Topeka State Journal*, September 25, 1908, 6.

67. "Out They Go."

68. Minutes of the school board of education, April 4, 1921.

69. "Court House Notes and Police Gossip," *Topeka Daily Capital*, October 13, 1929.

70. Mrs. Chas W. French to NAACP, October 14, 1929, NAACP Topeka Branch Office Files, Kansas State Historical Society Collection, Topeka.

71. Wilhemina Wright v. Board of Education of Topeka, 129 Kan. 852, p. 853.

72. The Fosters' attorney argued that the bus stop was four blocks away from their home and Buchanan School was three miles away. Similarly, Wilhemina Wright lived "a few blocks" from Randolph her neighborhood school, while Buchanan was "some 20 blocks" away from their residence.

73. Counter Abstract and Brief of Appellees, Wright v. Board of Education of Topeka (1930), p. 10, Kansas Supreme Court records, State Archives and Library, Kansas State Historical Society, Topeka.

74. Counter Abstract, Wright v. Board, p. 11.

75. Mrs. Chas W. French to NAACP, March 12, 1933, NAACP Topeka Branch Office Files, Kansas State Historical Society Collection, Topeka.

76. "Court House Notes."

77. Minutes of the school board of education, June 6, 1938.

78. Audra Simpson, "Consent's Revenge," *Cultural Anthropology* 31, no. 3 (2016): 330.

79. Minutes of the school board of education, February 8, 1946.

80. Sam Dicks, ed., "Eliza Bradshaw: An Exoduster Grandmother," *Kansas History: A Journal of the Central Plains* 26 (Summer 2003): 111, www.kshs.org/publicat/history/2003summer_dicks.pdf.

81. Dicks, "Eliza Bradshaw," 109.

82. Nathaniel Sawyer to Governor Henry Justin Allen, January 11, 1918, Correspondence of the Governor: Henry J. Allen, 1919–1923, Kansas State Archives, Kansas Historical Society Collection, Topeka.

83. Field Secretary to I. B. Taylor, April 17, 1922, NAACP Topeka Branch Office Files, Kansas State Historical Society Collection, Topeka; Mrs. I. B. Taylor to William Pickens, April 22, 1922, NAACP Topeka Branch Office Files, Kansas State Historical Society Collection, Topeka.

84. Minutes of the school board of education, December 6, 1937.

85. Minutes of the school board of education, January 10, 1938.

86. Minutes of the school board of education, February 7, 1938.

87. Simpson, "Consent's Revenge," 330.

88. Minutes of the school board of education, February 1, 1909, and April 12, 1909.

89. *Topeka Plaindealer*, September 3, 1920.

90. Lucinda Todd, interviewed by Ralph Crowder, MS 251, Brown v. Topeka Board of Education Oral History Collection, State Archives and Library, Kansas State Historical Society, Topeka (hereafter BOHC).

91. Minutes of the school board of education, June 5, 1935.

92. Sawyer to Allen, January 11, 1918.

93. Keith Weldon Medley, *We as Freeman: Plessy v. Ferguson* (Gretna, LA: Pelican, 2003), 17.

94. Medley, *We as Freeman*, 146.

95. Mark Golub, "Plessy as 'Passing': Judicial Responses to Ambiguously Raced Bodies in Plessy v. Ferguson," *Law & Society Review* 39, no. 3 (2005): 567.

96. American Studies scholar Lisa Marie Cacho explicates the relationship between racial ideologies and racist practices, paying particular attention to narratives of morality and worthiness. Lisa Marie Cacho, *Social Death: Racialized Rightlessness and the Criminalization of the Unprotected* (New York: NYU Press, 2012).

97. *Colored Citizen*, July 19, 1897.

98. Barbara Hollingsworth, "Papers from Desegregation Case Donated," *Augusta Chronicle*, July 4, 2008.

99. Martha Rose Beard, "Re-Thinking Oral History—a Study of Narrative Performance," *Rethinking History* 21, no. 4 (2017): 532.

100. Beard, "Re-Thinking Oral History," 530.

101. Todd, interview, BOHC.

102. Todd, interview, BOHC.

103. Thayer Brown Phillips, interviewed by Ralph Crowder, November 20, 1991, MS 251, BOHC.

104. Todd, interview, BOHC.

105. See Evelyn Brooks Higginbotham, *Righteous Discontent: The Women's Movement in the Black Baptist Church, 1880–1920* (Cambridge, MA: Harvard University Press, 1993).

106. Lucinda Todd, interviewed by Richard Kluger, in her home, October 22, 1970, folder 98, box 5, MS 759, Brown vs. Board of Education Collection, Manuscripts and Archives, Yale University Library, New Haven, CT.

107. Merrill Ross, interviewed by Richard Kluger in his home, folder 13, box 1, p. 2, MS 759, Brown vs. Board of Education Collection, Manuscripts and Archives, Yale University Library, New Haven, CT.

108. Todd, interview, BOHC.

109. Todd, interview, BOHC.

110. Todd, interview, BOHC.

111. Todd, interview, BOHC.

112. Hollingsworth, "Papers from Desegregation Case Donated."

113. Todd was not the first Black resident to raise concerns about Black students' lack of access to a music program. Hezekiah Brown offered to implement one in the city's segregated schools in 1939, but he was denied by the school board. The school board's affirmative response to Todd's complaint may have been timing. It occurred five years after the school board lost the *Graham* desegregation case. Also, Brown did not have the benefit of mainstream media evidencing the disparity like Todd.

114. Tina Campt, *Listening to Images* (Durham, NC: Duke University Press, 2017), 17.

Chapter Three

1. W. E. B. Du Bois, "A Philosophy of Race Segregation," MS 312, W. E. B. Du Bois Papers 1868–1963, Special Collections and University Archives, University of Massachusetts Amherst Libraries, https://credo.library.umass.edu/view/full/mums312-b197 -i071; W. E. B. Du Bois, *Dusk of Dawn: An Essay toward an Autobiography of a Race Concept* (New York: Harcourt, Brace, 1940), 201.

2. James D. Anderson, *The Education of Blacks in the South, 1860–1935* (Chapel Hill: University of North Carolina Press, 1988).

3. Pauline Lipman, "Segregation, the 'Black Spatial Imagination,' and Radical Social Transformation," *Democracy & Education* 26, no. 2 (2018): 2.

4. *Topeka Plaindealer*, September 3, 1920.

5. Dennis Kelly, "Roots of Integration: 'Brown v. Board' turns 40," *USA Today*, February 16, 1994.

6. Julia Etta Parks, interview by Jean Van Delinder, Oct. 16, 1992, MS 251, Brown v. Topeka Board of Education Oral History Collection, State Archives and Library, Kansas State Historical Society, Topeka (hereafter BOHC).

7. Jan Biles, "On the Front Line," *Topeka Capital-Journal*, May 9, 2004. Campbell became the first Black person elected to the Kansas State Board of Education in 2008.

8. Richard Ridley, interviewed by Jean Van Delinder, Jan. 21, 1992, MS 251, BOHC. Richard Ridley graduated from Monroe Elementary School in the early 1940s.

9. Jack Alexander, interviewed by Ralph Crowder, 1991, MS 251, BOHC.

10. For historical accounts of academically strong Jim Crow schools, see Thomas Sowell, "Black Excellence: The Case of Dunbar High School," *Public Interest* 35 (Spring 1974): 3–21; Vanessa Siddle Walker, *Their Highest Potential: An African American School Community in the Segregated South* (Chapel Hill: University of North Carolina Press, 1996); Vanessa Siddle Walker, "Valued Segregated Schools for African American Children in the South, 1935–1969: A Review of Common Themes and Characteristics," *Review of Educational Research* 70, no. 3 (Autumn 2000): 253–85; Hilton Kelly, "What Jim Crow's Teachers Could Do: Educational Capital and Teachers' Work in Under-Resourced Schools," *Urban Review* 42, no. 4 (2010): 329–50; and Matthew C. Whitaker, *Race Work: The Rise of Civil Rights in the Urban West* (Lincoln: University of Nebraska Press, 2005), 117. On positive alumni recollections of all-Black schools, see Thomas Sowell, "Patterns of Black Excellence," *Public Interest* 43 (Spring 1976): 26–58; Raymond Wolters, *Race and Education, 1954–2007* (Columbia: University of Missouri Press, 2008), 240; Faustine C. Jones-Wilson, *A Traditional Model of Educational Excellence: Dunbar High School of Little Rock, Arkansas* (Washington, DC: Howard University Press, 1981); Kelly Hilton, *Race, Remembering, and Jim Crow's Teachers* (New York: Routledge, 2009); and Vivian Gunn Morris and Curtis L. Morris, *Creating Caring and Nurturing Educational Environments for African American Children* (Westport, CT: Praeger, 2000).

11. Katherine McKittrick, *Demonic Grounds: Black Women and the Cartographies of Struggle* (Minneapolis: University of Minnesota Press, 2006), 11.

12. Bill Maxwell, "In Face of Jim Crow, All-Black School Instilled Discipline, Self-reliance in Our Lives," *Tampa Bay Times*, March 28, 2010, www.tampabay.com/opinion

/columns/in-face-of-jim-crow-all-Black-school-instilled-discipline-self-reliance-in /1082857.

13. William H. Chafe, *Remembering Jim Crow: African Americans Tell about Life in the Segregated South* (New York: New Press, 2001), 165.

14. Charles Baston, interview by Jean Van Delinder, May 14, 1992, MS 251, BOHC.

15. Lipman, "Segregation," 2.

16. Fred Moten, *The Universal Machine* (Durham, NC: Duke University Press, 2018), 201.

17. This quote is attributed to Ezekiel Ridley, long-standing principal at Washington Elementary School. Birdie Wilson Johnson, "Leadership, Struggles, and Challenges of Hortense Ridley Tate: A Twentieth Century African-American Woman's Legacy to Methodism and Community Service" (PhD diss., Drew University, Madison, NJ, 1998), 54.

18. *Colored Citizen*, December 14, 1878.

19. *Colored Citizen*, June 21, 1879.

20. "The Colored Schools, Pupils and Teachers," *A Centennial History of the Topeka Schools, Compiled by Retired Teachers of the School System, 1954*, 3, Kansas Collection, Center for Historical Research, Kansas State Historical Society, Topeka.

21. William Reynolds v. Board of Education of Topeka, depositions (1902): 139.

22. Graham v. Board of Education of Topeka, 153 Kan. 840 (1941).

23. Kelly, "Roots of Integration."

24. Leola Brown Montgomery, interview by Ralph Crowder, Nov. 15, 1991, MS 251, BOHC.

25. Zelma Henderson, interview by Ralph Crowder, Jan. 31, 1992, MS 251, BOHC.

26. Jan Biles, "On the Front Line."

27. Johnson, "Leadership, Struggles, and Challenges," 42.

28. Montgomery, interview.

29. Mary Clarkin, "Alice Lee: Living without Anger," *Topeka Capital Journal*, April 29, 2019, www.cjonline.com/story/news/education/2019/04/29/alice-lee-living-without -anger/5298296007/.

30. Ridley, interview.

31. Lena Burnett, interviewed by Richard Kluger, in her home, 1970, handwritten notes, folder 124, box 12, p. 330, MS 759, Brown vs. Board of Education Collection, Manuscripts and Archives, Yale University Library, New Haven, CT.

32. Emily Cowan, "McKinley Elementary School," *Abandoned KS*, February 11, 2021, https://abandonedks.com/mckinley-elementary-school/.

33. Parks, interview.

34. Montgomery, interview.

35. Alexander, interview.

36. Joe Douglas, interview by Ralph Crowder, Oct. 24, 1991, MS 251, BOHC.

37. Douglas, interview.

38. Ambrose Caliver, "The Negro Teacher and a Philosophy of Negro Education," *Journal of Negro Education* 2, no. 4 (1933): 438. Caliver was the US Office of Education's senior specialist in the education of Negroes.

39. Ridley, interview.

40. According to Adam Fairclough, in 1930 12 percent of Black teachers were college graduates, in 1940 35 percent Black teachers were college graduates, and by 1952 72 percent Black teachers were college graduates. Adam Fairclough, *Teaching Equality: Black Schools in the Age of Jim Crow* (Athens: University of Georgia Press, 2001), 50.

41. Ridley, interview.

42. Ridley, interview.

43. Richard Kluger, *Simple Justice: The History of* Brown v. Board of Education (New York: Vintage, 1977), 377.

44. Mamie Williams, "The Teaching Annals of Ella," 5, folder 111, box 6, Brown vs. Board of Education Collection, Manuscripts and Archives, Yale University Library, New Haven, CT. Williams submitted this autobiographical tale to the *Journal of Education* for a short story contest in 1940.

45. Mamie Williams, interviewed by Richard Kluger, in her home, October 24, 1970, transcript, folder 111, box 6, MS 759, Brown vs. Board of Education Collection, Manuscripts and Archives, Yale University Library, New Haven, CT.

46. Mamie Williams, "Retirement—They Five W's and H (How) of It," 2, folder 111, box 6, Brown vs. Board of Education Collection, Manuscripts and Archives, Yale University Library, New Haven, CT.

47. "Mamie Williams's Journal 1894–1976," box 1, MS 136, Mamie Luella Williams Papers, 1930–1979, Kansas State Archives, Kansas Historical Society Collection, Topeka.

48. Thayer Phillips, interview by Ralph Crowder, November 20, 1991, MS 251, BOHC.

49. Williams, interview.

50. Ida Norman, interview by Ralph Crowder, November 1, 1991, MS 251, BOHC.

51. Saidiya Hartman, "The Anarchy of Colored Girls Assembled in a Riotous Manner," *South Atlantic Quarterly* 117, no. 3 (2018): 467.

52. El Dorothy Scott, interview by Jean Van Delinder, Jan. 27, 1992, MS 251, BOHC.

53. Ridley, interview.

54. Hartman, "Anarchy of Colored Girls," 467.

55. Hartman, "Anarchy of Colored Girls," 467.

56. Saidiya V. Hartman, "Venus in Two Acts," *Small Axe: A Journal of Criticism* 26 (2008): 1.

57. Williams, interview.

58. Johanna Hall, "The African-American Community in Topeka, Kansas, 1940–1951: Crucial Years Before *Brown*" (master's thesis, University of Kansas, 1991), 56.

59. Hall, "African-American Community in Topeka," 56.

60. Mamie Williams, "Weekly Observations," *Plaindealer* (Topeka), January 6, 1933.

61. Williams, "Weekly Observations."

62. Williams, "Weekly Observations," December 9, 1932.

63. Williams, "Weekly Observations," March 31, 1933.

64. Williams, "Weekly Observations," February 24, 1933.

65. Mamie Williams, "The Challenge," *Of Merit, Achievement and Service: Studies in Negro Life Grade Six Book IV*, 9, folder 111, box 6, Brown vs. Board of Education Collection, Manuscripts and Archives, Yale University Library, New Haven, CT (hereafter *OMAS*).

66. Williams, "Challenge," *OMAS*, 9.

67. Parks, interview.

68. Kevin K. Gaines, *Uplifting the Race: Black Leadership, Politics, and Culture in the Twentieth Century* (Chapel Hill: University of North Carolina Press), 2.

69. The 1893 British case *Williams v. Eady* established the "in loco parentis" standard that continues to undergird corporal punishment in schools. Dr. Kim Teh outlined the debates over the use and utility of corporal punishment in educational settings in the United States, Britain, Canada, New Zealand, Australia, and Singapore in 2012. Mui Kim Teh, "Corporal Punishment: Archaic or Reasonable Discipline Method?" *International Journal of Law & Education* 17, no. 1 (2012): 73–86.

70. Ridley, interview.

71. Christina Jackson, interview by Jean Van Delinder, Sept. 20, 1991, MS 251, BOHC.

72. William Mitchell Jr., interview by Ralph Crowder, November 20, 1991, MS 251, BOHC.

73. For more on the European roots of spanking, see Stacey Patton, *Spare the Kids: Why Whupping Children Won't Save Black America* (Boston: Beacon Press), 2017. Researchers and writers have argued that Black American parents' disproportionate use of physical discipline for child behavior modification (relative to whites and Latinos) is a legacy of enslavement and is directly related to racial anxieties about Black children's vulnerability to anti-Black violence. For more on the relationship among parenting, punishment, and powerlessness, see Leon Litwack, *Trouble in Mind: Black Southerners in the Age of Jim Crow* (New York: Alfred A. Knopf, 1998), and Ta-Nehisi Coates, *Between the World and Me* (New York: Spiegel & Grau, 2015).

74. Sampada Aranke and Nikolas Oscar Sparks, "Reading and Feeling after Scenes of Subjection," *Women & Performance* (March 21, 2017): 1–6.

75. Williams, "Challenge," *OMAS*, 12.

76. Kluger, *Simple Justice*, 379. After *Graham* was decided in 1941, Williams wrote an editorial in a local Black newspaper, the *Plaindealer*.

77. Aranke and Sparks, "Reading and Feeling," 3.

78. Williams, interview.

79. David Wallace, "Fred Moten's Radical Critique of the Present," *New Yorker*, April 30, 2018, www.newyorker.com/culture/persons-of-interest/fred-motens-radical-critique-of-the-present.

80. Williams, interview.

81. Carole Mcgranahan, "Theorizing Refusal: An Introduction," *Cultural Anthropology* 31, no. 3 (2016): 322.

82. Johnson, "Leadership, Struggles, and Challenges," 39.

83. Johnson, "Leadership, Struggles, and Challenges," 28.

84. Johnson, "Leadership, Struggles, and Challenges," 37–38.

85. "Obituary," *Topeka Daily Capital*, October 5, 1960.

86. Kim Cary Warren discusses the evolution of the Industrial and Educational Institute. In the late nineteenth century white reformers' emphasized training Black students for the labor force. After the 1920s a new cohort of Black educators committed to racial uplift politics shifted the scholarly focus toward building a Black professional class. They introduced a broader, more classical curriculum that included Black studies

and changed the school's name to Kansas Vocational Institute to avoid confusion with the State Industrial School for Boys, a penal institution for male youth offenders. Kim Cary Warren, *The Quest for Citizenship African American and Native American Education in Kansas, 1880-1935* (Chapel Hill: University of North Carolina Press, 2010), 133–36.

87. Johnson, "Leadership, Struggles, and Challenges," 54–55.

88. Thelma D. Perry, *History of the American Teachers Association* (Washington, DC: National Education, 1975), 133–62.

89. Johnson, "Leadership, Struggles, and Challenges," 39.

90. *Topeka Daily Capital*, February 16, 1901, 5.

91. Fairclough, *Teaching Equality*, 43. Woodson founded the Association for the Study of Negro Life and History in 1915, the *Journal of Negro History* in 1916, and *Negro History Week* in 1926.

92. Douglas, interview.

93. Williams, "Weekly Observations," July 29, 1932, 7.

94. LaMerle McCoy, interview by Alice Fowler, Sherrie Tucker, and Leonard Monroe, March 8, 2004, Lawrence/Douglas County African American Oral History Centennial Project, www.lawrence.lib.ks.us/oralhistory/1mccoy.

95. Jackson, interview.

96. Marquis Bey, *The Problem of the Negro as a Problem for Gender* (Minneapolis: University of Minnesota Press, 2020).

97. Joseph C. Thompson, "Spirit of Washington School" (1940), Kansas Memory, Kansas State Historical Society, Topeka, www.kansasmemory.org/item/209841.

98. Caliver, "Negro Teacher," 444.

99. E. George Payne, "The Reorganization and Redirection of Negro Education: A Critical Analysis," *Journal of Negro Education* 5, no. 3 (1936): 529.

100. Myrtle R. Phillips, "The Negro Secondary School Teacher," *Journal of Negro Education* 9 (July 1940): 484.

101. Williams, interview.

102. Daniel S. Sawyer to Topeka Board of Education, September 13, 1948, Lucinda Todd Papers, Kansas State Historical Society, Topeka.

103. "Our Need," 4.

104. Williams, interview.

105. "Colored Schools, Pupils and Teachers," 10.

106. Williams, "Challenge," 5.

107. "Colored Schools, Pupils and Teachers," 10; J. S. Hunnicutt, "Dedication," *OMAS*, 3.

108. Hunnicutt, "Dedication," 3.

109. Willie Jamaal Wright, "The Morphology of Marronage," *Annals of the American Association of Geographers* 110, no. 4 (2020): 1135.

110. L. S. Turner, "Foreword," *OMAS*, 2.

111. Williams, interview.

112. "Our Need," 4.

113. Five out of its eight contributors were born before 1900, including Mamie Williams. The other three, Myrtle Graves, Althea Mcbrier, and J. B. Holland were born in 1902, 1903, and 1910, respectively.

114. Kluger, *Simple Justice*, 378.

115. Williams, "Challenge," 6.

116. Williams, "Challenge," 11. This quote is attributed to an October 2, 1943, article written by Virginia State college professor Luther P. Jackson and published in the *Norfolk Journal and Guide*.

117. Williams, "Challenge," 13.

118. W. E. B. Du Bois, "Criteria of Negro Art," *Crisis* 32 (1926): 295.

119. Fred Moten, "The Case of Blackness," *Criticism* 50, no. 2 (2008): 177.

120. Williams, "Challenge," 8–9.

121. Mamie Williams, "Africa, the Early Home of the Negro," OMAS, 15.

122. Williams, "Africa," 16–17.

123. Williams, "Weekly Observations," March 31, 1933.

124. Williams, "Africa," 18.

125. Fannie Patton, "From Africa to America," OMAS, 20. Williams had taught in Topeka public schools for over twenty years.

126. Several Black scholars took issue with white historians' scholarship on slavery at the turn of the twentieth century. See John David Smith, "A Different View of Slavery: Black Historians Attack the Proslavery Argument, 1890–1920," *Journal of Negro History* 65, no. 4 (1980): 298–311.

127. Williams, "Challenge," 6.

128. Patton, "From Africa to America," 21.

129. "Supplement," OMAS, 51.

130. Du Bois, "Criteria of Negro Art," 295.

131. "Supplement," 59.

132. Mamie Williams, "Challenge," 11. This quote is attributed to Luther P. Jackson, Virginia State college professor and columnist for the *Norfolk Journal and Guide*.

133. "Supplement," 72–73.

134. Moten, "The Case of Blackness," 178.

135. Caliver, "Negro Teacher," 443.

136. Brittney Cooper, *Beyond Respectability: The Intellectual Thought of Race Women* (Champaign: University of Illinois Press, 2017), 89.

137. Chafe, *Remembering Jim Crow*, 125.

138. For more on Lee, see Thomas Aiello, "Editing a Paper in Hell: Davis Lee and the Exigencies of Smalltime Black Journalism," *American Journalism* 33, no. 2 (2016): 144–68.

139. Davis Lee, "Should Teachers Gamble?" *Capital Plaindealer*, November 29, 1936.

140. Davis Lee, "Three Drunken Teachers," *Capital Plaindealer*, December 13, 1936.

141. Davis Lee, "Fighting at McKinley Stirs: Versions of Those Concerned Given by Interviewer," *Capital Plaindealer*, February 14, 1937.

142. Jane Rhodes, "Pedagogies of Respectability: Race, Media, and Black Womanhood in the Early 20th Century," *Souls* 18, no. 2–4 (2016): 202.

143. Rhodes, "Pedagogies of Respectability," 203.

144. "Fight Bill for Split Schools: Segregation Proposal in Education Led by William Towers," *Capital Plaindealer*, January 24, 1937, 1.

145. Davis Lee, "Uncle Tom Bradshaw Leads Boycott Move: The Truth Has Not Been Told Fox Ridley Plays a Secret Role," *Capital Plaindealer*, March 7, 1937, 8. Ridley was the subject of Lee's derision in three other editorials; two accused him of "sins of commission," or of recruiting teachers from outside of Topeka instead of the "sons and daughters of Shawnee County taxpayers." The other charged him with racial treason for having a harmonious relationship with school superintendent A. J. Stout, whom Lee alleged was plotting to bar Black students from attending the city's junior high schools. Davis Lee, "Mr. Stout and Mr. Ridley," *Capital Plaindealer*, 8.

146. Minutes of the school board of education, March 8, 1937.

147. *Capital Plaindealer*, July 30, 1937, 4.

148. Ridley, interview.

149. Martin Holbraad, "Ontography and Alterity: Defining Anthropological Truth," *Social Analysis* 53, no. 2 (2009): 82.

Chapter Four

1. W. E. B. Du Bois, "The Tragedy of 'Jim Crow,'" *Crisis* 26 (August 1923): 170.

2. Minutes of the school board of education, June 5, 1939.

3. *Capital Plaindealer*, December 19, 1902.

4. According to William Bradshaw Jr., Veale, a white real estate developer, was concerned about the dual education system's increased cost to taxpayers. Constance Sawyer, interview by Jean Van Delinder, March 5, 1992, MS 251, Brown v. Topeka Board of Education Oral History Collection, State Archives and Library, Kansas State Historical Society, Topeka.

5. "Court House Notes and Police Gossip," *Topeka Daily Capital*, October 13, 1929. NAACP Topeka Branch Office Files, Kansas State Historical Society Collection, Topeka.

6. As discussed in chapter 2, Mexican and Mexican American students were integrated with whites in the fourth grade. The city's junior high schools were open to students of Indigenous and Latinx descent.

7. See Michael Fultz, "African American Teachers in the South, 1890–1940: Powerlessness and the Ironies of Expectations and Protest," *History of Education Quarterly* 35, no. 4 (1995): 419–20.

8. Graham v. Board of Education 153 Kan. 840 (1941), 843.

9. Mrs. Chas W. French to NAACP, October 14, 1929, NAACP Topeka Branch Office Files, Kansas State Historical Society Collection, Topeka.

10. Court House Notes," *Topeka Daily Capital*, October 13, 1929.

11. Richard Kluger, *Simple Justice: The History of* Brown v. Board of Education *and Black America's Struggle for Equality* (New York: Vintage Books, 1977), 379. After *Graham* was decided in 1941, Williams wrote an editorial in a local Black newspaper, the *Capital Plaindealer*.

12. *Graham*, 93.

13. Mamie Williams, "The Teaching Annals of Ella," 3, folder 111, box 6, Brown vs. Board of Education Collection, Manuscripts and Archives, Yale University Library, New Haven, CT.

14. *Graham*, 160.

15. Kluger, *Simple Justice*, 379.

16. *Graham*, 147.

17. Audra Simpson, *Mohawk Interruptus* (Durham, NC: Duke University Press, 2014), 177.

18. *Graham*, 152.

19. *Graham*, 140.

20. George Berkin, "Hortense Tate, 104, Montclair Activist," *Star-Ledger* (Newark, NJ), September 10, 2003.

21. *Graham*, 231.

22. *Graham*, 229–30.

23. *Graham*, 203.

24. *Graham*, 188–89.

25. *Graham*, 203 and 191.

26. Minutes of the school board of education, February 5, 1940.

27. George Lipsitz, *The Possessive Investment in Whiteness: How White People Profit from Identity Politics* (Philadelphia: Temple University Press, 1998), 215.

28. Minutes of the school board, February 5, 1940.

29. "Kansas Citizens Charge School Board Is Unfair: Ask Fair Play in Topeka School Affairs," *Capitol Plaindealer* (Topeka), June 7, 1940.

30. Tracy Thompson was a substitute teacher because the school board barred married women from full employment.

31. Joseph C. Thompson, *Spirit of Washington, Washington School, Topeka, Kansas* (1940), Kansas Memory, Kansas State Historical Society, Topeka, www.kansasmemory .org/item/209841.

32. Minutes of the school board of education, May 5, 1941.

33. "Kansas Supreme Court Flays Educational Discrimination: Rule Pupil Can Attend White Junior High," *Capital Plaindealer* (Topeka), June 20, 1941.

34. "Counsel for Topeka Youth File Motion for Judgment in Jim-Crow School Case," *Capital Plaindealer* (Topeka), February 14, 1941.

35. William Pickens to Mrs. Charles W. French, March 7, 1933, NAACP Topeka Branch Office Files, Kansas State Historical Society Collection, Topeka.

36. Mrs. Chas W. French to NAACP, March 12, 1933, NAACP Topeka Branch Office Files, Kansas State Historical Society Collection, Topeka.

37. Joe Thompson, interviewed by Ralph Crowder, October 25, 1991, MS 251, Brown v. Topeka Board of Education Oral History Collection, State Archives and Library, Kansas State Historical Society, Topeka (hereafter BOHC).

38. Kluger, *Simple Justice*, 386.

39. *Times-Observer*, May 28, 1892.

40. Minutes of the school board of education, June 23, 1941.

41. Minutes of the school board, June 23, 1941.

42. Thom Rosenblum, "Unlocking the Schoolhouse Doors: Elisha Scott, 'Colored Lawyer, Topeka,'" *Kansas History: A Journal of the Central Plains* 36 (Spring 2013): 46.

43. Minutes of the school board, June 23, 1941.

44. Minutes of the school board, June 23, 1941.

45. Minutes of the school board, June 23, 1941.

46. "Equal Education Decision Causes Uproar in Topeka," *Capital Plaindealer* (Topeka), July 4, 1941.

47. "Militant," *Capitol Plaindealer* (Topeka), September 27, 1936, 1.

48. "Equal Education Decision Causes Uproar in Topeka."

49. Minutes of the school board of education, July 7, 1941.

50. Minutes of the school board of education, July 11, 1941.

51. Minutes of the school board of education, August 4, 1941.

52. Minutes of the school board of education, August 8, 1941.

53. Minutes of the school board, August 8, 1941. Industrial arts teacher Al Rouce was also reduced to part-time employment.

54. Constance Sawyer, interviewed by Jean Van Delinder, March 5, 1992, MS 251, BOHC; Chapter News, *Ivy Leaf* (December 1942): 13.

55. Daniel S. Sawyer to Topeka Board of Education, September 13, 1948, Mrs. Lucinda Todd Papers, State Archives and Library, Kansas State Historical Society, Topeka.

56. In his groundbreaking study of the modern civil rights movement, sociologist Aldon Morris defined a local movement center as an organization through which a dispossessed or disenfranchised people "mobilizes, organizes, and coordinates" a challenge to a dominant power structure. Aldon Morris, *The Origins of the Civil Rights Movement: Black Communities Organizing for Change* (New York: New Press, 1984), 40.

57. Raymond J. Reynolds to Roy Wilkins, September 2, 1941, NAACP Topeka Branch Office Files, Kansas State Historical Society, Topeka.

58. Sawyer to Topeka Board.

59. Sawyer to Topeka Board.

60. See also Mary L. Dudziak, "The Limits of Good Faith: Desegregation in Topeka, Kansas, 1950–1956," *Law and History Review* 5, no. 2 (Autumn 1987): 351–91. Caldwell is mentioned more substantively in a short 2004 article written by Kendra Hamilton. Kendra Hamilton, "The View from Topeka," *Black Issues in Higher Education* 21, no. 7 (2004): 32–37.

Chapter Five

1. Citizens Committee on Civil Rights, "The People Fight Back," 1948, box 1, Mrs. Lucinda Todd Papers, State Archives and Library, Kansas State Historical Society, Topeka. (Emphasis in original document.)

2. Citizens Committee on Civil Rights, "The People Fight Back," https://www.kansasmemory.org/item/213389.

3. Francis Ward, "Historic School Desegregation Case Still Open," *Los Angeles Times*, May 13, 1974.

4. Constance Sawyer, interview by Jean Van Delinder, March 5, 1992, MS 251, Brown v. Topeka Board of Education Oral History Collection, State Archives and Library, Kansas State Historical Society, Topeka (hereafter BOHC).

5. Mamie Williams, interviewed by Richard Kluger, in her home, October 24, 1970, transcript, 2–3, folder 111, box 6, MS 759, Brown vs. Board of Education Collection, Manuscripts and Archives, Yale University Library, New Haven, CT.

6. Merrill Ross, interviewed by Richard Kluger, in his home, 1970, transcript, 2, folder 88, box 5, MS 759, Brown vs. Board of Education Collection, Manuscripts and Archives, Yale University Library, New Haven, CT.

7. Lucinda Todd, interviewed by Richard Kluger, in her home, October 22, 1970, transcript, 4, folder 98, box 5, MS 759, Brown vs. Board of Education Collection, Manuscripts and Archives, Yale University Library, New Haven, CT.

8. Daniel S. Sawyer to Topeka Board of Education, September 13, 1948, Mrs. Lucinda Todd Papers, State Archives and Library, Kansas State Historical Society, Topeka.

9. Todd, interview.

10. Citizens Committee on Civil Rights.

11. Lucinda Todd, "Background for *Brown vs. Board of Education* School Case," (nd), Mrs. Lucinda Todd Papers, State Archives and Library, Kansas State Historical Society, Topeka.

12. Robert L. Jamieson Jr., "A History Lesson on Getting Along," *Seattle PI*, February 9, 2007.

13. Black Past and University of Washington websites feature the same Caldwell biography, which states that "he worked alongside others to aid desegregation efforts." See also "H. L. Caldwell, Principal of Roxhill, Dies," *Seattle Times*, September 4, 1964, 10.

14. Saidiya Hartman, "Venus in Two Acts," *Small Axe: A Journal of Criticism* 12, no. 2 (2008): 3.

15. For more on articulations of whiteness and anti-Black violence in Kansas during the nineteenth century, see Brent M. S. Campney, *This Is Not Dixie* (Champaign: University of Illinois Press), 2015.

16. Linda McMurray Edwards, "George Washington Carver," *Encyclopedia of Alabama*, March 2, 2007, http://encyclopediaofalabama.org/article/h-1064.

17. Gordon Parks, *The Learning Tree* (New York: Random House, 1963), 20. In the reminiscent poem "Kansas Land" Parks describes his childhood memories of the Plains state. He concludes, "Yes, all this I would miss—along with the fear, hatred and violence we Blacks had suffered upon this beautiful land."

18. Parks, *Voices in the Mirror: An Autobiography* (New York: Doubleday, 1990), 12.

19. The upgrade was not warranted by an increasing population. By state statute, cities of the first-class in Kansas were defined as those with a population of over 15,000. Fort Scott had a population of 12,000 in 1888. Chris J. Cluck, "Years before *Brown v. Board* There Was Crawford Case," *Ft. Scott Tribune*, July 2, 1997, 1–2.

20. Parks, *Learning Tree*, 20.

21. "A Race War Is on at Ft. Scott Schools," *Colored Citizen* (Fort Scott), September 21, 1900, 1. Privileging whiteness was expensive but worthwhile for white citizens. Providing a second Jim Crow school for Black students cost the district $2.50 per student, compared to neighborhood schools, which only cost eighty cents per student.

22. Lorraine Madway, "Documenting Art and History: The 'Back to Fort Scott' Materials in the Gordon Parks Papers," *Great Plains Quarterly* 36, no. 2 (2016): 86.

23. Parks, *Voices in the Mirror*, 2.

24. Rebekah Schilperoort, "Students Learn about Seattle's First Black Principal," *West Seattle Herald*, February 28, 2007.

25. The plaintiffs in *Thurman-Watts v. The Board of Education of Coffeyville* won their case because it was illegal to segregate high school students, not because the school board members' affiliation with a white supremacist organization established their racist intent to segregate Black schoolchildren.

26. Joe Douglas, interview by Ralph Crowder, October 24, 1991, MS 251, BOHC.

27. John Scott, interviewed by Richard Kluger, October 21, 1970, handwritten notes, folder 98, box 5, p. 311, MS 759, Brown vs. Board of Education Collection, Manuscripts and Archives, Yale University Library, New Haven, CT.

28. Berdyne Scott, interview by Ralph Crowder, November 24, 1991, MS 251, BOHC.

29. Douglas, interview.

30. Johanna Hall, "The African-American Community in Topeka, Kansas, 1940–1951: Crucial Years Before Brown" (master's thesis, University of Kansas, 1993), 35.

31. Jack Alexander, interviewed by Ralph Crowder, 1991, MS 251, BOHC.

32. Williams, interview.

33. Williams, interview.

34. Richard Kluger, *Simple Justice: The History of* Brown v. Board of Education *and Black America's Struggle for Equality* (New York: Vintage Books, 1977), 382.

35. Kluger, *Simple Justice*, 382.

36. Ross, interview, 1970.

37. Merrill Ross, interview by Jean Van Delinder, November 13, 1991, MS 251, BOHC.

38. Ross, interview, 1970.

39. Ross, interview, November 13, 1991.

40. Ross, interview, November 13, 1991.

41. Minutes of the school board of education, February 8, 1946, and April 8, 1946. Graham was fired again four days after his reinstatement.

42. Douglas, interview.

43. Douglas, interview.

44. Richard Ridley, interviewed by Jean Van Delinder, Jan. 21, 1992, MS 251, BOHC.

45. Kluger, *Simple Justice*, 383.

46. John Scott, interview.

47. Hall, "African-American Community," 68.

48. Linda Laird, "Todd Was Key Figure in Struggle," *Topeka Capital-Journal*, April 18, 1993.

49. Todd, interview; the *Daily Capital* broke its silence on Black educational issues when it revealed the conflict between the NAACP and Black school preservationists two weeks after Tabor's editorial. "Colored Groups Disagree on Their School Problems," *Topeka Daily Capital*, April 24, 1948, 6.

50. Milton Tabor, "Topeka Roundup," *Topeka Daily Capital*, April 11, 1948, 13A.

51. Mrs. Lucinda Todd Papers, State Archives and Library, Kansas State Historical Society, Topeka.

52. Milton Tabor to Arthur Capper, February 11, 1947, Kansas Memory, Kansas State Historical Society, Topeka, www.kshs.org/km/items/view/217653. During World War II, white Southerners feared an uprising among Black domestic workers as stories spread of their unionization and potential refusal to work in white homes. There were also rumors that these "Eleanor Clubs," inspired by labor and civil rights advocate Eleanor Roosevelt, conspired to have "a white woman in every kitchen by Christmas." Bryant Simon, "Fearing Eleanor: Racial Anxieties and Wartime Rumors in the American South, 1940–1945," in *Labor in the Modern South*, ed. Glenn T. Eskew (Athens: University of Georgia Press, 2001).

53. Lucinda Todd to Milton Tabor, April 11, 1948, folder 2, box 1, Mrs. Lucinda Todd Papers, State Archives and Library, Kansas State Historical Society, Topeka.

54. Laird, "Todd Was Key Figure."

55. The highest-paid administrator in Topeka public schools in 1952 was the Topeka High School principal, who had an annual salary of $7,500.

56. "Our Need," *Of Merit, Achievement and Service: Studies in Negro Life*, 4, folder 111, box 6, Brown vs. Board of Education Collection, Manuscripts and Archives, Yale University Library, New Haven, CT.

57. Harrison Caldwell, "Studies in Negro Life: A Report Presented to Dr Cloy Hobson, Professor of Education, the University of Kansas, Lawrence, KS" (Summer 1953): 12. Harrison L. Caldwell papers, 1942–64, University of Washington Libraries Manuscripts and Archives, Seattle.

58. Caldwell, "Studies in Negro Life," 12.

59. Caldwell, "Studies in Negro Life," 13.

60. Caldwell, "Studies in Negro Life," 38. Caldwell attributed the latter part of the quote to Tracy Thompson, former teacher and founder of the Kansas Colored Parent-Teacher Association.

61. "Negro's Skill Not Fully Utilized," newspaper and date unknown, Harrison Caldwell papers.

62. Lucinda Todd, fundraising speech (draft), Des Moines, IA, 1953. Lucinda Todd Collection, Kansas State Historical Society, Topeka.

63. Harrison Caldwell, "Sunday Meditation: Democracy and Christian Life" (1947), Harrison Caldwell papers, 1942–64, University of Washington Libraries Manuscripts and Archives, Seattle.

64. "Chapter News," *Ivy Leaf*, December 1943.

65. Ross, interview, 1970.

66. Minutes Topeka YMCA-George Washington Carver, February 21, 1949, State Archives and Library, Kansas State Historical Society, Topeka.

67. Mamie Williams and Mrs. Pearl Anderson, "Harrison Caldwell (Double Acrostic)," March 6, 1946, Harrison Caldwell papers, 1942–64, University of Washington Libraries Manuscripts and Archives, Seattle.

68. Ross, interview, 1970.

69. Louis R. Harlan and Raymond Smock, *Booker T. Washington in Perspective Essays of Louis R. Harlan* (Jackson: University of Mississippi, 1988), 151.

70. *Kansas City Call*, March 31, 1950.

71. "Audit Reports Criticize Improper Handling of School Funds, Warn Board Repeatedly," *Topeka Daily Capital*, March 25, 1951.

72. Caldwell, "Studies in Negro Life," 9.

73. "Pupils Bare Their Hearts," *Seattle Times*, November 5, 1956.

Chapter Six

1. Minutes of the school board of education, April 23, 1948.

2. "Colored Groups Disagree on Their School Problems," *Topeka Daily Capital*, April 24, 1948, 6.

3. Lucinda Todd, "Background for Brown vs. Board of Education School Case," (nd), Mrs. Lucinda Todd Papers, State Archives and Library, Kansas State Historical Society, Topeka.

4. Noliwe Rooks, *Cutting School: Privatization, Segregation, and the End of Public Education* (New York: New Press, 2017), 93.

5. Richard Ridley, interviewed by Jean Van Delinder, Jan. 21, 1992, MS 251, Brown v. Topeka Board of Education Oral History Collection, State Archives and Library, Kansas State Historical Society, Topeka (hereafter BOHC).

6. Minutes of the school board of education, April 23, 1948.

7. James C. Scott, "Infrapolitics and Mobilizations: A Response by James C. Scott," *Revue française d'études américaines* 131, no. 1 (2012): 112–17.

8. Ewa Majewski, "On Weakness, Solidarity, and Non-Heroic Resistance. The Weak Avant-Garde: A Feminist Analysis Lecture by Ewa Majewska," filmed March 16, 2016, at Museum of Modern Art in Warsaw, video, 1:41:51, https://artmuseum.pl/en/doc/video-muzeum-otwarte-o-slabosci-solidarnosci-i-nie-heroicznym.

9. Kansas assistant attorney general Paul Wilson also relies upon this narrative in his autobiography. Paul Wilson, *A Time to Lose: Representing Kansas in Brown v. Board of Education* (Lawrence: University of Kansas, 1995).

10. Richard Kluger, *Simple Justice: The History of Brown v. Board of Education and Black America's Struggle for Equality* (New York: Vintage Books, 1977), 375.

11. John Scott, interviewed by Richard Kluger, October 21, 1970, handwritten notes, 311, folder 124, box 12, MS 759, Brown vs. Board of Education Collection, Manuscripts and Archives, Yale University Library, New Haven, CT.

12. Bolivar Watkins to Lucille Black, February 18, 1946, NAACP Topeka Branch Office Files, Kansas State Historical Society Collection, Topeka.

13. Lucinda Todd, interview by Richard Kluger, in her home, October 22, 1970, transcript, 4, folder 98, box 5, MS 759, Brown vs. Board of Education Collection, Manuscripts and Archives, Yale University Library, New Haven, CT.

14. Maurita Davis, interviewed by Jean Van Delinder, July 15, 1994, MS 251, BOHC.

15. Davis, interview.

16. Lena Burnett, interview by Richard Kluger, in her home, transcript, 3, folder 13, box 1, MS 759, Brown vs. Board of Education Collection, Manuscripts and Archives, Yale University Library, New Haven, CT.

17. Davis, interview.

18. Burnett, interview.

19. Burnett, interview.

20. Burnett, interview.

21. David Long, "Topekan Meets with Carter," Topeka newspaper unknown, May 29, 1977, Lucinda Todd Papers, Kansas State Historical Society, Topeka.

22. Lucinda Todd, interviewed by Ralph Crowder, MS 251, BOHC.

23. Todd, interview, n.d.

24. Linda Laird, "Todd Was Key Figure in Struggle," *Topeka Capital-Journal*, April 18, 1993.

25. Todd, interview, n.d.

26. Kluger, *Simple Justice*, 393.

27. Lucille Black to Vera Forbes, October 20, 1949, NAACP Topeka Branch Office Files, Kansas State Historical Society Collection, Topeka.

28. Lucinda Todd, fundraising speech, Des Moines, IA (1953), Mrs. Lucinda Todd Papers, State Archives and Library, Kansas State Historical Society, Topeka.

29. Mamie Williams, interviewed by Richard Kluger, in her home, October 24, 1970, transcript, 2–3, folder 111, box 6, MS 759, Brown vs. Board of Education Collection, Manuscripts and Archives, Yale University Library, New Haven, CT.

30. Constance Sawyer, interview by Jean Van Delinder, March 5, 1992, MS 251, Brown v. Topeka Board of Education Oral History Collection, State Archives and Library, Kansas State Historical Society, Topeka.

31. Williams, interview; Todd, interview, October 22, 1970.

32. Todd, "Background."

33. Citizens Committee on Civil Rights, "The People Fight Back," 1948, box 1, Mrs. Lucinda Todd Papers, State Archives and Library, Kansas State Historical Society, Topeka.

34. Todd, fundraising speech.

35. Todd, "Background."

36. Citizens Committee on Civil Rights, "The People Fight Back." (Emphasis in original document.)

37. Daniel S. Sawyer to Topeka Board of Education, September 13, 1948, Kansas Memory, Kansas State Historical Society, Topeka, www.kshs.org/index.php?url=km/items/view/213393.

38. Counter Abstract and Brief of Appellees, Wright v. Board of Education of Topeka (1930), p. 10, Kansas Supreme Court records, State Archives and Library, Kansas State Historical Society, Topeka.

39. Minutes of the school board of education, September 13, 1948.

40. Minutes of the school board, September 13, 1948.

41. John Scott, interviewed by Richard Kluger, October 21, 1970, folder 98, box 5, MS 759, Brown vs. Board of Education Collection, Manuscripts and Archives, Yale University Library, New Haven, CT.

42. Todd, fundraising speech.

43. Todd, fundraising speech.

44. Sawyer, interview.

45. McKinley Burnett to Walter White, May 24, 1948, NAACP Topeka Branch Office Files, Kansas State Historical Society Collection, Topeka.

46. Todd, interview, October 22, 1970.

47. Burnett to White.

48. Todd, interview, October 22, 1970.

49. Williams, interview.

50. Gloster B. Current to McKinley Burnett, June 3, 1948, NAACP Topeka Branch Office Files, Kansas State Historical Society Collection, Topeka.

51. Williams, interview.

52. The highest-paid administrator in Topeka public schools in 1952 was the Topeka High School principal, who had an annual salary of $7,500.

53. Berdyne Scott, interview by Ralph Crowder, November 24, 1991, MS 251, BOHC.

54. Todd, interview, n.d.

55. Ridley, interview.

56. Ridley, interview.

57. Burnett, interview.

58. Charles Baston, interview by Jean Van Delinder, May 14, 1992, MS 251, BOHC.

59. Baston, interview.

60. McKinley Burnett to Walter White, September 1, 1950, Mrs. Lucinda Todd Papers, State Archives and Library, Kansas State Historical Society, Topeka.

61. Minutes of the school board of education, August 7, 1950.

62. "Petro New Head of School Board," *Topeka Daily Capital*, August 8, 1950, 2.

63. Kluger, *Simple Justice*, 394.

64. Minutes of the school board of education, August 7, 1950.

65. Todd, "Background."

66. Lucinda Todd to Walter White, August 29, 1950, Mrs. Lucinda Todd Papers, State Archives and Library, Kansas State Historical Society, Topeka.

67. Williams, interview.

68. Williams, interview.

69. Davis, interview.

70. Nancy Stoetzer, "35 Years Ago the Fight for This Classroom Began," *Topeka Capital Journal*, May 14, 1989.

71. Leola Brown Montgomery, interview by Ralph Crowder, Nov. 15, 1991, MS 251, BOHC.

72. Joe Douglas, interview by Ralph Crowder, Oct. 24, 1991, MS 251, BOHC.

73. Those women were Dorothy (Page) Crawford, Ada Mae Eggleston, Althea McBrier, Eva Montgomery, Mildred North, Fannie O. Patton, Myrtle (Graves) Starns, Ethel Williams, and Mamie Williams.

74. Williams, interview.

75. Jack Greenberg to Charles E. Bledsoe, May 25, 1951, Charles S. Scott Collection, The Kansas Collection, University of Kansas Spencer Research Library, University of Kansas, Lawrence.

76. Abstract of Pleadings/Statement of Facts/Brief of Evidence, Brown v. Board of Education of Topeka (1951), Charles S. Scott Collection, The Kansas Collection, University of Kansas Spencer Research Library, University of Kansas.

77. "The Superintendents," 168, Brown vs. Board of Education Collection, folder 124, box 12, MS 759, Manuscripts and Archives, Yale University Library, New Haven.

78. Wilson, *A Time to Lose*, 86.

79. Robert L. Carter to Herbert Bell, September 14, 1951, Mrs. Lucinda Todd Papers, State Archives and Library, Kansas State Historical Society, Topeka.

80. Todd, interview, October 22, 1970.

81. "North Topeka West Topeka, KS Neighborhood Plan," the North Topeka West Neighborhood Improvement Association & Topeka Planning Department, February 16, 2016, https://s3.amazonaws.com/cot-wp-uploads/wp-content/uploads/planning/1NTW2015NHPlanFinal-Approved2-16-16.pdf.

82. Minutes of the school board of education, November 5, 1951.

83. Todd, interview, October 22, 1970.

84. Jacqueline Trescott, "Reflections on a Milestone Past: 25 Years Since the Brown Decision," *Washington Post*, May 17, 1979.

85. Berdyne Scott, interview.

86. Kluger, *Simple Justice*, 393.

87. Mamie Williams to Richard Kluger, February 28, 1975, MS 759, Brown vs. Board of Education Collection, Manuscripts and Archives, Yale University Library, New Haven, CT.

88. The Todd family received a veiled threat from a white citizen by mail after the *Brown* decision. Lucinda Todd kept a handwritten note on a newspaper picture of Linda Brown and Lucinda Todd that read, "There's trouble in every school where niggers and whites are mixed. Niggers are animals." Folder 61, box 1, Mrs. Lucinda Todd Papers, State Archives and Library, Kansas State Historical Society, Topeka.

89. Montgomery, interview.

90. Charles Bennett, the school board member who challenged McKinley Burnett to a physical fight, was one of the school board members who voted in favor of firing newly hired Black teachers.

91. "Sparks Fly Over Dismissal of 6 Negro Teachers," *Kansas American*, April 10, 1953, 1.

92. Wendell Godwin to Darla Buchanan, March 13, 1953, Charles S. Scott Collection, The Kansas Collection, University of Kansas Spencer Research Library, University of Kansas.

93. Robert Carter to McKinley Burnett, March 31, 1953, Mrs. Lucinda Todd Papers, State Archives and Library, Kansas State Historical Society, Topeka.

94. J. B. Holland, interview by Richard Kluger, in his home, folder 124, box 12, MS 759, Brown vs. Board of Education Collection, Manuscripts and Archives, Yale University Library, New Haven, CT.

95. Lucinda Todd to Lucille Black, August 14, 1953, NAACP Topeka Branch Office Files, Kansas State Historical Society Collection, Topeka.

96. St. John African Methodist Episcopal Church, National Register of Historic Places Registration Form, October 16, 2008, www.kshs.org/resource/national_register/nominationsNRDB/Shawnee_StJohnAfricanMethodistEpiscopalChurchNR.pdf.

97. Zelma Henderson, interview by Ralph Crowder, January 31, 1992, MS 251, BOHC.

98. Jan Biles, "Plaintiffs Fought Discrimination: Some Students Felt Comfortable in Segregated Schools but Lost Out on Education," *Topeka Capital-Journal*, May 9, 2004.

99. Sawyer, interview.

100. Todd, interview, n.d. Among the teachers who were members of St. John AME were Ezekiel Ridley, Ruth Ridley, El Dorothy Scott, Katherine King, Diantha Booker Reynolds, Lilian Craw, Othella Oglesby, Hester Hardeman, Loyce Abbott, and Jeanette Temple.

101. E. B. Hicks, interview by Jean Van Delinder, November 22, 1991, MS 251, BOHC.

102. Williams, interview.

103. Burnett, interview; Francis Ward, "Historic School Desegregation Case Still Open," *Los Angeles Times*, May 13, 1974.

104. Lucinda Todd to Lucille Black, June 3, 1953, NAACP Topeka Branch Office Files, Kansas State Historical Society Collection, Topeka.

105. Lucinda Todd to Lucille Black, August 14, 1953, NAACP Topeka Branch Office Files, Kansas State Historical Society Collection, Topeka.

106. Johanna Hall, "The African-American Community in Topeka, Kansas, 1940–1951: Crucial Years Before Brown" (master's thesis, University of Kansas, 1991), 77.

107. Jeanette Dandridge, interviewed by Jean Van Delinder, June 14, 1992, MS 251, BOHC.

108. Lucinda Todd, interviewed by Ralph Crowder, MS 251, BOHC.

109. During that same time period, the Topeka school board employed forty Black women as schoolteachers; half of those teachers could be confirmed as AKAs.

110. Flossie Holland, basileus/president; Emma Cooper, anti-basileus/vice president; Dorothy Bradshaw, grammateus/recording secretary; Katherine King, epistoleus/corresponding secretary; Dorothy Crawford, dean of pledges; Geraldine Harmon, parlimentarian; undergraduate advisors: Ada Eggleston, Mattie Bradshaw, Ada Brock, Hester Hardemann, Barbara Jackson (Ross), Eva Montgomery, Myrtle Starnes, Jeanette Temple, and Ethel Williams.

111. Stoetzer, "35 Years Ago."

112. Deborah Dandridge, interviewed by Jean Van Delinder, July 26, 1994, MS 251, BOHC.

113. J. Dandridge, interview; Louise and Berdyne Scott, the wives of *Brown* attorneys John and Charles Scott, were members of Delta Sigma Theta, as was Harrison Caldwell's wife, Valeria.

114. Nancy Todd Noches to *Ebony* magazine, April 11, 2004, Mrs. Lucinda Todd Papers, State Archives and Library, Kansas State Historical Society, Topeka.

115. D. Dandridge, interview.

116. Davis, interview.

117. Brown v. Board of Education of Topeka, 347 U.S. 483 (1954).

Conclusion

1. William Barry Furlong, "The Case of Linda Brown: Now a High-School Senior, a Girl Who Made History at 9 Looks Back on the Trying Days of 'Brown vs. the Board of Education,'" *New York Times*, February 12, 1961.

2. Richard Kluger, *Simple Justice: The History of* Brown v. Board of Education *and Black America's Struggle for Equality* (New York: Vintage Books, 1977), 4.

3. Mamie Williams, interviewed by Richard Kluger, in her home, October 24, 1970, folder 111, box 6, MS 759, Brown vs. Board of Education Collection, Manuscripts and Archives, Yale University Library, New Haven, CT.

4. Kluger, *Simple Justice*, 379.

5. Stanley Stalter, July 27, 1994, MS 251, Brown v. Topeka Board of Education Oral History Collection, State Archives and Library, Kansas State Historical Society, Topeka (hereafter BOHC).

6. Minutes of the school board of education, September 8, 1953.

7. Lucinda Todd, interviewed by Ralph Crowder, MS 251, BOHC.

8. Minutes of the school board of education, June 5, 1935.

9. Carolyn L. Wims Campbell, interview by Eric Sexton, March 25, 2022, Kansas Oral History Project Inc., Kansas Oral History Collection, Topeka, https://ksoralhistory .org/interview/interview-of-carolyn-l-wims-campbell-by-eric-sexton-march-25-2022 /?sf_data=all&_sfm_interviewee_details_interviewee_political_party=Democrat& _sfm_interviewee_details_interviewee_gender=Female&_sfm_tags_significant _years=2770.

10. Zelma Henderson, interview by Ralph Crowder, January 31, 1992, MS 251, BOHC.

11. Jan Biles, "On the Front Line," *Topeka Capital-Journal*, May 9, 2004.

12. Leola Brown Montgomery, interview by Ralph Crowder, Nov. 15, 1991, MS 251, BOHC.

13. Dennis Kelly, "Roots of Integration: 'Brown v. Board' turns 40," *USA Today*, February 16, 1994.

14. J. B. Holland, interview by Richard Kluger, in his home, folder 124, box 12, MS 759, Brown vs. Board of Education Collection, Manuscripts and Archives, Yale University Library, New Haven, CT.

15. La Vonne I. Neal and Alicia L. Moore, "Their Cries Went up Together: *Brown et al. v. Board of Education* Then and Now," *Journal of Curriculum and Supervision* 20, no. 1 (Fall 2004): 11.

16. Katherine L. Sawyer, "Legacy of Brown: Topeka Resident Recalls Testifying as a Child," *Topeka Capital-Journal*, May 10, 2014.

17. Kendra Hamilton, "The View from Topeka," *Black Issues in Higher Education*, May 20, 2004, 35. According to Joan Preston Cerstvik, white students used to all-white schools also experienced "a certain level of discomfort" with the sudden integration of Black students in their classrooms. "A wariness or suspicion of others was apparent on both sides," she said. Joan Preston Cerstvik, "Wisdom, Hindsight Render *Brown's* Goals 'Incomplete,'" *Black Issues in Higher Education*, May 20, 2004, 36.

18. Hamilton, "View from Topeka," 35.

19. Deborah Scott, interviewed by Jean Van Delinder, November 15, 1991, MS 251, BOHC.

20. "Kansas Begins Purge of Negro Teachers," *Kansas City Call*, April 10, 1953.

21. Minutes of the school board of education, October 21, 1953.

22. "Pupils Bare Their Hearts," *Seattle Times*, November 5, 1956.

23. Anna Mary Murphy, "Major Problem in Kansas: Negro Teachers Hit by Deseg-regation," *Topeka Capital*, January 29, 1956.

24. "Case Is a Paradox," *Kansas City Star*, May 17, 1954.

25. Sawyer, "Legacy of Brown."

26. NAACP Legal and Educational Fund to Foundations, "Program to Protect Negro Teachers from Dismissal as a Result of Integration of Public Schools," 1955, folder 13, box 9, John W. Davis Papers, Howard University Moorland-Spingarn Research Center, Washington, DC.

27. Barbara Ross, interviewed by Jean Van Delinder, Nov. 13, 1991, MS 251, BOHC.

28. Holland, interview. Kappa Alpha Psi members Raymond Reynolds and Elisha Scott were also critical civil rights attorneys who paved the road to *Brown*.

29. Adam Fairclough, *Teaching Equality: Black Schools in the Age of Jim Crow* (Athens: University of Georgia Press, 2001), 66.

30. Graham v. Board of Education 153 Kan. 840 (1941), 203.

31. Holland, interview.

32. El Dorothy Scott, interview by Jean Van Delinder, Jan. 27, 1992, MS 251, BOHC.

33. Minutes of the school board of education, March 7, 1955.

34. Minutes of the school board of education, January 18, 1956.

35. Holland, interview.

36. Deborah Dandridge, interviewed by Jean Van Delinder, July 26, 1994, MS 251, BOHC.

37. Pamela G. Hollie, "A Look at the *Brown* Case 25 Years Later," *New York Times*, May 16, 1979.

38. Dandridge, interview.

39. Thayer Brown Phillips, interviewed by Ralph Crowder, November 20, 1991, MS 251, BOHC.

40. Beryl Ann New, "Legacy of *Brown*: Topeka Neighborhood Helped Shape Long-time Educator," *Topeka Capital-Journal*, May 10, 2014.

41. Minutes of the school board of education, January 18, 1956, and June 20, 1956.

42. Minutes of the school board of education, February 4, 1957.

43. Fred Rausch, interviewed by Cheryl Brown Henderson, October 12, 1994, MS 251, BOHC.

44. Minutes of the school board of education, June 3, 1957.

45. Phil Anderson, "In 1954, Students Felt Impact of Integration in Topeka Elemen-tary Schools," *Topeka Capital-Journal*, April 28, 2019, 37.

46. Minutes of the school board of education, September 3, 1957.

47. "Negro Teachers Faced Hard Task," *Topeka Daily Capital*, August 7, 1961.

48. Minutes of the school board of education, June 4, 1956.

49. Stalter, interview.

50. Frank Wilson, October 12, 1994, MS 251, BOHC.

51. Stalter, interview.

52. Anderson, "In 1954, Students Felt Impact," 37.

53. Brent Green, "A Heroic Black Teacher in an All-White School," *Medium*, August 20, 2021, https://boomermarketing.medium.com/how-a-Black-superhero-teacher-defeated-jim-crow-in-an-all-white-school-bf32d7169d98.

54. Wilson, interview.

55. Holland, interview.

56. W. E. B. Du Bois, "Strivings of the Negro People," *Atlantic*, August 1897, www .theatlantic.com/magazine/archive/1897/08/strivings-of-the-negro-people/305446/.

57. B. Ross, interview.

58. Linda Tillman, "African American Principals and the Legacy of *Brown*," *Review of Research in Education* 28 (2004): 112; in 1976, educator and civil rights advocate J. Rupert Picott reported that the number of Black principals in the South dropped 90 percent between 1964 and 1973. J. Picott, "A Quarter Century of the Black Experience in Elementary and Secondary Education, 1950–1974," *Negro Educational Review* (1976): 45.

59. E. Scott, interview.

60. Furlong, "The Case of Linda Brown."

61. B. Ross, interview.

62. Merrill Ross, interviewed by Jean Van Delinder, Nov. 13, 1991, MS 251, BOHC.

63. B. Ross, interview.

64. M. Ross, interview.

65. Richard Ridley, interviewed by Jean Van Delinder, Jan. 21, 1992, MS 251, BOHC.

66. Hollie, "A Look at the *Brown* Case."

67. B. Ross, interview.

68. Brown v. Board of Education of Topeka, 347 US 483 (1954).

69. Hollie, "A Look at the *Brown* Case."

70. Thurgood Marshall, "Justice Thurgood Marshall's Opinion in the *Bakke* Case," *Crisis* 86, no. 2 (1979): 45.

71. Mamie Williams, "Weekly Observations," *Plaindealer* (Topeka), December 9, 1932.

72. Donna Haraway, "Situated Knowledges: The Science Question in Feminism and the Privilege of Partial Perspective," *Feminist Studies* 14, no. 3 (1988): 575–99.

73. According to the National Center for Education Statistics, 26 percent of Black students were enrolled in charters schools in 2016, and 15 percent were enrolled in traditional public schools. "School Choice in the United States: 2019," National Center for Education Statistics, access date July 20, 2022, https://nces.ed.gov/programs /schoolchoice/ind_02.asp.

74. Derrell Bradford, "Bradford: For Black Families Focused on Education, the NAACP Just Committed 'the Worst Kind of Betrayal,'" *The 74*, July 27, 2017, www .the74million .org/article/bradford-for-Black-families-focused-on-education-the -naacp-just-committed-the-worst-kind-of-betrayal/.

75. Howard Fuller, "Fuller: NAACP's Attack on Charter Schools Hurts Black Students," *Milwaukee Journal Sentinel*, August 3, 2017.

76. Lori Higgins, "In Detroit, a Push to Use African-American History and Culture to Help Students Succeed," *Chalkbeat Detroit*, March 26, 2019.

77. Kristen A. Graham, "Philly's Black-Led Charter Schools Are Treated Unfairly, New Group Says," *Philadelphia Inquirer*, November 24, 2020.

78. Jerome Morris, "Closures of Black K-12 Schools across the Nation Threaten Neighborhood Stability," *Conversation*, June 25, 2021. For more on Farragut Elementary

as a valued Black school, see Jerome E. Morris, "A 'Communally Bonded' School for African American Students, Families, and a Community," *Phi Delta Kappan* 84, no. 3 (2002): 230–34.

79. Interestingly, both schools were all white prior to *Brown*. White resistance to desegregation in both neighborhoods capitulated once the racial demographics shifted to predominantly Black. Farragut admitted Black students in 1956 and Whitefoord in 1961.

80. Bryce Huffman, "Loss of African-Centered Schools in Detroit Hurts Black Children the Most," *Michigan Radio*, February 15, 2019, www.michiganradio.org /education/2019-02-15/loss-of-african-centered-schools-in-detroit-hurts-Black-chil dren-the-most.

81. Graham, "Philly's Black-Led Charter Schools."

82. James T. Patterson, Brown v. Board of Education: *A Civil Rights Milestone and Its Troubled Legacy* (Oxford: Oxford University Press, 2001), 168.

83. Graham, "Philly's Black-Led Charter Schools."

84. "Resolution: Calling for Moratorium on Charter School Expansion and Strengthening of Oversight in Governance and Practice," NAACP, 2016, https://naacp.org /resources/calling-moratorium-charter-school-expansion-and-strengthening -oversight-governance-and.

85. Beryl Ann New, "Legacy of *Brown*."

Index

Note: Pages in *italics* refer to illustrative matter.

Abbott, Loyce, 199
abolitionist movement, 17–18, 23–24, 70, 215n27
accommodationism, racial, 28, 50, 74, 75, 91, 123, 127, 137, 141–46, 148, 154–55
affirmative action, 30, 202
African American Charter School Coalition (AACSC), 207
Akua, Chike, 205
Aldridge, Ira, 96
Alexander, Jack, 31, 32, 71, 77, 138–39
alien land laws, 22–23
Allen, Henry J., 22
Alpha Iota Omega sorority, 178, 179
Alpha Kappa Alpha (AKA) sorority, 66, 107, 126, 147, 157, 178–79, 240n109
alternative historical narrative, 6–13, 102–3
AME Church. *See* St. John AME Church
American Civil Liberties Union (ACLU), 26
Anderson, Marian, 95, 146
anti-Asian racism, 22. *See also* racism
anti-Black racism. *See* racism
anti-Black violence, 23–25. *See also* racism
anti-immigrant racism, 22. *See also* Mexicans and Mexican Americans; racism
anti-integration school activism, 1–12; between 1918–1942, 44–49; Black Topekans v. Topeka Board of Education, 49–56; Black Topekans v. Topeka school boards, 56–61; *Graham* case and, 102–7, 130–34; racial

subjectivities in, 67–68; roots of, 70–78. *See also* Black school preservationism; *Graham v. Board of Education of Topeka*; school integration, overview; separate-but-equal standard
antisegregation school activism, 14, 39–41, 150–52. See also *Brown v. Board of Education of Topeka*; school integration, overview; separate-but-equal standard
anti-slavery movement. *See* abolitionist movement
Argentine, Kansas, 45–46
Arn, Edward, 16
athletics, 30–31
Atlanta, Georgia, 206

Bagley, W. C., 80
Barbour, Ethel, *166*
Barker, Katherine, 84
basketball, 30, 31–32, 139–40
Baston, Charles, 33, 72, 168, 217n76
benevolent whiteness, 19–21, 22, 70, 131. *See also* whiteness-as-property
Bennett, Charles, 151, 158, 159
Bethune, Mary McLeod, 95, 146
Black, Lucille, 175
Black churches, 66, 176–77, 187, 213n34
Black educators: 1937–38, attacks against, 97–100; *Brown* case's effects on, 174–75, 186–200; under Caldwell, 137–45; economic and educational concerns of, 164–67; educational degrees of, 108, 192, 226n40; as *Graham* case witnesses, 107–15;

Black educators (cont.)
  salaries of, 50, 78, 91, 145, 165,
  221n45; on segregated schools, 69,
  72–78. See also *names of specific
  persons*; principalships
Black futurities, 67, 70, 92, 100, 108,
  141, 154, 203
Black geographies, 82
Blackness, 20–21, 27, 50, 51, 65, 83–86,
  203
Black Panther Party, 205
Black Parent-Teacher Association, 103–4
Black refusal, 26–30
Black school preservationism, 15, 103,
  114–15, 118–19, 121, 123, 124, 130,
  133, 151–54, 162, 172–75. *See also*
  anti-integration school activism
Black sociality, 30–32, 176–80
Black studies curriculum, 90–92,
  128–29. See also *Of Merit, Achievement
  and Service (OMAS)*
bleeding Kansas, as term, 3, 16, 17, 21,
  59
Booth, Marthella, 162
Boswell Junior High School, 102
Bousfield, Maudelle Brown, 95
Bradford, Derrell, 205
Bradshaw, Dorothy, 55, *166*
Bradshaw, Eliza, 58–59
Bradshaw, Mattie, 58–59, 99, 107, 111,
  116, 125, 179
Bradshaw, Maytie, 99, 107, 116, 125,
  126, 170, 179
Bradshaw, William: on *Foster* case,
  121–22, 156–57; on *Graham* case,
  105–12, 157; segregationist activism
  by, 57, 58–59, 62, 68, 99; as Topeka
  NAACP member, 116
Branner Annex School, 46–49, 112
Branner Elementary School, 46–47, 112
Brewer Normal School, 79
Briggs v. Elliott, 183
Brown, Hezekiah, 223n113
Brown, John W., 72
Brown, Linda, 10, 71, 75, 171, 181–85

Brown, Oliver, 75, 171, 177, 198
Brown, Osawatomie, 21
Brown, Terry Lynn, 181, 182, 183, *184*
Brown v. Board of Education of Topeka:
  alternative historical narrative of,
  6–13; Black schools after, 204–7; filing
  and case detail of, 171–75, 180; LDF
  strategy in, 1; *LIFE* magazine feature
  after, 181–85; moral of, 207–9; as
  result of decade-long struggle, 5;
  Topeka's transition after, 185–200;
  white supremacy in post-*Brown* era,
  200–204. *See also* Topeka Board of
  Education; Topeka NAACP
Brown v. Topeka Board of Education
  Oral History Collection, Kansas State
  Historical Society, 13, 64
Buchanan, Darla, 179
Buchanan Elementary School, 56,
  59–60, 61–67, 70–71, 79, 187, 198–99
*Buford Crawford v. Ft. Scott Board of
  Education*, 135–36
Bunten, Bill, 31
Burnett, Lena, 27, 76, 156, 167, 173–74
Burnett, McKinley, 5, 27, 29, 76,
  99–100, 130, 150, 155–57, 163,
  168–69, 191

Cacho, Lisa Marie, 223n96
Caldwell, George and Henrietta, 134–35
Caldwell, Harrison, 5, *166*; 1909–35, life
  and work of, 134–37; 1950–56, work
  of, 148–49; actions by, as instigator of
  Brown, 130–31, 159–60; board
  directorship of, 137–45; description
  of, 138; principalships of, 149, 165,
  170, 189, 190; racial uplift politics of,
  145–48; "A Reign of Terror" by,
  162–64; response to *Brown* case by,
  189, 194; salary of, 145, 165; as
  superintendent, 90, 129
Caliver, Ambrose, 89
Campbell, Carolyn, 71, 76, 187
Campney, Brent M. S., 18, 23
Campt, Tina, 67

Capital Federal Savings and Loan, 217n76

Capital Plaindealer (publication), 98–99, 104

Carper, Katherine, 190

Carper, Lena Mae, 188

Carter, Robert L., 1, 172, 175, 207

Carver, George Washington, 87, 135, 146, 147

Carver YMCA, 147–48, 162

Casey, Marlin S., 124

Central Park Elementary School, 199

"The Challenge" (Williams), 95

charter schools, 205–9, 243n73

Christianity, 94. *See also* Black churches

Citizens Committee on Civil Rights, 130, 161

Civil Rights Act (1875), 19

Civil War, 19

Clara Barton Elementary School, 46

Cloud, F. J., 18

collective shame, 16

Collins, Ercelle, 194

"The Colored World Within," as concept, 72

colorism, 62–66, 82, 138. *See also* racism

Comité des Citoyens, 62–63

Committee on Indian Affairs, 42

Conrad, Harold, 40

Cooper, Emma, 125, 177, 179

corporal punishment, 84, 203, 227n69

Crawford, Dorothy, 166

Creoles, 62–63

Crowder, Ralph, 64, 66

Current, Gloster B., 164

Curtis, Charles, 173

Dandridge, Deborah, 30, 179, 180, 192

Dandridge, Jeanette, 178, 179, 193

Dandridge, Milburn, 193

Davidson, William, 50, 74

Davis, Maurita Burnett, 27–28, 29, 30, 180, 217n58

Dawson, William L., 96

Delaware, 3

Delci, Helen Espinoza, 48

desegregation campaign. *See* antisegregation school activism

desegregation case. *See Brown v. Board of Education of Topeka*

Detroit, Michigan, 206

Dett, R. Nathaniel, 95

Dickinson, J. A., 40

discipline in parenting, physical, 36–37, 84, 227n73

Double V Campaign, 146–47

Douglas, Aaron, 96

Douglas, Joseph, 36, 77, 88

Douglas, Joseph, Jr., 76, 77, 171

Douglas Elementary School, 50, 52

Douglass, Frederick, 95

Dred Scott v. Sanford, 25

Du Bois, W. E. B., 10, 21, 26, 69, 72, 88, 96, 103, 197

Dunbar, Paul Lawrence, 95, 146

Dwyer, Owen J., 51

economic crash, 22

Ecord, Allen, 47

Eggleston, Ada, 166

8-1-3 attendance policy, 72, 104

Eleanor Clubs, 144, 235n52

Elliott, Roderick W., 183

emancipatory schools, 105–12

embodied whiteness, 48. *See also* whiteness-as-property

embodiment of racial consciousness, 3

Emerson, Claude, 29, 30, 37

Emerson Elementary School, 45–46

employment discrimination, 27–28, 30, 145, 165–66

enslaved persons, 94–95. *See also* slavery

equal, defining, 71–72

erasure, 8–10, 85

Etchison, Nicole, 18

Exodusters movement, 14, 20, 23, 43, 61, 64, 73, 86, 117, 135, 173

Farragut Elementary School, 206, 244n79

Fatzer, Harold, 18, 39, 40, 189–90

Fifteenth Amendment, US Constitution, 19
50CAN advocacy group, 205
Forbes Air Force Base, 156
forced removal of immigrants, 22
Fort Scott, Kansas, 31, 134–37, 139, 233n19
Foster v. Board of Education, 50, 55, 56, 105, 121–22, 157
Fourteenth Amendment, US Constitution, 20
Foust, Edward S., 176–77
Franklin, C. A., 93
Free State narrative, 18, 22, 42
French, Galena, 56–57

Gage Elementary School, 55, 112
Garfield Elementary School, 53, 54
Garvey, Marcus, 88–89
gender and work, 80–81, 139, 231n30
Gibson, Barbara, 28
Gilliam, Geraldine, 166
Godwin, Wendell, 172, 175, 186–87, 195, 196
Gone with the Wind (film), 96
Gooden, Lillian, 34
Graham, Edward, 58, 140, 234n41
Graham, Oaland, 102, 104–5, 108, 112–13
Graham, Ulysses, 104–5
Graham v. Board of Education of Topeka, 4; case details of, 50, 75, 102–5; emancipatory schools and, 105–7, 220n20; Topeka NAACP v. Black political activists on, 118–23; Topeka school board's response to, 112–15, 123–26; witness testimonies in, 107–12
Grant, Arnold and Dorothy, 194
Great Depression, 22, 35, 36
Great Railroad Strike (1922), 35, 156
Green, Brent, 197
Greenberg, Jack, 171
Guy, James H., 117

Hall, Jacqueline Dowd, 152
Hallmark Cards, 27–28

Handy, W. C., 96
Hansen, Chris, 26
Haraway, Donna, 204
Hardeman, Hester, 177, 179
Harrison, G. L., 149
Hartman, Saidiya, 81, 134
Haskell, Dudley Chase, 42
Heart Mountain incarceration camp, 183
Henderson, Wilmer, 138
Henderson, Zelma, 75, 176, 178, 187
Herd, E. Bernard, 177
heteropatriarchy, 5, 80, 136
Hicks, E. B., 37, 195
Higginbotham, Evelyn, 66
Highland Park, Topeka, 23
Highland Presbyterian Mission, 41
Hill, P. H., 177
historical narrative, alternative, 6–13, 102–3
Holland, Flossie, 198
Holland, J. B., 166; *Brown* case and, 195–98; on Caldwell, 139; on integration, 191; on segregated school's effects, 188; on teacher's qualifications, 108, 192; Todd's request for, 67
Hollie, Pamela G., 192–93, 202
Horne, Lena, 95, 96
housing discrimination, 32–38, 183, 189
Howard, Bill, 135
How Race is Made (Molina), 47
Hughes, Langston, 146
Hunnicutt, J. S., 91

I. C. Norcom High School, 72
immigrant laborers, 22, 35–36. *See also* Mexicans and Mexican Americans
Indian Removal Act (1830), 21
integrated neighborhoods, 35–37
Ipsen, Avaren, 11
Iwasaki, Hikaru "Carl," 181–85

Jackson, Christina, 84, 89
Jackson, R. S., 99–100
Jackson, Samuel C., 142

Jacobson, Matthew Frye, 218n83
Japanese American internment, 183
Johnson, James Weldon, 88
Johnson, J. Rosamond, 96
Jones, John Paul, 51
Jones, Nancy, 195
Journal of Negro Education, 90

Kansas Colored Parent-Teacher
    Association, 148, 162
Kansas Congress of Colored Parents
    and Teachers, 162
Kansas Freedman's Relief Association,
    23
Kansas Industrial and Educational
    Institute, 87, 117, 227n86
"Kansas Land" (Parks), 233n17
Kansas State Teachers Association,
    42–43, 147
Kappa Alpha Psi fraternity, 122, 190
Kaw Mission, 41
Kaw Nation, 173
Kelly, C. K., 44
Kelly, Eugene H., Jr., 177
Ketchum, Omar B., 25
Kiene, Julia, 61
Kilpatrick, William Heard, 79
King, Katherine, 166
Kluger, Richard, 7–9, 10, 27, 66, 80,
    129
Ku Klux Klan, 86

Lang, Maurice J., III, 37, 218n94
Law and Order League, 87
Lawton, Maude, 178
The Learning Tree (Parks), 136
Lee, Alice, 76
Lee, Davis, 98, 230n145
Lee, Thelma Chiles, 104
lending discrimination, 217n76
LIFE magazine, 181–85
Lincoln Elementary School, 53–54
Lipsitz, George, 21, 52
The Long Civil Rights Movement, as
    phrase, 152

Long Movement, 6
Louisiana, 62–63
Love, Doris, 166
Lowe, Robert, 7
Lowman Hill Elementary School, 44,
    50–51, 60, 61, 74, 187, 191
lynchings, 24, 84, 118, 135

Machiavellianism, 148–49
Magaw, W. S., 54–55
Marshall, Thurgood, 202–3
Massachusetts Emigrant Aid Society,
    23
Massey family, 193–94
Matzeliger, Jan E., 95
Maxwell, Bill, 71
Maynor, Dorothy, 96
McBrier, Althea, 166
McClure, James, 60, 104, 112, 123–24
McCoy, LaMerle, 88
McDaniels, Hattie, 96
McFarland, Kenneth, 90–92, 127, 128,
    131–34, 137, 139, 149, 159
McKinley Elementary School, 70–71, 75,
    172–73
McLaurin v. Oklahoma, 1
Methodism. *See* St. John AME Church
Mexicanness, 22, 28–29, 49–50
Mexicans and Mexican Americans,
    22, 28–29, 35, 44–49, 56, 70, 112,
    143–44, 156, 215n25, 217n52,
    221n44
migration, 22, 23
Ming, William, 190
Ministerial Alliance Group, 194
Missouri, 219n6
Missouri Compromise, 17
Mitchell, William, Jr., 27, 28, 36, 84
Mitchell, William, Sr., 25, 27
Molina, Natalia, 47
Monroe Elementary School, 70–71, 74,
    91, 184, 185
Montgomery, Leola Brown, 75, 76, 174,
    178, 188
Montgomery bus boycott, 10, 103

Moore, George, 33
Morris, Aldon, 232n56
Moten, Fred, 31, 73, 96–97
movement against school integration.
    See anti-integration school activism
movie theaters, 28–30, 157
Murphy, Lance, 30
music programs, 67, 111, 142, 157–58,
    160, 223n113

NAACP. *See* Topeka NAACP
NAACP Education Committee, 127–29,
    132
NAACP Legal Defense Fund, 1, 171, 175,
    190, 207
National Association of Colored
    Women's motto, 148
Native Americans, 44, 173
Naylor, Frank, 54
"Negro National Anthem" (song), 88,
    200
Neiswanger, Isabel, 104, 124–25
New, Beryl, 209
New England Emigrant Aid Society, 17
Noches, Ramon, 64
Norman, Ida, 81, *166*, 194
normative whiteness, 23–26. *See also*
    embodied whiteness
North, Mildred, *166*

Oden, Don, 32
Oertel, Kristen Tegtmeier, 18
Of Merit, Achievement and Service
    (OMAS), 91–97, 128–29, 145, 146
Oklahoma, 1
Oliphant, Nat, 24
Ortega, Raymond, 143
othering, 3

Palton, Fannie, *166*
Parkdale Elementary School, 199
parks, 28
Parks, Gordon, 23, 26, 135–36, 233n17
Parks, Julia Etta, 71, 76–77, 83
Parks, Rosa, 10, 103

Pasadena, California, 220n34
paternalism, 8
Patterson, Julia, *166*
Patton, Fannie, 94
Payne, E. George, 90
"The People Fight Back" (petition), 160
Perez, Lupe, 41, 45, 47, 49
Philadelphia, Pennsylvania, 207
Phillips, Myrtle, 90
Phillips, Stacy, 207
Phillips, Thayer Brown, 80, 193
Phillips, U. B., 95
"Philosophy of Race Segregation" (Du
    Bois), 69
Pickens, William, 116
Plessy, Homer, 63
Plessy v. Ferguson, 1, 7, 52, 62, 70, 180.
    See also separate-but-equal standard
political structures, 2–5
political subjectivities, 2–5, 19–21
possessive investment in whiteness, as
    phrase, 21
Potawatomi Trail of Death, 21
Pottawatomie Massacre, 21
preservationism, Black school, 15, 103,
    114–15, 118–19, 121, 123, 124, 130,
    133, 151–54, 162, 172–75. *See also*
    anti-integration school activism
Price, Jean, 195
principalships, 79, 125, 128, 134, 149,
    170, 196, 198, 221n45, 238n52,
    243n58. *See also* Black educators

Quakers, 86
Quinton, Eugene S., 55

racial accommodationism. *See* accom-
    modationism, racial
racial formation, 17–19, 22, 32–33
racial geographies, 2, 11, 14, 62–63, 79,
    103, 142
racial liberalism, 8–10
racial passing, 5, 27–28
racial self-determination, 7–8. *See also*
    anti-integration school activism

racial subjectivities, 2–5, 10–11, 67–68
racial uplift politics, 5, 66, 73, 83, 87,
  145–48, 203, 213n37
racism: after Kansas statehood, 19–21;
  after school integration, 152, 239n88;
  in early twentieth century, 22–30; in
  employment, 27–28, 30, 145, 165–66;
  in lending, 217n76; in neighborhood
  and housing, 32–38; paternalism, 8;
  structures of, 2–5. *See also* colorism
Raines, C. P., 194
Ramblers (basketball team), 31–32, 129,
  139–41
Rangel, Ed, 29, 49
Rangel, Jane, 36
Rausch, Fred, 195
Reconstruction, 23
Red Summer, 24–25
residential segregation, 32–38, 183,
  189
respectability politics, 5, 66, 83, 84,
  96–97, 98, 104, 141, 146, 157, 174,
  185, 197, 203
restaurants, 28–29, 30
retribution, 124–26, 173, 179–80
Reynolds, Earl, 121–22
Reynolds, Raymond, 24, 33, 121, 124
Reynolds, R. J., 58
Reynolds, William, 51–53, 121
Reynolds v. Board of Education, 50–53,
  56, 121
Rhodes, Jane, 98
Rich, Adrienne, 219n2
Ridley, Ezekiel, 5, 76, 77, 86–89, 99,
  100, 110, 116, 118–19, 147–48, 177
Ridley, Fox, 230n145
Ridley, Frances, 33
Ridley, Hortense, 110
Ridley, Richard, 4, 28, 32, 71, 76, 100,
  140, 152, 166–67
Ridley, Ruth, 110–11, 177
Robinson, H. H., 18
Robinson, Jeffrey, 207
Rodriguez, Tom, 35
Roosevelt, Eleanor, 235n52

Ross, Barbara, 166, 190, 197, 200
Ross, Merrill, 31, 34, 66, 132, 139–40,
  166, 190, 199
Rotary Club, 146–47
Russian immigrants, 35–36

salaries, 50, 78, 91, 145, 165, 221n45,
  235n55, 238n52. *See also*
  principalships
Sand Town, Kansas, 173
Santa Fe Railway, 34, 35, 45, 54
Sawyer, Annabel, 116, 125–26, 170, 179
Sawyer, Cyrene, 177
Sawyer, Daniel, 59, 60–61, 90, 111–12,
  120–28, 132, 161, 190–91
Sawyer, Grace, 127
Sawyer, Katherine Carper, 188
Sawyer, Nathaniel, 62, 105
Sawyer, Theata, 160–61
school integration, overview, 1–15,
  181–209. *See also* anti-integration
  school activism; antisegregation
  school activism; separate-but-equal
  standard
school matrons, 104
Scott, Berdyne, 35, 36
Scott, Charles S., Sr., 37, 169, 172, 188
Scott, Deborah, 37, 188
Scott, Dorothy, 191, 198
Scott, El Dorothy, 81
Scott, Elisha, 99, 100, 117–18, 119–20, 123
Scott, James C., 29
Scott, John, 137–38, 169, 172, 173
separate-but-equal standard, 1, 4,
  28–32. *See also* anti-integration school
  activism; *Plessy v. Ferguson*; school
  integration, overview
Separate Car Act (1890), 63
sexuality, 81
Sex Working in the Bible (Ipsen), 11
Seymour Foods, 35
Shawnee County Bar Association, 105
Shawnee Manual Labor School, 41–42
Sheldon, Charles, 43, 61, 117
Siddle Walker, Vanessa, 15

Simple Justice (Kluger), 7–9, 85, 174, 197
Simpson, Audra, 57–58
Singleton, Benjamin "Pap," 23, 176
6-3-3 attendance policy, 72
slavery, 3, 17–21, 94–95. *See also*
    enslaved persons
Smith, Dean, 31
Snyder, Harry, 24–25, 47, 216n35
sociality, 30–32, 176–80
songs, 88
South Carolina, 3
The Spirit of Washington (film), 89, 114,
    121
Starnes, Myrtle, 166, 195–98
"Star-Spangled Banner" (song), 88
State Industrial School for Boys,
    228n86
Statler, Stanley, 186, 196
St. John AME Church, 66, 176–77,
    240n100
St. Mark's AME Church, 187
Stout, A. J., 61, 99, 112–15, 124, 127,
    131
Struggles before Brown (Van Delinder),
    9–10
St. Simon's Episcopal Church, 82, 117
Studies in Negro Life curriculum. See
    Of Merit, Achievement and Service
    (OMAS)
"Sunday Meditation" (Caldwell), 147
Sutton, Georgia, 97
Sweatt v. Painter, 1
swimming pools, 28

Tabor, Milton, 142–44
Tanner, Henry Ossawa, 96
Teacher Transformation Institute, 205
temporal and spatial dynamics, 2–3
Tennessee, 176
Tennessee Town, Kansas, 14, 33, 37,
    43, 61–62, 87, 117, 176, 187
Texas, 1
Thompson, Joe, 114, 120–21, 162
Thompson, Tracy, 114, 148, 162,
    231n30, 235n60

Thurman-Watts v. The Board of Education
    of Coffeyville, 118, 234n25
Tillotson, D. C., 73
Todd, Alvin, 64, 65, 158
Todd, Lucinda, 5, 29, 41, 64–67, 132,
    143–45, 157–58, 187, 223n113
Todd, Nancy, 65, 67, 158
Topeka Board of Education, 1, 3, 42–44,
    49–56, 70, 90–91, 169. See also *Brown*
    v. Board of Education of Topeka
Topeka Compromise (1942), 142
Topeka Council of Colored Parents and
    Teachers, 113, 148, 153, 163–64
Topeka Country Club, 26
Topeka High School, 30–32, 142, 211n2
Topeka NAACP, 1–2, 12–13, 115–23;
    1941–49, work of, 154–62; 1950–53,
    Black opposition to, 171–78; on
    Graham, 75; response to anti-
    integration by, 164–70. See also
    Brown v. Board of Education of Topeka
Townsend, Prentice A., 161
Turner, L. S., 91, 92

Underground Railroad, 23
United States Indian Industrial Training
    School, 42
US Constitution, 19, 20

Vance, Edna, 166
Van Delinder, Jean, 9–10, 129
Veale, Tinkham, 105, 230n4
Veterans Administration hospital,
    Topeka, 156
Virginia, 3
Voting Rights Act (1965), 6

Walker, Eva, 166
War Relocation Authority, 183
Warren, Earl, 7, 180, 183
Warren, Kim Cary, 219n13
Washington, Booker T., 83, 87, 119,
    146, 148
Washington, DC, 3
Washington, Minerva, 166

Washington Elementary School, 70, 78, 86–89, 114, 170
Watkins, Bolivar E., 155
Wells, Elaine, 205
Wheatley, Phyllis, 96
White, Walter, 33, 164, 168
white civility, 26–30
Whitefoord Elementary School, 206
white male subjectivities, 17
whiteness. *See* embodied whiteness; whiteness-as-property
whiteness-as-property, 11, 17–27, 32, 34, 36, 40–41, 48, 63, 72, 107, 135. *See also* benevolent whiteness; embodied whiteness
white supremacy, 5, 16–18, 80, 200–204, 214n14
Whitson, Mose J., 194, 199
Wilkins, Roy, 25, 126
Williams, Bert, 96

Williams, Mamie Luella, 5, 78–82, *166*, *185*; about, 7; on all-Black schools, 7–8, 85–86, 185–86; Black studies curriculum by, 92–93; on Caldwell, 138–39; *Graham* case and, 107–10, 170; on McFarland, 132; as principal, 170; salary of, 145, 165; teaching career of, 79, 229n125
Williams, Vance, 194, 195
Williams v. Eady, 227n69
Wilmarth, L. C., 43
Wilson, Charles, 65
Wilson, Frank, 196
Wilson, Paul, 39
Wilson, William H., 51
Winter, Jacob, 43
Woodson, Carter G., 88, 91–92
Worswick, Mike, 196–97
Wright v. Board of Education, 50, 55, 56, 75, 222n72

www.ingramcontent.com/pod-product-compliance
Lightning Source LLC
Chambersburg PA
CBHW032346280326
41935CB00008B/472